Natural Right and History

By

LEO STRAUSS

THE UNIVERSITY OF CHICAGO PRESS
CHICAGO & LONDON

CHARLES R. WALGREEN FOUNDATION LECTURES

ISBN: 0-226-77692-1 (clothbound); 0-226-77694-8 (paperbound)

Library of Congress Catalog Card Number: 53-12840

THE UNIVERSITY OF CHICAGO PRESS, CHICAGO 60637

The University of Chicago Press, Ltd., London

FOREWORD

✿

FOR many years the political philosophy of responsible government has been a neglected field in American political science. Characteristic of this period was the complete rejection of natural law, the standard by which, traditionally, government relations were judged. Law and rights emanated from the states. Under democratic regimes it was held that majority will created law and granted rights. Beyond these, no restrictions of law could bind the sovereign state. In recent years that peculiar twentieth-century phenomenon—the totalitarian regime—revived among political philosophers the study of the traditionalist natural law doctrine, with its insistence upon limited state authority.

This work of Professor Strauss, based upon his Walgreen Foundation lectures, presents a keen analysis of the philosophy of natural right. It is a critique of certain modern political theories and an able presentation of basic principles of the traditionalist point of view.

JEROME KERWIN
Chairman of the Walgreen Foundation

v

PREFACE TO THE 7th IMPRESSION (1971)

*

IT almost goes without saying that if I were to write this book again, I would write it differently. But I have been assured from various quarters that the book as written was useful and continues to be useful.

Since the time when I wrote the book, I have, I believe, deepened my understanding of "natural right and history." This applies in the first place to "modern natural right." My view was confirmed by the study of Vico's *La scienza nuova seconda* which is devoted to a reconsideration of natural right and which is not properly approached and understood by those who take "the historical consciousness" for granted. Since I have not written anything on Vico, I can refer the interested reader only to what I wrote in the meantime on Hobbes and Locke in my articles "On the Basis of Hobbes' Political Philosophy" and "Locke's Doctrine of Natural Law"; both articles have been republished in *What Is Political Philosophy?* (The Free Press of Glencoe, 1959). I refer particularly to what I wrote on the nerve of Hobbes' argument (p. 176n).

In the last ten years I have concentrated on the study of "classic natural right," and in particular on "Socrates." I have dealt with this subject in some books published since 1964, and in one entitled *Xenophon's Socrates,* which is almost ready for publication.

Nothing that I have learned has shaken my inclination to prefer "natural right," especially in its classic form, to the reigning relativism, politivist or historicist. To avoid a common misunderstanding, I should add the remark that the appeal to a higher law, if that law is understood in terms of "our" tradition as distinguished from "nature," is historicist in character, if not in intention. The case is obviously different if appeal is made to the divine law; still, the divine law is not the natural law, let alone natural right.

L. S.

SEPTEMBER, 1970
ST. JOHN'S COLLEGE, ANNAPOLIS, MD.

vii

TABLE OF CONTENTS

❊

There were two men in one city; the one rich, and the other poor. The rich man had exceeding many flocks and herds: But the poor man had nothing, save one little ewe lamb, which he had bought and nourished up: and it grew up together with him, and with his children: it did eat of his own meat, and drank of his own cup, and lay in his bosom, and was unto him as a daughter. And there came a traveller unto the rich man, and he spared to take of his own flock and of his own herd, to dress for the wayfaring man that was come unto him; but took the poor man's lamb, and dressed it for the man that was come to him.

Naboth the Jezreelite had a vineyard which was in Jezreel, hard by the palace of Ahab king of Samaria. And Ahab spake unto Naboth, saying, Give me thy vineyard, that I may have it for a garden of herbs, because it is near unto my house: and I will give thee for it a better vineyard than it; or, if it seem good to thee, I will give thee the worth of it in money. And Naboth said to Ahab, The Lord forbid it to me, that I should give the inheritance of my fathers unto thee.

INTRODUCTION

✳

IT IS proper for more reasons than the most obvious one that I should open this series of Charles R. Walgreen Lectures by quoting a passage from the Declaration of Independence. The passage has frequently been quoted, but, by its weight and its elevation, it is made immune to the degrading effects of the excessive familiarity which breeds contempt and of misuse which breeds disgust. "We hold these truths to be self-evident, that all men are created equal, that they are endowed by their Creator with certain unalienable Rights, that among these are Life, Liberty, and the pursuit of Happiness." The nation dedicated to this proposition has now become, no doubt partly as a consequence of this dedication, the most powerful and prosperous of the nations of the earth. Does this nation in its maturity still cherish the faith in which it was conceived and raised? Does it still hold those "truths to be self-evident"? About a generation ago, an American diplomat could still say that "the natural and the divine foundation of the rights of man . . . is self-evident to all Americans." At about the same time a German scholar could still describe the difference between German thought and that of Western Europe and the United States by saying that the West still attached decisive importance to natural right, while in Germany the very terms "natural right" and "humanity" "have now become almost incomprehensible . . . and have lost altogether their original life and color." While abandoning the idea of natural right and through abandoning it, he continued, German thought has "created the historical sense," and thus was led eventually

1

to unqualified relativism.[1] What was a tolerably accurate description of German thought twenty-seven years ago would now appear to be true of Western thought in general. It would not be the first time that a nation, defeated on the battlefield and, as it were, annihilated as a political being, has deprived its conquerors of the most sublime fruit of victory by imposing on them the yoke of its own thought. Whatever might be true of the thought of the American people, certainly American social science has adopted the very attitude toward natural right which, a generation ago, could still be described, with some plausibility, as characteristic of German thought. The majority among the learned who still adhere to the principles of the Declaration of Independence interpret these principles not as expressions of natural right but as an ideal, if not as an ideology or a myth. Present-day American social science, as far as it is not Roman Catholic social science, is dedicated to the proposition that all men are endowed by the evolutionary process or by a mysterious fate with many kinds of urges and aspirations, but certainly with no natural right.

Nevertheless, the need for natural right is as evident today as it has been for centuries and even millennia. To reject natural right is tantamount to saying that all right is positive right, and this means that what is right is determined exclusively by the legislators and the courts of the various countries. Now it is obviously meaningful, and sometimes even necessary, to speak of "unjust" laws or "unjust" decisions. In passing such judgments we imply that there is a standard of right and wrong independent of positive right and higher than positive right: a standard with reference to which we are able to judge of positive right. Many people today hold the view that the standard in question is in the best case nothing but the

1. "Ernst Troeltsch on Natural Law and Humanity," in Otto Gierke, *Natural Law and the Theory of Society*, translated with Introduction by Ernest Barker, I (Cambridge: At the University Press, 1934), 201–22.

ideal adopted by our society or our "civilization" and embodied in its way of life or its institutions. But, according to the same view, all societies have their ideals, cannibal societies no less than civilized ones. If principles are sufficiently justified by the fact that they are accepted by a society, the principles of cannibalism are as defensible or sound as those of civilized life. From this point of view, the former principles can certainly not be rejected as simply bad. And, since the ideal of our society is admittedly changing, nothing except dull and stale habit could prevent us from placidly accepting a change in the direction of cannibalism. If there is no standard higher than the ideal of our society, we are utterly unable to take a critical distance from that ideal. But the mere fact that we can raise the question of the worth of the ideal of our society shows that there is something in man that is not altogether in slavery to his society, and therefore that we are able, and hence obliged, to look for a standard with reference to which we can judge of the ideals of our own as well as of any other society. That standard cannot be found in the needs of the various societies, for the societies and their parts have many needs that conflict with one another: the problem of priorities arises. This problem cannot be solved in a rational manner if we do not have a standard with reference to which we can distinguish between genuine needs and fancied needs and discern the hierarchy of the various types of genuine needs. The problem posed by the conflicting needs of society cannot be solved if we do not possess knowledge of natural right.

It would seem, then, that the rejection of natural right is bound to lead to disastrous consequences. And it is obvious that consequences which are regarded as disastrous by many men and even by some of the most vocal opponents of natural right do follow from the contemporary rejection of natural right. Our social science may make us very wise or clever as regards the means for any objectives we might choose. It admits being unable to help us in discriminating between legitimate and illegitimate, between just and unjust, objectives. Such a science is instrumental and nothing but instrumental: it is born to be the handmaid of any powers or any interests that be. What Machiavelli did apparently, our social science would actually do if it did not prefer—only God knows why—generous liberalism to consistency: namely, to give advice with equal competence and alacrity to tyrants as well as to free peoples.[2] According to our social science, we can be or become wise in all matters of secondary importance, but we have to be resigned to utter ignorance in the most important respect: we cannot have any knowledge regarding the ultimate principles of our choices, i.e., regarding their soundness or unsoundness; our ultimate principles have no other support than our arbitrary and hence blind preferences. We are then in the position of beings who are sane and sober when engaged in trivial business and who gamble like madmen when confronted with serious issues—retail sanity and wholesale madness. If our principles have no other support than our blind preferences, everything a man is willing to dare will be per-

2. "Vollends sinnlos ist die Behauptung, dass in der Despotie keine Rechtsordnung bestehe, sondern Willkür des Despoten herrsche . . . stellt doch auch der despotisch regierte Staat irgendeine Ordnung menschlichen Verhaltens dar. . . . Diese Ordnung ist eben die Rechtsordnung. Ihr den Charakter des Rechts abzusprechen, ist nur eine naturrechtliche Naivität oder Überhebung. . . . Was als Willkür gedeutet wird, ist nur die rechtliche Möglichkeit des Autokraten, jede Entscheidung an sich zu ziehen, die Tätigkeit der untergeordneten Organe bedingungslos zu bestimmen und einmal gesetzte Normen jederzeit mit allgemeiner oder nur besonderer Geltung aufzuheben oder abzuändern. Ein solcher Zustand ist ein Rechtszustand, auch wenn er als nachteilig empfunden wird. Doch hat er auch seine guten Seiten. Der im modernen Rechtsstaat gar nicht seltene Ruf nach Diktatur zeigt dies ganz deutlich" (Hans Kelsen, *Allgemeine Staatslehre* [Berlin, 1925], pp. 335-36). Since Kelsen has not changed his attitude toward natural right, I cannot imagine why he has omitted this instructive passage from the English translation (*General Theory of Law and State* [Cambridge: Harvard University Press, 1949], p. 300).

missible. The contemporary rejection of natural right leads to nihilism—nay, it is identical with nihilism.

In spite of this, generous liberals view the abandonment of natural right not only with placidity but with relief. They appear to believe that our inability to acquire any genuine knowledge of what is intrinsically good or right compels us to be tolerant of every opinion about good or right or to recognize all preferences or all "civilizations" as equally respectable. Only unlimited tolerance is in accordance with reason. But this leads to the admission of a rational or natural right of every preference that is tolerant of other preferences or, negatively expressed, of a rational or natural right to reject or condemn all intolerant or all "absolutist" positions. The latter must be condemned because they are based on a demonstrably false premise, namely, that men can know what is good. At the bottom of the passionate rejection of all "absolutes," we discern the recognition of a natural right or, more precisely, of that particular interpretation of natural right according to which the one thing needful is respect for diversity or individuality. But there is a tension between the respect for diversity or individuality and the recognition of natural right. When liberals became impatient of the absolute limits to diversity or individuality that are imposed even by the most liberal version of natural right, they had to make a choice between natural right and the uninhibited cultivation of individuality. They chose the latter. Once this step was taken, tolerance appeared as one value or ideal among many, and not intrinsically superior to its opposite. In other words, intolerance appeared as a value equal in dignity to tolerance. But it is practically impossible to leave it at the equality of all preferences or choices. If the unequal rank of choices cannot be traced to the unequal rank of their objectives, it must be traced to the unequal rank of the acts of choosing; and this means eventually that genuine choice, as distinguished from spurious or despicable choice, is nothing but resolute or deadly serious decision. Such a decision, however, is akin to intolerance rather than to tolerance. Liberal relativism has its roots in the natural right tradition of tolerance or in the notion that everyone has a natural right to the pursuit of happiness as he understands happiness; but in itself it is a seminary of intolerance.

Once we realize that the principles of our actions have no other support than our blind choice, we really do not believe in them any more. We cannot wholeheartedly act upon them any more. We cannot live any more as responsible beings. In order to live, we have to silence the easily silenced voice of reason, which tells us that our principles are in themselves as good or as bad as any other principles. The more we cultivate reason, the more we cultivate nihilism: the less are we able to be loyal members of society. The inescapable practical consequence of nihilism is fanatical obscurantism.

The harsh experience of this consequence has led to a renewed general interest in natural right. But this very fact must make us particularly cautious. Indignation is a bad counselor. Our indignation proves at best that we are well meaning. It does not prove that we are right. Our aversion to fanatical obscurantism must not lead us to embrace natural right in a spirit of fanatical obscurantism. Let us beware of the danger of pursuing a Socratic goal with the means, and the temper, of Thrasymachus. Certainly, the seriousness of the need of natural right does not prove that the need can be satisfied. A wish is not a fact. Even by proving that a certain view is indispensable for living well, one proves merely that the view in question is a salutary myth: one does not prove it to be true. Utility and truth are two entirely different things. The fact that reason compels us to go beyond the ideal of our society does not yet guarantee that in taking this step we shall not be confronted with a void or with a multiplicity of incompatible and equally justifiable principles of "natural right." The gravity of the issue imposes upon us the duty of a detached, theoretical, impartial discussion.

The problem of natural right is today a matter of recollection rather than of actual knowledge. We are therefore in need of historical studies in order to familiarize ourselves with the whole complexity of the issue. We have for some time to become students of what is called the "history of ideas." Contrary to a popular notion, this will aggravate rather than remove the difficulty of impartial treatment. To quote Lord Acton: "Few discoveries are more irritating than those which expose the pedigree of ideas. Sharp definitions and unsparing analysis would displace the veil beneath which society dissembles its divisions, would make political disputes too violent for compromise and political alliances too precarious for use, and would embitter politics with all the passions of social and religious strife." We can overcome this danger only by leaving the dimension in which politic restraint is the only protection against the hot and blind zeal of partisanship.

The issue of natural right presents itself today as a matter of party allegiance. Looking around us, we see two hostile camps, heavily fortified and strictly guarded. One is occupied by the liberals of various descriptions, the other by the Catholic and non-Catholic disciples of Thomas Aquinas. But both armies and, in addition, those who prefer to sit on the fences or hide their heads in the sand are, to heap metaphor on metaphor, in the same boat. They all are modern men. We all are in the grip of the same difficulty. Natural right in its classic form is connected with a teleological view of the universe. All natural beings have a natural end, a natural destiny, which determines what kind of operation is good for them. In the case of man, reason is required for discerning these operations: reason determines what is by nature right with ultimate regard to man's natural end. The teleological view of the universe, of which the teleological view of man forms a part, would seem to have been destroyed by modern natural science. From the point of view of Aristotle—and who could dare to claim to be a better judge in this matter than Aristotle?—the issue between the mechanical and the teleological conception of the universe is decided by the manner in which the problem of the heavens, the heavenly bodies, and their motion is solved.[3] Now in this respect, which from Aristotle's own point of view was the decisive one, the issue seems to have been decided in favor of the nonteleological conception of the universe. Two opposite conclusions could be drawn from this momentous decision. According to one, the nonteleological conception of the universe must be followed up by a nonteleological conception of human life. But this "naturalistic" solution is exposed to grave difficulties: it seems to be impossible to give an adequate account of human ends by conceiving of them merely as posited by desires or impulses. Therefore, the alternative solution has prevailed. This means that people were forced to accept a fundamental, typically modern, dualism of a nonteleological natural science and a teleological science of man. This is the position which the modern followers of Thomas Aquinas, among others, are forced to take, a position which presupposes a break with the comprehensive view of Aristotle as well as that of Thomas Aquinas himself. The fundamental dilemma, in whose grip we are, is caused by the victory of modern natural science. An adequate solution to the problem of natural right cannot be found before this basic problem has been solved.

Needless to say, the present lectures cannot deal with this problem. They will have to be limited to that aspect of the problem of natural right which can be clarified within the confines of the social sciences. Present-day social science rejects natural right on two different, although mostly combined, grounds; it rejects it in the name of History and in the name of the distinction between Facts and Values.

3. *Physics* 196ª25 ff., 199ª3–5.

I

NATURAL RIGHT AND THE HISTORICAL APPROACH

✳

THE attack on natural right in the name of history takes, in most cases, the following form: natural right claims to be a right that is discernible by human reason and is universally acknowledged; but history (including anthropology) teaches us that no such right exists; instead of the supposed uniformity, we find an indefinite variety of notions of right or justice. Or, in other words, there cannot be natural right if there are no immutable principles of justice, but history shows us that all principles of justice are mutable. One cannot understand the meaning of the attack on natural right in the name of history before one has realized the utter irrelevance of this argument. In the first place, "consent of all mankind" is by no means a necessary condition of the existence of natural right. Some of the greatest natural right teachers have argued that, precisely if natural right is rational, its discovery presupposes the cultivation of reason, and therefore natural right will not be known universally: one ought not even to expect any real knowledge of natural right among savages.[1] In other words, by proving that there is no principle of justice that has not been denied somewhere or at some time, one has not yet proved that any given denial was justified or reasonable. Furthermore, it has always been known that different notions of jus-

---

1. Consider Plato *Republic* 456^{b}12–^{c}2, 452^{a}7–8 and ^{c}6–^{d}1; *Laches* 184^{d}1–185^{a}3; Hobbes, *De cive*, II, 1; Locke, *Two Treatises of Civil Government*, Book II, sec. 12, in conjunction with *An Essay on the Human Understanding*, Book I, chap. iii. Compare Rousseau, *Discours sur l'origine de l'inégalité*, Preface; Montesquieu, *De l'esprit des lois*, I, 1–2; also Marsilius *Defensor pacis* ii. 12. 8.

tice obtain at different times and in different nations. It is absurd to claim that the discovery of a still greater number of such notions by modern students has in any way affected the fundamental issue. Above all, knowlege of the indefinitely large variety of notions of right and wrong is so far from being incompatible with the idea of natural right that it is the essential condition for the emergence of that idea: realization of the variety of notions of right is *the* incentive for the quest for natural right. If the rejection of natural right in the name of history is to have any significance, it must have a basis other than historical evidence. Its basis must be a philosophic critique of the possibility, or of the knowability, of natural right—a critique somehow connected with "history."

The conclusion from the variety of notions of right to the nonexistence of natural right is as old as political philosophy itself. Political philosophy seems to begin with the contention that the variety of notions of right proves the nonexistence of natural right or the conventional character of all right.[2] We shall call this view "conventionalism." To clarify the meaning of the present-day rejection of natural right in the name of history, we must first grasp the specific difference between conventionalism, on the one hand, and "the historical sense" or "the historical consciousness" characteristic of nineteenth- and twentieth-century thought, on the other.[3]

2. Aristotle *Eth. Nic.* 1134b24–27.

3. The legal positivism of the nineteenth and twentieth centuries cannot be simply identified with either conventionalism or historicism. It seems, however, that it derives its strength ultimately from the generally accepted historicist premise (see particularly Karl Bergbohm, *Jurisprudenz und Rechtsphilosophie*, I [Leipzig, 1892], 409 ff.). Bergbohm's strict argument against the possibility of natural right (as distinguished from the argument that is meant merely to show the disastrous consequences of natural right for the positive legal order) is based on "the undeniable truth that nothing eternal and absolute exists except the One Whom man cannot comprehend, but only divine in a spirit of faith" (p. 416 n.), that is, on the assumption that "the standards with reference to which we pass judgment on the historical, positive law . . . are themselves absolutely the progeny of their time and are always historical and relative" (p. 450 n.).

Conventionalism presupposed that the distinction between nature and convention is the most fundamental of all distinctions. It implied that nature is of incomparably higher dignity than convention or the fiat of society, or that nature is the norm. The thesis that right and justice are conventional meant that right and justice have no basis in nature, that they are ultimately against nature, and that they have their ground in arbitrary decisions, explicit or implicit, of communities: they have no basis but some kind of agreement, and agreement may produce peace but it cannot produce truth. The adherents of the modern historical view, on the other hand, reject as mythical the premise that nature is the norm; they reject the premise that nature is of higher dignity than any works of man. On the contrary, either they conceive of man and his works, his varying notions of justice included, as equally natural as all other real things, or else they assert a basic dualism between the realm of nature and the realm of freedom or history. In the latter case they imply that the world of man, of human creativity, is exalted far above nature. Accordingly, they do not conceive of the notions of right and wrong as fundamentally arbitrary. They try to discover their causes; they try to make intelligible their variety and sequence; in tracing them to acts of freedom, they insist on the fundamental difference between freedom and arbitrariness.

What is the significance of the difference between the old and the modern view? Conventionalism is a particular form of classical philosophy. There are obviously profound differences between conventionalism and the position taken by Plato, for example. But the classical opponents agree in regard to the most fundamental point: both admit that the distinction between nature and convention is fundamental. For this distinction is implied in the idea of philosophy. Philosophizing means to ascend from the cave to the light of the sun, that is, to the truth. The cave is the world of opinion as opposed to knowledge. Opinion is essentially variable. Men cannot live, that is, they cannot live together, if opinions are not stabilized by social fiat. Opinion thus becomes authoritative opinion or public dogma or Weltanschauung. Philosophizing means, then, to ascend from public dogma to essentially private knowledge. The public dogma is originally an inadequate attempt to answer the question of the all-comprehensive truth or of the eternal order.[4] Any inadequate view of the eternal order is, from the point of view of the eternal order, accidental or arbitrary; it owes its validity not to its intrinsic truth but to social fiat or convention. The fundamental premise of conventionalism is, then, nothing other than the idea of philosophy as the attempt to grasp the eternal. The modern opponents of natural right reject precisely this idea. According to them, all human thought is historical and hence unable ever to grasp anything eternal. Whereas, according to the ancients, philosophizing means to leave the cave, according to our contemporaries all philosophizing essentially belongs to a "historical world," "culture," "civilization," "Weltanschauung," that is, to what Plato had called the cave. We shall call this view "historicism."

We have noted before that the contemporary rejection of natural right in the name of history is based, not on historical evidence, but on a philosophic critique of the possibility or knowability of natural right. We note now that the philosophic critique in question is not particularly a critique of natural right or of moral principles in general. It is a critique of human thought as such. Nevertheless, the critique of natural right played an important role in the formation of historicism.

Historicism emerged in the nineteenth century under the protection of the belief that knowledge, or at least divination, of the eternal is possible. But it gradually undermined the belief which had sheltered it in its infancy. It suddenly appeared

4. Plato *Minos* 314b10–315b2.

within our lifetime in its mature form. The genesis of historicism is inadequately understood. In the present state of our knowledge, it is difficult to say at what point in the modern development the decisive break occurred with the "unhistorical" approach that prevailed in all earlier philosophy. For the purpose of a summary orientation it is convenient to start with the moment when the previously subterraneous movement came to the surface and began to dominate the social sciences in broad daylight. That moment was the emergence of the historical school.

The thoughts that guided the historical school were very far from being of a purely theoretical character. The historical school emerged in reaction to the French Revolution and to the natural right doctrines that had prepared that cataclysm. In opposing the violent break with the past, the historical school insisted on the wisdom and on the need of preserving or continuing the traditional order. This could have been done without a critique of natural right as such. Certainly, premodern natural right did not sanction reckless appeal from the established order, or from what was actual here and now, to the natural or rational order. Yet the founders of the historical school seemed to have realized somehow that the acceptance of any universal or abstract principles has necessarily a revolutionary, disturbing, unsettling effect as far as thought is concerned and that this effect is wholly independent of whether the principles in question sanction, generally speaking, a conservative or a revolutionary course of action. For the recognition of universal principles forces man to judge the established order, or what is actual here and now, in the light of the natural or rational order; and what is actual here and now is more likely than not to fall short of the universal and unchangeable norm.[5] The recognition of universal principles thus tends to

5. ". . . [les] imperfections [des États], s'ils en ont, comme la seule diversité, qui est entre eux suffit pour assurer que plusieurs en ont . . ." (Descartes, *Discours de la méthode*, Part II).

prevent men from wholeheartedly identifying themselves with, or accepting, the social order that fate has allotted to them. It tends to alienate them from their place on the earth. It tends to make them strangers, and even strangers on the earth.

By denying the significance, if not the existence, of universal norms, the eminent conservatives who founded the historical school were, in fact, continuing and even sharpening the revolutionary effort of their adversaries. That effort was inspired by a specific notion of the natural. It was directed against both the unnatural or conventional and the supranatural or otherworldly. The revolutionists assumed, we may say, that the natural is always individual and that therefore the uniform is unnatural or conventional. The human individual was to be liberated or to liberate himself so that he could pursue not just his happiness but his own version of happiness. This meant, however, that one universal and uniform goal was set up for all men: the natural right of each individual was a right uniformly belonging to every man as man. But uniformity was said to be unnatural and hence bad. It was evidently impossible to individualize rights in full accordance with the natural diversity of individuals. The only kinds of rights that were neither incompatible with social life nor uniform were "historical" rights: rights of Englishmen, for example, in contradistinction to the rights of man. Local and temporal variety seemed to supply a safe and solid middle ground between antisocial individualism and unnatural universality. The historical school did not discover the local and temporal variety of notions of justice: the obvious does not have to be discovered. The utmost one could say is that it discovered the value, the charm, the inwardness of the local and temporal or that it discovered the superiority of the local and temporal to the universal. It would be more cautious to say that, radicalizing the tendency of men like Rousseau, the historical school asserted that the local and the temporal have a higher value than the universal. As a consequence, what claimed to be universal appeared eventually as derivative from something locally and temporally confined, as the local and temporal *in statu evanescendi*. The natural law teaching of the Stoics, for example, was likely to appear as a mere reflex of a particular temporal state of a particular local society—of the dissolution of the Greek city.

The effort of the revolutionists was directed against all otherworldliness[6] or transcendence. Transcendence is not a preserve of revealed religion. In a very important sense it was implied in the original meaning of political philosophy as the quest for the natural or best political order. The best regime, as Plato and Aristotle understood it, is, and is meant to be, for the most part, different from what is actual here and now or beyond all actual orders. This view of the transcendence of the best political order was profoundly modified by the way in which "progress" was understood in the eighteenth century, but it was still preserved in that eighteenth-century notion. Otherwise, the theorists of the French Revolution could not have condemned all or almost all social orders which had ever been in existence. By denying the significance, if not the existence, of universal norms, the historical school destroyed the only solid basis of all efforts to transcend the actual. Historicism can therefore be described as a much more extreme form of modern this-worldliness than the French radicalism of the eighteenth century had been. It certainly acted as if it intended to make men absolutely at home in "this world."

[handwritten margin note: historicism denies man's ability to transcend]

6. As regards the tension between the concern with the history of the human race and the concern with life after death, see Kant's "Idea for a universal history with cosmopolitan intent," proposition 9 (*The Philosophy of Kant*, ed. C. J. Friedrich ["Modern Library"], p. 130). Consider also the thesis of Herder, whose influence on the historical thought of the nineteenth century is well known, that "the five acts are in this life" (see M. Mendelssohn, *Gesammelte Schriften, Jubiläums-Ausgabe*, III, 1, pp. xxx–xxxii.)

Since any universal principles make at least most men potentially homeless, it depreciated universal principles in favor of historical principles. It believed that, by understanding their past, their heritage, their historical situation, men could arrive at principles that would be as objective as those of the older, prehistoricist political philosophy had claimed to be and, in addition, would not be abstract or universal and hence harmful to wise action or to a truly human life, but concrete or particular—principles fitting the particular age or particular nation, principles relative to the particular age or particular nation.

In trying to discover standards which, while being objective, were relative to particular historical situations, the historical school assigned to historical studies a much greater importance than they had ever possessed. Its notion of what one could expect from historical studies was, however, not the outcome of historical studies but of assumptions that stemmed directly or indirectly from the natural right doctrine of the eighteenth century. The historical school assumed the existence of folk minds, that is, it assumed that nations or ethnic groups are natural units, or it assumed the existence of general laws of historical evolution, or it combined both assumptions. It soon appeared that there was a conflict between the assumptions that had given the decisive impetus to historical studies and the results, as well as the requirements, of genuine historical understanding. In the moment these assumptions were abandoned, the infancy of historicism came to its end.

Historicism now appeared as a particular form of positivism, that is, of the school which held that theology and metaphysics had been superseded once and for all by positive science or which identified genuine knowledge of reality with the knowledge supplied by the empirical sciences. Positivism proper had defined "empirical" in terms of the procedures of the natural sciences. But there was a glaring contrast between the manner in which historical subjects were treated by positivism proper and the manner in which they were treated by the historians who really proceeded empirically. Precisely in the interests of empirical knowledge it became necessary to insist that the methods of natural science be not considered authoritative for historical studies. In addition, what "scientific" psychology and sociology had to say about man proved to be trivial and poor if compared with what could be learned from the great historians. Thus history was thought to supply the only empirical, and hence the only solid, knowledge of what is truly human, of man as man: of his greatness and misery. Since all human pursuits start from and return to man, the empirical study of humanity could seem to be justified in claiming a higher dignity than all other studies of reality. History—history divorced from all dubious or metaphysical assumptions—became the highest authority.

But history proved utterly unable to keep the promise that had been held out by the historical school. The historical school had succeeded in discrediting universal or abstract principles; it had thought that historical studies would reveal particular or concrete standards. Yet the unbiased historian had to confess his inability to derive any norms from history: no objective norms remained. The historical school had obscured the fact that particular or historical standards can become authoritative only on the basis of a universal principle which imposes an obligation on the individual to accept, or to bow to, the standards suggested by the tradition or the situation which has molded him. Yet no universal principle will ever sanction the acceptance of every historical standard or of every victorious cause: to conform with tradition or to jump on "the wave of the future" is not obviously better, and it is certainly not always better than to burn what one has worshiped or to resist the "trend of history." Thus all standards suggested by history as such proved to be fundamentally ambiguous and therefore unfit to be considered standards. To the unbiased historian, "the historical process" revealed itself as the meaningless web spun by what men did, produced, and thought, no more than by unmitigated chance—a tale told by an idiot. The historical standards, the standards thrown up by this meaningless process, could no longer claim to be hallowed by sacred powers behind that process. The only standards that remained were of a purely subjective character, standards that had no other support than the free choice of the individual. No objective criterion henceforth allowed the distinction between good and bad choices. Historicism culminated in nihilism. The attempt to make man absolutely at home in this world ended in man's becoming absolutely homeless.

The view that "the historical process" is a meaningless web or that there is no such thing as the "historical process" was not novel. It was fundamentally the classical view. In spite of considerable opposition from different quarters, it was still powerful in the eighteenth century. The nihilistic consequence of historicism could have suggested a return to the older, prehistoricist view. But the manifest failure of the practical claim of historicism, that it could supply life with a better, a more solid, guidance than the prehistoricist thought of the past had done, did not destroy the prestige of the alleged theoretical insight due to historicism. The mood created by historicism and its practical failure was interpreted as the unheard-of experience of the true situation of man as man—of a situation which earlier man had concealed from himself by believing in universal and unchangeable principles. In opposition to the earlier view, the historicists continued to ascribe decisive importance to that view of man that arises out of historical studies, which as such are particularly and primarily concerned not with the permanent and universal but with the variable and unique. History as history seems to present to us the depressing spectacle of a disgraceful variety of thoughts and beliefs and, above all, of the passing-away of every thought and belief ever held by men. It seems to show that all human thought is dependent on unique historical contexts that are preceded by more or less different contexts and that emerge out of their antecedents in a fundamentally unpredictable way: the foundations of human thought are laid by unpredictable experiences or decisions. Since all human thought belongs to specific historical situations, all human thought is bound to perish with the situation to which it belongs and to be superseded by new, unpredictable thoughts.

The historicist contention presents itself today as amply supported by historical evidence, or even as expressing an obvious fact. But if the fact is so obvious, it is hard to see how it could have escaped the notice of the most thoughtful men of the past. As regards the historical evidence, it is clearly insufficient to support the historicist contention. History teaches us that a given view has been abandoned in favor of another view by all men, or by all competent men, or perhaps only by the most vocal men; it does not teach us whether the change was sound or whether the rejected view deserved to be rejected. Only an impartial analysis of the view in question—an analysis that is not dazzled by the victory or stunned by the defeat of the adherents of the view concerned—could teach us anything regarding the worth of the view and hence regarding the meaning of the historical change. If the historicist contention is to have any solidity, it must be based not on history but on philosophy: on a philosophic analysis proving that all human thought depends ultimately on fickle and dark fate and not on evident principles accessible to man as man. The basic stratum of that philosophic analysis is a "critique of reason" that allegedly proves the impossibility of theoretical metaphysics and of philosophic ethics or natural right. Once all metaphysical and ethical views can be assumed to be, strictly speaking, untenable, that is, untenable as regards their claim to be simply true, their historical fate necessarily appears to be deserved. It then becomes a plausible, although not very important, task to trace the prevalence, at different times, of different metaphysical and ethical views, to the times at which they prevailed. But this leaves still intact the authority of the positive sciences. The second stratum of the philosophical analysis underlying historicism is the proof that the positive sciences rest on metaphysical foundations.

Taken by itself, this philosophic critique of philosophic and scientific thought—a continuation of the efforts of Hume and of Kant—would lead to skepticism. But skepticism and historicism are two entirely different things. Skepticism regards itself as, in principle, coeval with human thought; historicism regards itself as belonging to a specific historical situation. For the skeptic, all assertions are uncertain and therefore essentially arbitrary; for the historicist, the assertions that prevail at different times and in different civilizations are very far from being arbitrary. Historicism stems from a nonskeptical tradition—from that modern tradition which tried to define the limits of human knowledge and which therefore admitted that, within certain limits, genuine knowledge is possible. In contradistinction to all skepticism, historicism rests at least partly on such a critique of human thought as claims to articulate what is called "the experience of history."

No competent man of our age would regard as simply true the complete teaching of any thinker of the past. In every case experience has shown that the originator of the teaching took things for granted which must not be taken for granted or that he did not know certain facts or possibilities which were discovered in a later age. Up to now, all thought has proved to be in need of radical revisions or to be incomplete or limited in decisive respects. Furthermore, looking back at the past, we seem to observe that every progress of thought in one direction was bought at the price of a retrogression of thought in another respect: when a given limitation was overcome by a progress of thought, earlier important insights were invariably forgotten as a consequence of that progress. On the whole, there was then no progress, but merely a change from one type of limitation to another type. Finally, we seem to observe that the most important limitations of earlier thought were of such a nature that they could not possibly have been overcome by any effort of the earlier thinkers; to say nothing of other considerations, any effort of thought which led to the overcoming of specific limitations led to blindness in other respects. It is reasonable to assume that what has invariably happened up to now will happen again and again in the future. Human thought is essentially limited in such a way that its limitations differ from historical situation to historical situation and that the limitation characteristic of the thought of a given epoch cannot be overcome by any human effort. There always have been and there always will be surprising, wholly unexpected, changes of outlook which radically modify the meaning of all previously acquired knowledge. No view of the whole, and in particular no view of the whole of human life, can claim to be final or universally valid. Every doctrine, however seemingly final, will be superseded sooner or later by another doctrine. There is no reason to doubt that earlier thinkers had insights which are wholly inaccessible to us and which cannot become accessible to us, however carefully we might study their works, because our limitations prevent us from even suspecting the possibility of the insights in question. Since the limitations of human thought are essentially unknowable, it makes no sense to conceive of them in terms of social, economic, and other conditions, that is, in terms of knowable or analyzable phenomena: the limitations of human thought are set by fate.

The historicist argument has a certain plausibility which can easily be accounted for by the preponderance of dogmatism in the past. We are not permitted to forget Voltaire's complaint: "nous avons des bacheliers qui savent tout ce que ces grands hommes ignoraient."[7] Apart from this, many thinkers of the first rank have propounded all-comprehensive doctrines which they regarded as final in all important respects—doctrines which invariably have proved to be in need of radical revision. We ought therefore to welcome historicism as an ally in our fight against dogmatism. But dogmatism—or the inclination "to identify the goal of our thinking with the point at which we have become tired of thinking"[8]—is so natural to man that it is not likely to be a preserve of the past. We are forced to suspect that historicism is the guise in which dogmatism likes to appear in our age. It seems to us that what is called the "experience of history" is a bird's-eye view of the history of thought, as that history came to be seen under the combined influence of the belief in necessary progress (or in the impossibility of returning to the thought of the past) and of the belief in the supreme value of diversity or uniqueness (or of the equal right of all epochs or civilizations). Radical historicism does not seem to be in need of those beliefs any more. But it has never examined whether the "experience" to which it refers is not an outcome of those questionable beliefs.

When speaking of the "experience" of history, people imply that this "experience" is a comprehensive insight which arises out of historical knowledge but which cannot be reduced to historical knowledge. For historical knowledge is always extremely fragmentary and frequently very uncertain, whereas the alleged experience is supposedly global and certain. Yet it can hardly be doubted that the alleged experience ultimately rests on a number of historical observations. The question, then, is whether these observations entitle one to assert that the acquisition of new important insights necessarily leads to

7. "Âme," *Dictionnaire philosophique*, ed. J. Benda, I, 19.
8. See Lessing's letter to Mendelssohn of January 9, 1771.

the forgetting of earlier important insights and that the earlier thinkers could not possibly have thought of fundamental possibilities which came to the center of attention in later ages. It is obviously untrue to say, for instance, that Aristotle could not have conceived of the injustice of slavery, for he did conceive of it. One may say, however, that he could not have conceived of a world state. But why? The world state presupposes such a development of technology as Aristotle could never have dreamed of. That technological development, in its turn, required that science be regarded as essentially in the service of the "conquest of nature" and that technology be emancipated from any moral and political supervision. Aristotle did not conceive of a world state because he was absolutely certain that science is essentially theoretical and that the liberation of technology from moral and political control would lead to disastrous consequences: the fusion of science and the arts together with the unlimited or uncontrolled progress of technology has made universal and perpetual tyranny a serious possibility. Only a rash man would say that Aristotle's view—that is, his answers to the questions of whether or not science is essentially theoretical and whether or not technological progress is in need of strict moral or political control—has been refuted. But whatever one might think of his answers, certainly the fundamental questions to which they are the answers are identical with the fundamental questions that are of immediate concern to us today. Realizing this, we realize at the same time that the epoch which regarded Aristotle's fundamental questions as obsolete completely lacked clarity about what the fundamental issues are.

Far from legitimizing the historicist inference, history seems rather to prove that all human thought, and certainly all philosophic thought, is concerned with the same fundamental themes or the same fundamental problems, and therefore that there exists an unchanging framework which persists in all changes of human knowledge of both facts and principles. This inference is obviously compatible with the fact that clarity about these problems, the approach to them, and the suggested solutions to them differ more or less from thinker to thinker or from age to age. If the fundamental problems persist in all historical change, human thought is capable of transcending its historical limitation or of grasping something trans-historical. This would be the case even if it were true that all attempts to solve these problems are doomed to fail and that they are doomed to fail on account of the "historicity" of "all" human thought.

To leave it at this would amount to regarding the cause of natural right as hopeless. There cannot be natural right if all that man could know about right were the problem of right, or if the question of the principles of justice would admit of a variety of mutually exclusive answers, none of which could be proved to be superior to the others. There cannot be natural right if human thought, in spite of its essential incompleteness, is not capable of solving the problem of the principles of justice in a genuine and hence universally valid manner. More generally expressed, there cannot be natural right if human thought is not capable of acquiring genuine, universally valid, final knowledge within a limited sphere or genuine knowledge of specific subjects. Historicism cannot deny this possibility. For its own contention implies the admission of this possibility. By asserting that all human thought, or at least all relevant human thought, is historical, historicism admits that human thought is capable of acquiring a most important insight that is universally valid and that will in no way be affected by any future surprises. The historicist thesis is not an isolated assertion: it is inseparable from a view of the essential structure of human life. This view has the same trans-historical character or pretension as any natural right doctrine.

The historicist thesis is then exposed to a very obvious difficulty which cannot be solved but only evaded or obscured by considerations of a more subtle character. Historicism asserts that all human thoughts or beliefs are historical, and hence deservedly destined to perish; but historicism itself is a human thought; hence historicism can be of only temporary validity, or it cannot be simply true. To assert the historicist thesis means to doubt it and thus to transcend it. As a matter of fact, historicism claims to have brought to light a truth which has come to stay, a truth valid for all thought, for all time: however much thought has changed and will change, it will always remain historical. As regards the decisive insight into the essential character of all human thought and therewith into the essential character or limitation of humanity, history has reached its end. The historicist is not impressed by the prospect that historicism may be superseded in due time by the denial of historicism. He is certain that such a change would amount to a relapse of human thought into its most powerful delusion. Historicism thrives on the fact that it inconsistently exempts itself from its own verdict about all human thought. The historicist thesis is self-contradictory or absurd. We cannot see the historical character of "all" thought—that is, of all thought with the exception of the historicist insight and its implications—without transcending history, without grasping something trans-historical.

If we call all thought that is radically historical a "comprehensive world view" or a part of such a view, we must say: historicism is not itself a comprehensive world view but an analysis of all comprehensive world views, an exposition of the essential character of all such views. Thought that recognizes the relativity of all comprehensive views has a different character from thought which is under the spell of, or which adopts, a comprehensive view. The former is absolute and neutral; the latter is relative and committed. The former is a theoretical insight that transcends history; the latter is the outcome of a fateful dispensation.

The radical historicist refuses to admit the trans-historical character of the historicist thesis. At the same time he recognizes the absurdity of unqualified historicism as a theoretical thesis. He denies, therefore, the possibility of a theoretical or objective analysis, which as such would be trans-historical, of the various comprehensive views or "historical worlds" or "cultures." This denial was decisively prepared by Nietzsche's attack on nineteenth-century historicism, which claimed to be a theoretical view. According to Nietzsche, the theoretical analysis of human life that realizes the relativity of all comprehensive views and thus depreciates them would make human life itself impossible, for it would destroy the protecting atmosphere within which life or culture or action is alone possible. Moreover, since the theoretical analysis has its basis outside of life, it will never be able to understand life. The theoretical analysis of life is noncommittal and fatal to commitment, but life means commitment. To avert the danger to life, Nietzsche could choose one of two ways: he could insist on the strictly esoteric character of the theoretical analysis of life—that is, restore the Platonic notion of the noble delusion—or else he could deny the possibility of theory proper and so conceive of thought as essentially subservient to, or dependent on, life or fate. If not Nietzsche himself, at any rate his successors adopted the second alternative.[9]

The thesis of radical historicism can be stated as follows. All understanding, all knowledge, however limited and "scientific," presupposes a frame of reference; it presupposes a horizon, a comprehensive view within which understanding and knowing take place. Only such a comprehensive vision

9. For the understanding of this choice, one has to consider its connection with Nietzsche's sympathy with "Callicles," on the one hand, and his preferring the "tragic life" to the theoretical life, on the other (see Plato *Gorgias* 481ᵈ and 502ᵇ ff., and *Laws* 658ᵈ2–5; compare Nietzsche's *Vom Nutzen und Nachteil der Historie für das Leben* [Insel-Bücherei ed.], p. 73). This passage reveals clearly the fact that Nietzsche adopted what one may consider the fundamental premise of the historical school.

makes possible any seeing, any observation, any orientation. The comprehensive view of the whole cannot be validated by reasoning, since it is the basis of all reasoning. Accordingly, there is a variety of such comprehensive views, each as legitimate as any other: we have to choose such a view without any rational guidance. It is absolutely necessary to choose one; neutrality or suspension of judgment is impossible. Our choice has no support but itself; it is not supported by any objective or theoretical certainty; it is separated from nothingness, the complete absence of meaning, by nothing but our choice of it. Strictly speaking, we cannot choose among different views. A single comprehensive view is imposed on us by fate: the horizon within which all our understanding and orientation take place is produced by the fate of the individual or of his society. All human thought depends on fate, on something that thought cannot master and whose workings it cannot anticipate. Yet the support of the horizon produced by fate is ultimately the choice of the individual, since that fate has to be accepted by the individual. We are free in the sense that we are free either to choose in anguish the world view and the standards imposed on us by fate or else to lose ourselves in illusory security or in despair.

The radical historicist asserts, then, that only to thought that is itself committed or "historical" does other committed or "historical" thought disclose itself, and, above all, that only to thought that is itself committed or "historical" does the true meaning of the "historicity" of all genuine thought disclose itself. The historicist thesis expresses a fundamental experience which, by its nature, is incapable of adequate expression on the level of noncommitted or detached thought. The evidence of that experience may indeed be blurred, but it cannot be destroyed by the inevitable logical difficulties from which all expressions of such experiences suffer. With a view to his fundamental experience, the radical historicist denies that the final and, in this sense, trans-historical character of the historicist thesis makes doubtful the content of that thesis. The final and irrevocable insight into the historical character of all thought would transcend history only if that insight were accessible to man as man and hence, in principle, at all times; but it does not transcend history if it essentially belongs to a specific historic situation. It belongs to a specific historic situation: that situation is not merely the condition of the historicist insight but its source.[10]

All natural right doctrines claim that the fundamentals of justice are, in principle, accessible to man as man. They presuppose, therefore, that a most important truth can, in principle, be accessible to man as man. Denying this presupposition, radical historicism asserts that the basic insight into the essential limitation of all human thought is not accessible to man as man, or that it is not the result of the progress or the labor of human thought, but that it is an unforeseeable gift of unfathomable fate. It is due to fate that the essential dependence of thought on fate is realized now, and was not realized in earlier times. Historicism has this in common with all other thought, that it depends on fate. It differs from all other thought in this, that, thanks to fate, it has been given to realize the radical dependence of thought on fate. We are absolutely ignorant of the surprises which fate may have in store for later generations, and fate may in the future again conceal what it has revealed to us; but this does not impair the truth of that revelation. One does not have to transcend history in order to see the historical character of all thought: there is a privileged moment, an absolute moment in the historical process, a moment in which the essential character of all thought becomes transparent. In exempting itself from its own verdict,

10. The distinction between "condition" and "source" corresponds to the difference between Aristotle's "history" of philosophy in the first book of the *Metaphysics* and historicist history.

historicism claims merely to mirror the character of historical reality or to be true to the facts; the self-contradictory character of the historicist thesis should be charged not to historicism but to reality.

The assumption of an absolute moment in history is essential to historicism. In this, historicism surreptitiously follows the precedent set in a classic manner by Hegel. Hegel had taught that every philosophy is the conceptual expression of the spirit of its time, and yet he maintained the absolute truth of his own system of philosophy by ascribing absolute character to his own time; he assumed that his own time was the end of history and hence the absolute moment. Historicism explicitly denies that the end of history has come, but it implicitly asserts the opposite: no possible future change of orientation can legitimately make doubtful the decisive insight into the inescapable dependence of thought on fate, and therewith into the essential character of human life; in the decisive respect the end of history, that is, of the history of thought, has come. But one cannot simply assume that one lives or thinks in the absolute moment; one must show, somehow, how the absolute moment can be recognized as such. According to Hegel, the absolute moment is the one in which philosophy, or quest for wisdom, has been transformed into wisdom, that is, the moment in which the fundamental riddles have been fully solved. Historicism, however, stands or falls by the denial of the possibility of theoretical metaphysics and of philosophic ethics or natural right; it stands or falls by the denial of the solubility of the fundamental riddles. According to historicism, therefore, the absolute moment must be the moment in which the insoluble character of the fundamental riddles has become fully manifest or in which the fundamental delusion of the human mind has been dispelled.

But one might realize the insoluble character of the fundamental riddles and still continue to see in the understanding of these riddles the task of philosophy; one would thus merely replace a nonhistoricist and dogmatic philosophy by a non-historicist and skeptical philosophy. Historicism goes beyond skepticism. It assumes that philosophy, in the full and original sense of the term, namely, the attempt to replace opinions about the whole by knowledge of the whole, is not only incapable of reaching its goal but absurd, because the very idea of philosophy rests on dogmatic, that is, arbitrary, premises or, more specifically, on premises that are only "historical and relative." For clearly, if philosophy, or the attempt to replace opinions by knowledge, itself rests on mere opinions, philosophy is absurd.

The most influential attempts to establish the dogmatic and hence arbitrary or historically relative character of philosophy proper proceed along the following lines. Philosophy or the attempt to replace opinions about the whole by knowledge of the whole, presupposes that the whole is knowable, that is, intelligible. This presupposition leads to the consequence that the whole as it is in itself is identified with the whole in so far as it is intelligible or in so far as it can become an object; it leads to the identification of "being" with "intelligible" or "object"; it leads to the dogmatic disregard of everything that cannot become an object, that is, an object for the knowing subject, or the dogmatic disregard of everything that cannot be mastered by the subject. Furthermore, to say that the whole is knowable or intelligible is tantamount to saying that the whole has a permanent structure or that the whole as such is unchangeable or always the same. If this is the case, it is, in principle, possible to predict how the whole will be at any future time: the future of the whole can be anticipated by thought. The presupposition mentioned is said to have its root in the dogmatic identification of "to be" in the highest sense with "to be always," or in the fact that philosophy understands "to be" in such a sense that "to be" in the highest sense must mean "to be always." The dogmatic character of the basic premise of philosophy is said to have been revealed by the discovery of history or of the "historicity" of human life. The meaning of that discovery can be expressed in theses like these: what is called the whole is actually always incomplete and therefore not truly a whole; the whole is essentially changing in such a manner that its future cannot be predicted; the whole as it is in itself can never be grasped, or it is not intelligible; human thought essentially depends on something that cannot be anticipated or that can never be an object or that can never be mastered by the subject; "to be" in the highest sense cannot mean—or, at any rate, it does not necessarily mean—"to be always."

We cannot even attempt to discuss these theses. We must leave them with the following observation. Radical historicism compels us to realize the bearing of the fact that the very idea of natural right presupposes the possibility of philosophy in the full and original meaning of the term. It compels us at the same time to realize the need for unbiased reconsideration of the most elementary premises whose validity is presupposed by philosophy. The question of the validity of these premises cannot be disposed of by adopting or clinging to a more or less persistent tradition of philosophy, for it is of the essence of traditions that they cover or conceal their humble foundations by erecting impressive edifices on them. Nothing ought to be said or done which could create the impression that unbiased reconsideration of the most elementary premises of philosophy is a merely academic or historical affair. Prior to such reconsideration, however, the issue of natural right can only remain an open question.

For we cannot assume that the issue has been finally settled by historicism. The "experience of history" and the less ambiguous experience of the complexity of human affairs may blur, but they cannot extinguish, the evidence of those simple experiences regarding right and wrong which are at the bottom of the philosophic contention that there is a natural right. Historicism either ignores or else distorts these experiences. Furthermore, the most thoroughgoing attempt to establish historicism culminated in the assertion that if and when there are no human beings, there may be *entia*, but there cannot be *esse*, that is, that there can be *entia* while there is no *esse*. There is an obvious connection between this assertion and the rejection of the view that "to be" in the highest sense means "to be always." Besides, there has always been a glaring contrast between the way in which historicism understands the thought of the past and genuine understanding of the thought of the past; the undeniable possibility of historical objectivity is explicitly or implicitly denied by historicism in all its forms. Above all, in the transition from early (theoretical) to radical ("existentialist") historicism, the "experience of history" was never submitted to critical analysis. It was taken for granted that it is a genuine experience and not a questionable interpretation of experience. The question was not raised whether what is really experienced does not allow of an entirely different and possibly more adequate interpretation. In particular, the "experience of history" does not make doubtful the view that the fundamental problems, such as the problems of justice, persist or retain their identity in all historical change, however much they may be obscured by the temporary denial of their relevance and however variable or provisional all human solutions to these problems may be. In grasping these problems as problems, the human mind liberates itself from its historical limitations. No more is needed to legitimize philosophy in its original, Socratic sense: philosophy is knowledge that one does not know; that is to say, it is knowledge of what one does not know, or awareness of the fundamental problems and, therewith, of the fundamental alternatives regarding their solution that are coeval with human thought.

If the existence and even the possibility of natural right must remain an open question as long as the issue between historicism and nonhistoricist philosophy is not settled, our most urgent need is to understand that issue. The issue is not understood if it is seen merely in the way in which it presents itself from the point of view of historicism; it must also be seen in the way in which it presents itself from the point of view of nonhistoricist philosophy. This means, for all practical purposes, that the problem of historicism must first be considered from the point of view of classical philosophy, which is nonhistoricist thought in its pure form. Our most urgent need can then be satisfied only by means of historical studies which would enable us to understand classical philosophy exactly as it understood itself, and not in the way in which it presents itself on the basis of historicism. We need, in the first place, a nonhistoricist understanding of nonhistoricist philosophy. But we need no less urgently a nonhistoricist understanding of historicism, that is, an understanding of the genesis of historicism that does not take for granted the soundness of historicism.

Historicism assumes that modern man's turn toward history implied the divination and eventually the discovery of a dimension of reality that had escaped classical thought, namely, of the historical dimension. If this is granted, one will be forced in the end into extreme historicism. But if historicism cannot be taken for granted, the question becomes inevitable whether what was hailed in the nineteenth century as a discovery was not, in fact, an invention, that is, an arbitrary interpretation of phenomena which had always been known and which had been interpreted much more adequately prior to the emergence of "the historical consciousness" than afterward. We have to raise the question whether what is called the "discovery" of history is not, in fact, an artificial and makeshift solution to a problem that could arise only on the basis of very questionable premises.

I suggest this line of approach. "History" meant throughout the ages primarily political history. Accordingly, what is called the "discovery" of history is the work, not of philosophy in general, but of political philosophy. It was a predicament peculiar to eighteenth-century political philosophy that led to the emergence of the historical school. The political philosophy of the eighteenth century was a doctrine of natural right. It consisted in a peculiar interpretation of natural right, namely, the specifically modern interpretation. Historicism is the ultimate outcome of the crisis of modern natural right. The crisis of modern natural right or of modern political philosophy could become a crisis of philosophy as such only because in the modern centuries philosophy as such had become thoroughly politicized. Originally, philosophy had been the humanizing quest for the eternal order, and hence it had been a pure source of humane inspiration and aspiration. Since the seventeenth century, philosophy has become a weapon, and hence an instrument. It was this politicization of philosophy that was discerned as the root of our troubles by an intellectual who denounced the treason of the intellectuals. He committed the fatal mistake, however, of ignoring the essential difference between intellectuals and philosophers. In this he remained the dupe of the delusion which he denounced. For the politicization of philosophy consists precisely in this, that the difference between intellectuals and philosophers—a difference formerly known as the difference between gentlemen and philosophers, on the one hand, and the difference between sophists or rhetoricians and philosophers, on the other—becomes blurred and finally disappears.

II

NATURAL RIGHT AND THE DISTINCTION
BETWEEN FACTS AND VALUES

✻

THE historicist contention can be reduced to the assertion
that natural right is impossible because philosophy in the
full sense of the term is impossible. Philosophy is possible only
if there is an absolute horizon or a natural horizon in contradistinction to the historically changing horizons or the caves.
In other words, philosophy is possible only if man, while incapable of acquiring wisdom or full understanding of the
whole, is capable of knowing what he does not know, that is
to say, of grasping the fundamental problems and therewith
the fundamental alternatives, which are, in principle, coeval
with human thought. But the possibility of philosophy is
only the necessary and not the sufficient condition of natural
right. The possibility of philosophy does not require more
than that the fundamental problems always be the same; but
there cannot be natural right if the fundamental problem of
political philosophy cannot be solved in a final manner.

If philosophy in general is possible, political philosophy in
particular is possible. Political philosophy is possible if man
is capable of understanding the fundamental political alternative which is at the bottom of the ephemeral or accidental
alternatives. Yet if political philosophy is limited to understanding the fundamental political alternative, it is of no practical value. It would be unable to answer the question of what
the ultimate goal of wise action is. It would have to delegate
the crucial decision to blind choice. The whole galaxy of political philosophers from Plato to Hegel, and certainly all ad-

35

herents of natural right, assumed that the fundamental political problem is susceptible of a final solution. This assumption ultimately rested on the Socratic answer to the question of how man ought to live. By realizing that we are ignorant of the most important things, we realize at the same time that the most important thing for us, or the one thing needful, is quest for knowledge of the most important things or quest for wisdom. That this conclusion is not barren of political consequences is known to every reader of Plato's *Republic* or of Aristotle's *Politics*. It is true that the successful quest for wisdom might lead to the result that wisdom is not the one thing needful. But this result would owe its relevance to the fact that it is the result of the quest for wisdom: the very disavowal of reason must be reasonable disavowal. Regardless of whether this possibility affects the validity of the Socratic answer, the perennial conflict between the Socratic and the anti-Socratic answer creates the impression that the Socratic answer is as arbitrary as its opposite, or that the perennial conflict is insoluble. Accordingly, many present-day social scientists who are not historicists or who do admit the existence of fundamental and unchanging alternatives deny that human reason is capable of solving the conflict between these alternatives. Natural right is then rejected today not only because all human thought is held to be historical but likewise because it is thought that there is a variety of unchangeable principles of right or of goodness which conflict with one another, and none of which can be proved to be superior to the others.

Substantially, this is the position taken by Max Weber. Our discussion will be limited to a critical analysis of Weber's view. No one since Weber has devoted a comparable amount of intelligence, assiduity, and almost fanatical devotion to the basic problem of the social sciences. Whatever may have been his errors, he is the greatest social scientist of our century.

Weber, who regarded himself as a disciple of the historical

school[1] came very close to historicism, and a strong case can be made for the view that his reservations against historicism were halfhearted and inconsistent with the broad tendency of his thinking. He parted company with the historical school, not because it had rejected natural norms, i.e., norms that are both universal and objective, but because it had tried to establish standards that were particular and historical indeed, but still objective. He objected to the historical school not because it had blurred the idea of natural right but because it had preserved natural right in a historical guise, instead of rejecting it altogether. The historical school had given natural right a historical character by insisting on the ethnic character of all genuine right or by tracing all genuine right to unique folk minds, as well as by assuming that the history of mankind is a meaningful process or a process ruled by intelligible necessity. Weber rejected both assumptions as metaphysical, i.e., as based on the dogmatic premise that reality is rational. Since Weber assumed that the real is always individual, he could state the premise of the historical school also in these terms: the individual is an emanation from the general or from the whole. According to Weber, however, individual or partial phenomena can be understood only as effects of other individual or partial phenomena, and never as effects of wholes such as folk minds. To try to explain historical or unique phenomena by tracing them to general laws or to unique wholes means to assume gratuitously that there are mysterious or unanalyzable forces which move the historical actors.[2] There is no "meaning" of history apart from the "subjective" meaning or the intentions which animate the historical actors. But these intentions are of such limited power that the actual out-

1. *Gesammelte politische Schriften*, p. 22; *Gesammelte Aufsätze zur Wissenschaftslehre*, p. 208.

2. *Wissenschaftslehre*, pp. 13, 15, 18, 19, 28, 35–37, 134, 137, 174, 195, 230; *Gesammelte Aufsätze zur Sozial- und Wirtschaftsgeschichte*, p. 517.

come is in most cases wholly unintended. Yet the actual out-come—historical fate—which is not planned by God or man, molds not only our way of life but our very thoughts, and especially does it determine our ideals.[3] Weber was, however, still too much impressed by the idea of science to accept historicism without qualification. In fact, one is tempted to suggest that the primary motive of his opposition to the historical school and to historicism in general was devotion to the idea of empirical science as it prevailed in his generation. The idea of science forced him to insist on the fact that all science as such is independent of Weltanschauung: both natural and social science claim to be equally valid for Westerners and for Chinese, i.e., for people whose "world views" are radically different. The historical genesis of modern science—the fact that it is of Western origin—is wholly irrelevant as regards its validity. Nor did Weber have any doubt that modern science is absolutely superior to any earlier form of thinking orientation in the world of nature and society. That superiority can be established objectively, by reference to the rules of logic.[4] There arose, however, in Weber's mind this difficulty in regard to the social sciences in particular. He insisted on the objective and universal validity of social science in so far as it is a body of true propositions. Yet these propositions are only a part of social science. They are the results of scientific investigation or the answers to questions. The questions which we address to social phenomena depend on the direction of our interest or on our point of view, and these on our value ideas. But the value ideas are historically relative. Hence the substance of social science is radically historical; for it is the value ideas and the direction of interest which determine the whole conceptual framework of the social sciences. Accordingly, it does not

3. *Wissenschaftslehre*, pp. 152, 183, 224 n.; *Politische Schriften*, pp. 19, 437; *Gesammelte Aufsätze zur Religionssoziologie*, I, 82, 524.

4. *Wissenschaftslehre*, pp. 58–60, 97, 105, 111, 155, 160, 184.

make sense to speak of a "natural frame of reference" or to expect a final system of the basic concepts: all frames of reference are ephemeral. Every conceptual scheme used by social science articulates the basic problems, and these problems change with the change of the social and cultural situation. Social science is necessarily the understanding of society from the point of view of the present. What is trans-historical are merely the findings regarding the facts and their causes. More precisely, what is trans-historical is the validity of these findings; but the importance or significance of any findings depends on value ideas and hence on historically changeable principles. Ultimately, this applies to every science. All science presupposes that science is valuable, but this presupposition is the product of certain cultures, and hence historically relative.[5] However, the concrete and historical value ideas, of which there is an indefinitely large variety, contain elements of a trans-historical character: the ultimate values are as timeless as the principles of logic. It is the recognition of timeless values that distinguishes Weber's position most significantly from historicism. Not so much historicism as a peculiar notion of timeless values is the basis of his rejection of natural right.[6]

Weber never explained what he understood by "values." He was primarily concerned with the relations of values to facts. Facts and values are absolutely heterogeneous, as is shown directly by the absolute heterogeneity of questions of fact and questions of value. No conclusion can be drawn from any fact as to its valuable character, nor can we infer the factual character of something from its being valuable or desirable. Neither time-serving nor wishful thinking is supported by reason. By proving that a given social order is the goal of the historical process, one does not say anything as to the value or desirable character of that order. By showing that

5. *Ibid.*, pp. 60, 152, 170, 184, 206–9, 213–14, 259, 261–62.
6. *Ibid.*, pp. 60, 62, 152, 213, 247, 463, 467, 469, 472; *Politische Schriften*, pp. 22, 60.

certain religious or ethical ideas had a very great effect or no effect, one does not say anything about the value of those ideas. To understand a factual or possible evaluation is something entirely different from approving or forgiving that evaluation. Weber contended that the absolute heterogeneity of facts and values necessitates the ethically neutral character of social science: social science can answer questions of facts and their causes; it is not competent to answer questions of value. He insisted very strongly on the role played by values in social science: the objects of social science are constituted by "reference to values." Without such "reference," there would be no focus of interest, no reasonable selection of themes, no principles of distinction between relevant and irrelevant facts. Through "reference to values" the objects of the social sciences emerge out of the ocean or morass of facts. But Weber insisted no less strongly on the fundamental difference between "reference to values" and "value judgments": by saying that something is relevant with regard to political freedom, for example, one does not take a stand for or against political freedom. The social scientist does not evaluate the objects constituted by "reference to values"; he merely explains them by tracing them to their causes. The values to which social science refers and among which acting man chooses are in need of clarification. This clarification is the function of social philosophy. But even social philosophy cannot solve the crucial value problems. It cannot criticize value judgments that are not self-contradictory.[7]

Weber contended that his notion of a "value-free" or ethically neutral social science is fully justified by what he re-

7. *Wissenschaftslehre*, pp. 90, 91, 124, 125, 150, 151, 154, 155, 461–65, 469–73, 475, 545, 550; *Gesammelte Aufsätze zur Soziologie und Sozialpolitik*, pp. 417–18, 476–77, 482. As regards the connection between the limitation of social science to the study of facts and the belief in the authoritative character of natural science, see *Soziologie und Sozialpolitik*, p. 478.

garded as the most fundamental of all oppositions, namely, the opposition of the Is and the Ought, or the opposition of reality and norm or value.[8] But the conclusion from the radical heterogeneity of the Is and the Ought to the impossibility of an evaluating social science is obviously not valid. Let us assume that we had genuine knowledge of right and wrong, or of the Ought, or of the true value system. That knowledge, while not derived from empirical science, would legitimately direct all empirical social science; it would be the foundation of all empirical social science. For social science is meant to be of practical value. It tries to find means for given ends. For this purpose it has to understand the ends. Regardless of whether the ends are "given" in a different manner from the means, the end and the means belong together; therefore, "the end belongs to the same science as the means."[9] If there were genuine knowledge of the ends, that knowledge would naturally guide all search for means. There would be no reason to delegate knowledge of the ends to social philosophy and the search for the means to an independent social science. Based on genuine knowledge of the true ends, social science would search for the proper means to those ends; it would lead up to objective and specific value judgments regarding policies. Social science would be a truly policy-making, not to say architectonic, science rather than a mere supplier of data for the real policy-makers. The true reason why Weber insisted on the ethically neutral character of social science as well as of social philosophy was, then, not his belief in the fundamental opposition of the Is and the Ought but his belief that there cannot be any genuine knowledge of the Ought. He denied to man any science, empirical or rational, any knowledge, scientific or philosophic, of the true value system: the true value system does not exist; there is a variety of values which are of the same

8. *Wissenschaftslehre*, pp. 32, 40 n., 127 n., 148, 401, 470–71, 501, 577.

9. Aristotle *Physics* 194ª26–27.

rank, whose demands conflict with one another, and whose conflict cannot be solved by human reason. Social science or social philosophy can do no more than clarify that conflict and all its implications; the solution has to be left to the free, non-rational decision of each individual.

I contend that Weber's thesis necessarily leads to nihilism or to the view that every preference, however evil, base, or insane, has to be judged before the tribunal of reason to be as legitimate as any other preference. An unmistakable sign of this necessity is supplied by a statement of Weber about the prospects of Western civilization. He saw this alternative: either a spiritual renewal ("wholly new prophets or a powerful renaissance of old thoughts and ideals") or else "mechanized petrifaction, varnished by a kind of convulsive sense of self-importance," i.e., the extinction of every human possibility but that of "specialists without spirit or vision and voluptuaries without heart." Confronted with this alternative, Weber felt that the decision in favor of either possibility would be a judgment of value or of faith, and hence beyond the competence of reason.[10] This amounts to an admission that the way of life of "specialists without spirit or vision and voluptuaries without heart" is as defensible as the ways of life recommended by Amos or by Socrates.

To see this more clearly and to see at the same time why Weber could conceal from himself the nihilistic consequence of his doctrine of values, we have to follow his thought step by step. In following this movement toward its end we shall inevitably reach a point beyond which the scene is darkened by the shadow of Hitler. Unfortunately, it does not go without saying that in our examination we must avoid the fallacy that in the last decades has frequently been used as a substitute for the *reductio ad absurdum:* the *reductio ad Hitlerum.* A view is not

10. Compare *Religionssoziologie*, I, 204, with *Wissenschaftslehre*, pp. 469–70 and 150–51.

refuted by the fact that it happens to have been shared by Hitler.

Weber started out from a combination of the views of Kant as they were understood by certain neo-Kantians and of the views of the historical school. From neo-Kantianism he took over his general notion of the character of science, as well as of "individual" ethics. Accordingly, he rejected utilitarianism and every form of eudemonism. From the historical school he took over the view that there is no possible social or cultural order which can be said to be *the* right or rational order. He combined the two positions by means of the distinction between moral commands (or ethical imperatives) and cultural values. Moral commands appeal to our conscience, whereas cultural values appeal to our feelings: the individual ought to fulfil his moral duties, whereas it depends entirely on his arbitrary will whether he wishes to realize cultural ideals or not. Cultural ideals or values lack the specific obligatory character of the moral imperatives. These imperatives have a dignity of their own, with whose recognition Weber seemed to be greatly concerned. But, precisely because of the fundamental difference between moral commands and cultural values, ethics proper is silent in regard to cultural and social questions. Whereas gentlemen, or honest men, necessarily agree as to things moral, they legitimately disagree in regard to such things as Gothic architecture, private property, monogamy, democracy, and so on.[11]

One is thus led to think that Weber admitted the existence of absolutely binding rational norms, namely, the moral imperatives. Yet one sees immediately afterward that what he said about the moral commands is not much more than the residue of a tradition in which he was brought up and which, indeed, never ceased to determine him as a human being. What

11. *Politische Schriften*, p. 22; *Religionssoziologie*, I, 33–35; *Wissenschaftslehre*, pp. 30, 148, 154, 155, 252, 463, 466, 471; *Soziologie und Sozialpolitik*, p. 418.

he really thought was that ethical imperatives are as subjective as cultural values. According to him, it is as legitimate to reject ethics in the name of cultural values as it is to reject cultural values in the name of ethics, or to adopt any combination of both types of norm which is not self-contradictory.[12] This decision was the inevitable consequence of his notion of ethics. He could not reconcile his view that ethics is silent about the right social order with the undeniable ethical relevance of social questions, except by "relativizing" ethics. It was on this basis that he developed his concept of "personality" or of the dignity of man. The true meaning of "personality" depends on the true meaning of "freedom." Provisionally, one may say that human action is free to the extent to which it is not affected by external compulsion or irresistible emotions but is guided by rational consideration of means and ends. Yet true freedom requires ends of a certain kind, and these ends have to be adopted in a certain manner. The ends must be anchored in ultimate values. Man's dignity, his being exalted far above everything merely natural or above all brutes, consists in his setting up autonomously his ultimate values, in making these values his constant ends, and in rationally choosing the means to these ends. The dignity of man consists in his autonomy, i.e., in the individual's freely choosing his own values or his own ideals or in obeying the injunction: "Become what thou art."[13]

At this stage, we still have something resembling an objective norm, a categoric imperative: "Thou shalt have ideals." That imperative is "formal"; it does not determine in any way the content of the ideals, but it might still seem to establish an intelligible or nonarbitrary standard that would allow us to distinguish in a responsible manner between human excel-

12. *Wissenschaftslehre*, pp. 38, n. 2, 40–41, 155, 463, 466–69; *Soziologie und Sozialpolitik*, p. 423.

13. *Wissenschaftslehre*, pp. 38, 40, 132–33, 469–70, 533–34, 555.

lence and depravity. Therewith it might seem to create a universal brotherhood of all noble souls; of all men who are not enslaved by their appetites, their passions, and their selfish interests; of all "idealists"—of all men who can justly esteem or respect one another. Yet this is only a delusion. What seems at first to be an invisible church proves to be a war of everybody against everybody or, rather, pandemonium. Weber's own formulation of his categoric imperative was "Follow thy demon" or "Follow thy god or demon." It would be unfair to complain that Weber forgot the possibility of evil demons, although he may have been guilty of underestimating them. If he had thought only of good demons, he would have been forced to admit an objective criterion that would allow him to distinguish in principle between good and evil demons. His categoric imperative actually means "Follow thy demon, regardless of whether he is a good or evil demon." For there is an insoluble, deadly conflict between the various values among which man has to choose. What one man considers following God another will consider, with equal right, following the Devil. The categoric imperative has then to be formulated as follows: "Follow God or the Devil as you will, but, whichever choice you make, make it with all your heart, with all your soul, and with all your power."[14] What is absolutely base is to follow one's appetites, passions, or self-interest and to be indifferent or lukewarm toward ideals or values, toward gods or devils.

Weber's "idealism," i.e., his recognition of all "ideal" goals or of all "causes," seems to permit of a nonarbitrary distinction between excellence and baseness or depravity. At the same time, it culminates in the imperative "Follow God or the Devil," which means, in nontheological language, "Strive resolutely for excellence or baseness." For if Weber meant to say that choosing value system A in preference to

14. *Ibid.*, pp. 455, 466–69, 546; *Politische Schriften*, pp. 435–36.

value system B is compatible with genuine respect for value system B or does not mean rejecting value system B as base, he could not have known what he was talking about in speaking of a choice between God and Devil; he must have meant a mere difference of tastes while talking of a deadly conflict. It thus appears that for Weber, in his capacity as a social philosopher, excellence and baseness completely lost their primary meaning. Excellence now means devotion to a cause, be it good or evil, and baseness means indifference to all causes. Excellence and baseness thus understood are excellence and baseness of a higher order. They belong to a dimension that is exalted far above the dimension of action. They can be seen only after one has completely broken away from the world in which we have to make decisions, although they present themselves as preceding any decision. They are the correlates of a purely theoretical attitude toward the world of action. That theoretical attitude implies equal respect for all causes; but such respect is possible only for him who is not devoted to any cause. Now if excellence is devotion to a cause and baseness indifference to all causes, the theoretical attitude toward all causes would have to be qualified as base. No wonder, then, that Weber was driven to question the value of theory, of science, of reason, of the realm of the mind, and therewith of both the moral imperatives and the cultural values. He was forced to dignify what he called "purely 'vitalistic' values" to the same height as the moral commands and the cultural values. The "purely 'vitalistic' values" may be said to belong entirely to "the sphere of one's own individuality," being, that is, purely personal and in no way principles of a cause. Hence they are not, strictly speaking, values. Weber contended explicitly that it is perfectly legitimate to take a hostile attitude toward all impersonal and supra-personal values and ideals, and therewith toward every concern with "personality" or the dignity of man as previously defined; for, according to him, there is only one way to become a "personality," namely, through absolute devotion to a cause. At the moment when the "vitalistic" values are recognized as of equal rank with cultural values, the categoric imperative "Thou shalt have ideals" is being transformed into the command "Thou shalt live passionately." Baseness no longer means indifference to any of the incompatible great objects of humanity, but being engrossed with one's comfort and prestige. But with what right except that of arbitrary whim can one reject the way of life of the philistine in the name of "vitalistic" values, if one can reject the moral commands in the name of "vitalistic" values? It was in tacit recognition of the impossibility of stopping on the downward path that Weber frankly admitted that it is merely a subjective judgment of faith or value if one despises "specialists without spirit or vision and voluptuaries without heart" as degraded human beings. The final formulation of Weber's ethical principle would thus be "Thou shalt have preferences"—an Ought whose fulfilment is fully guaranteed by the Is.[15]

One last obstacle to complete chaos seems to remain. Whatever preferences I may have or choose, I must act rationally: I must be honest with myself, I must be consistent in my adherence to my fundamental objectives, and I must rationally choose the means required by my ends. But why? What difference can this still make after we have been reduced to a condition in which the maxims of the heartless voluptuary as well as those of the sentimental philistine have to be regarded as no less defensible than those of the idealist, of the gentleman, or of the saint? We cannot take seriously this belated insistence on responsibility and sanity, this inconsistent concern with consistency, this irrational praise of rationality. Can one not very easily make out a stronger case for inconsistency than Weber has made out for preferring cultural values to the moral

15. *Wissenschaftslehre*, pp. 61, 152, 456, 468–69, 531; *Politische Schriften*, pp. 443–44.

imperatives? Does one not necessarily imply the depreciation of rationality in every form at the moment in which one declares it legitimate to make "vitalistic" values one's supreme values? Weber would probably have insisted that, whatever preference one adopts, one has to be honest, at least with one's self, and especially that one must not make the dishonest attempt to give one's preferences an objective foundation which would necessarily be a sham foundation. But, should he have done so, he would merely have been inconsistent. For, according to him, it is equally legitimate to will or not to will truth, or to reject truth in favor of the beautiful and the sacred.[16] Why, then, should one not prefer pleasing delusions or edifying myths to the truth? Weber's regard for "rational self-determination" and "intellectual honesty" is a trait of his character which has no basis but his nonrational preference for "rational self-determination" and "intellectual honesty."

One may call the nihilism to which Weber's thesis leads "noble nihilism." For that nihilism stems not from a primary indifference to everything noble but from the alleged or real insight into the baseless character of everything thought to be noble. Yet one cannot make a distinction between noble and base nihilism except if one has some knowledge of what is noble and what is base. But such knowledge transcends nihilism. In order to be entitled to describe Weber's nihilism as noble, one must have broken with his position.

One could make the following objection to the foregoing criticism. What Weber really meant cannot be expressed in terms of "values" or "ideals" at all; it is much more adequately expressed by his quotation "Become what thou art," i.e., "Choose thy fate." According to this interpretation, Weber rejected objective norms because objective norms are incompatible with human freedom or with the possibility of acting. We must leave it open whether this reason for rejecting

16. *Wissenschaftslehre*, pp. 60–61, 184, 546, 554.

objective norms is a good reason and whether the nihilistic consequence would be avoided by this interpretation of Weber's view. It is sufficient to remark that its acceptance would require a break with the notions of "value" and "ideal" on which Weber's actual doctrine is built and that it is that actual doctrine, and not the possible interpretation mentioned, which dominates present-day social science.

Many social scientists of our time seem to regard nihilism as a minor inconvenience which wise men would bear with equanimity, since it is the price one has to pay for obtaining that highest good, a truly scientific social science. They seem to be satisfied with any scientific findings, although they cannot be more than "barren truths which generate no conclusion," the conclusions being generated by purely subjective value judgments or arbitrary preferences. We have to consider, therefore, whether social science as a purely theoretical pursuit, but still as a pursuit leading to the understanding of social phenomena, is possible on the basis of the distinction between facts and values.

We remind ourselves again of Weber's statement about the prospects of Western civilization. As we observed, Weber saw the following alternative: either a spiritual renewal or else "mechanized petrifaction," i.e., the extinction of every human possibility except that of "specialists without spirit or vision and voluptuaries without heart." He concluded: "But by making this statement we enter the province of judgments of value and faith with which this purely historical presentation shall not be burdened." It is not proper, then, for the historian or social scientist, it is not permissible, that he truthfully describe a certain type of life as spiritually empty or describe specialists without vision and voluptuaries without heart as what they are. But is this not absurd? Is it not the plain duty of the social scientist truthfully and faithfully to present social phenomena? How can we give a causal explanation of a social phenomenon if we do not first see it as what it is? Do we not know petrifaction or spiritual emptiness when we see it? And if someone is incapable of seeing phenomena of this kind, is he not disqualified by this very fact from being a social scientist, just as much as a blind man is disqualified from being an analyst of painting?

Weber was particularly concerned with the sociology of ethics and of religion. That sociology presupposes a fundamental distinction between "ethos" and "techniques of living" (or "prudential" rules). The sociologist must then be able to recognize an "ethos" in its distinctive character; he must have a feel for it, an appreciation of it, as Weber admitted. But does such appreciation not necessarily imply a value judgment? Does it not imply the realization that a given phenomenon is a *genuine* "ethos" and not a *mere* "technique of living"? Would one not laugh out of court a man who claimed to have written a sociology of art but who actually had written a sociology of trash? The sociologist of religion must distinguish between phenomena which have a religious character and phenomena which are a-religious. To be able to do this, he must know what religion is, he must have understanding of religion. Now, contrary to what Weber suggested, such understanding enables and forces him to distinguish between genuine and spurious religion, between higher and lower religions: those religions are higher in which the specifically religious motivations are effective to a higher degree. Or shall we say that the sociologist is permitted to note the presence or absence of religion or of "ethos"—for this would be merely factual observation—but must not dare to pronounce on the degree to which it is present, i.e., on the rank of the particular religion or "ethos" he is studying? The sociologist of religion cannot help noting the difference between those who try to gain the favor of their gods by flattering and bribing them and those who try to gain it by a change of heart. Can he see this difference without seeing at the same time the difference of rank which it implies, the difference between a mercenary and a nonmercenary attitude? Is he not forced to realize that the attempt to bribe the gods is tantamount to trying to be the lord or employer of the gods and that there is a fundamental incongruity between such attempts and what men divine when speaking of gods? In fact, Weber's whole sociology of religion stands or falls by such distinctions as those between "ethics of intention" and "priestly formalism" (or "petrified maxims"); "sublime" religious thought and "pure sorcery"; "the fresh source of a really, and not merely apparently, profound insight" and "a maze of wholly unintuitive, symbolistic images"; "plastic imagination" and "bookish thinking." His work would be not merely dull but absolutely meaningless if he did not speak almost constantly of practically all intellectual and moral virtues and vices in the appropriate language, i.e., in the language of praise and blame. I have in mind expressions like these: "grand figures," "incomparable grandeur," "perfection that is nowhere surpassed," "pseudo-systematics," "this laxity was undoubtedly a product of decline," "absolutely unartistic," "ingenious explanations," "highly educated," "unrivaled majestic account," "power, plasticity, and precision of formulation," "sublime character of the ethical demands," "perfect inner consistency," "crude and abstruse notions," "manly beauty," "pure and deep conviction," "impressive achievement," "works of art of the first rank." Weber paid some attention to the influence of Puritanism on poetry, music, and so on. He noted a certain negative effect of Puritanism on these arts. This fact (if it is a fact) owes its relevance exclusively to the circumstance that a genuinely religious impulse of a very high order was the cause of the decline of art, i.e., of the "drying-up" of previously existing genuine and high art. For, clearly, no one in his senses would voluntarily pay the slightest attention to a case in which a languishing superstition caused the production of trash. In the case studied by Weber, the cause was a genuine and high religion, and the effect was the decline of art: both the cause and the effect become visible only on the basis of value judgments as distinguished from mere reference to values. Weber had to choose between blindness to the phenomena and value judgments. In his capacity as a practicing social scientist, he chose wisely.[17]

The prohibition against value judgments in social science would lead to the consequence that we are permitted to give a strictly factual description of the overt acts that can be observed in concentration camps and perhaps an equally factual analysis of the motivation of the actors concerned: we would not be permitted to speak of cruelty. Every reader of such a description who is not completely stupid would, of course, see that the actions described are cruel. The factual description would, in truth, be a bitter satire. What claimed to be a straightforward report would be an unusually circumlocutory report. The writer would deliberately suppress his better knowledge, or, to use Weber's favorite term, he would commit an act of intellectual dishonesty. Or, not to waste any moral ammunition on things that are not worthy of it, the whole procedure reminds one of a childish game in which you lose if you pronounce certain words, to the use of which you are constantly incited by your playmates. Weber, like every other man who ever discussed social matters in a relevant manner, could not avoid speaking of avarice, greed, unscrupulousness, vanity, devotion, sense of proportion, and similar things, i.e., making value judgments. He expressed indignation against people who did not see the difference between Gretchen and a

17. *Ibid.*, pp. 380, 462, 481–83, 486, 493, 554; *Religionssoziologie*, I, 33, 82, 112 n., 185 ff., 429, 513; II, 165, 167, 173, 242 n., 285, 316, 370; III, 2 n., 118, 139, 207, 209–10, 221, 241, 257, 268, 274, 323, 382, 385 n.; *Soziologie und Sozialpolitik*, p. 469; *Wirtschaft und Gesellschaft*, pp. 240, 246, 249, 266.

prostitute, i.e., who failed to see the nobility of sentiment present in the one but absent from the other. What Weber implied can be formulated as follows: prostitution is a recognized subject of sociology; this subject cannot be seen if the degrading character of prostitution is not seen at the same time; if one sees the fact "prostitution," as distinguished from an arbitrary abstraction, one has already made a value judgment. What would become of political science if it were not permitted to deal with phenomena like narrow party spirit, boss rule, pressure groups, statesmanship, corruption, even moral corruption, i.e., with phenomena which are, as it were, constituted by value judgments? To put the terms designating such things in quotation marks is a childish trick which enables one to talk of important subjects while denying the principles without which there cannot be important subjects—a trick which is meant to allow one to combine the advantages of common sense with the denial of common sense. Or can one say anything relevant on public opinion polls, for example, without realizing the fact that many answers to the questionnaires are given by unintelligent, uninformed, deceitful, and irrational people, and that not a few questions are formulated by people of the same caliber—can one say anything relevant about public opinion polls without committing one value judgment after another?[18]

Or let us look at an example that Weber himself discussed at some length. The political scientist or historian has, for example, to explain actions of statesmen and generals, i.e., he has to trace their actions to their causes. He cannot do this without answering the question of whether the action concerned was caused by rational consideration of means and ends or by emotional factors, for example. For this purpose he has to construct the model of a perfectly

18. *Wissenschaftslehre*, p. 158; *Religionssoziologie*, I, 41, 170 n.; *Politische Schriften*, pp. 331, 435–36.

rational action in the given circumstances. Only thus will he be able to see which nonrational factors, if any, deflected the action from the strictly rational course. Weber admitted that this procedure implies evaluation: we are forced to say that the actor in question made this or that mistake. But, Weber argued, the construction of the model and the ensuing value judgment on the deviation from the model are merely a transitional stage in the process of causal explanation.[19] As good children, we are then to forget as soon as possible what, in passing by, we could not help noticing but were not supposed to notice. But, in the first place, if the historian shows, by objectively measuring the action of a statesman against the model of "rational action in the circumstances," that the statesman made one blunder after another, he makes an objective value judgment to the effect that the statesman was singularly inept. In another case the historian arrives by the same procedure at the equally objective value judgment that a general showed unusual resourcefulness, resolution, and prudence. It is impossible to understand phenomena of this kind without being aware of the standard of judgment that is inherent in the situation and accepted as a matter of course by the actors themselves; and it is impossible not to make use of that standard by actually evaluating. In the second place, one may wonder whether what Weber regarded as merely incidental or transitional—namely, the insight into the ways of folly and wisdom, of cowardice and bravery, of barbarism and humanity, and so on—is not more worthy of the interest of the historian than any causal explanation along Weberian lines. As for the question whether the inevitable and unobjectionable value judgments should be expressed or suppressed, it is really the question of how they should be expressed, "where, when, by whom, and toward whom"; it belongs, therefore, before another tribunal than that of the methodology of the social sciences.

19. *Wissenschaftslehre*, pp. 125, 129–30, 337–38; *Soziologie und Sozialpolitik*, p. 483.

Social science could avoid value judgments only by keeping strictly within the limits of a purely historical or "interpretive" approach. The social scientist would have to bow without a murmur to the self-interpretation of his subjects. He would be forbidden to speak of "morality," "religion," "art," "civilization," and so on, when interpreting the thought of peoples or tribes who are unaware of such notions. On the other hand, he would have to accept as morality, religion, art, knowledge, state, etc., whatever claimed to be morality, religion, art, etc. As a matter of fact, there exists a sociology of knowledge according to which everything that pretends to be knowledge—even if it is notorious nonsense—has to be accepted as knowledge by the sociologist. Weber himself identified the types of legitimate rule with what are thought to be types of legitimate rule. But this limitation exposes one to the danger of falling victim to every deception and every self-deception of the people one is studying; it penalizes every critical attitude; taken by itself, it deprives social science of every possible value. The self-interpretation of a blundering general cannot be accepted by the political historian, and the self-interpretation of a silly rhymer cannot be accepted by the historian of literature. Nor can the social scientist afford to rest content with the interpretation of a given phenomenon that is accepted by the group within which it occurs. Are groups less liable to deceive themselves than individuals? It was easy for Weber to make the following demand: "What is alone important [for describing a given quality as charismatic] is how the individual is actually regarded by those subject to charismatic authority, by his 'followers' or 'disciples.' " Eight lines later, we read: "Another type [of charismatic leader] is that of Joseph Smith, the founder of Mormonism, who, however, cannot be classified in this way with absolute certainty since there is a possibility that he was a very sophisticated type of swindler," i.e., that he merely pretended to have a charisma. It would be unfair to insist on the fact that the German original is, to say the least, much less explicit and emphatic than the English translation; for the problem implicitly raised by the translator—namely, the problem concerning the difference between genuine and pretended charisma, between genuine prophets and pseudo-prophets, between genuine leaders and successful charlatans—cannot be disposed of by silence.[20] The sociologist cannot be obliged to abide by the legal fictions which a given group never dared to regard as legal fictions; he is forced to make a distinction between how a given group actually conceives of the authority by which it is ruled and the true character of the authority in question. On the other hand, the strictly historical approach, which limits itself to understanding people in the way in which they understand themselves, may be very fruitful if kept in its place. By realizing this, we grasp a legitimate motive underlying the demand for a nonevaluating social science.

Today it is trivial to say that the social scientist ought not to judge societies other than his own by the standards of his society. It is his boast that he does not praise or blame, but understands. But he cannot understand without a conceptual framework or a frame of reference. Now his frame of reference is more likely than not to be a mere reflection of the way in which his own society understands itself in his time. Accordingly, he will interpret societies other than his own in terms that are wholly alien to those societies. He will force these societies into the Procrustean bed of his conceptual scheme. He will not understand these societies as they understand themselves. Since the self-interpretation of a society is an essential element of its being, he will not understand these societies as they really are. And since one cannot understand one's own society adequately if one does not understand other societies, he will not even be able really to understand his own

20. *The Theory of Social and Economic Organization* (Oxford University Press, 1947), pp. 359, 361; compare *Wirtschaft und Gesellschaft*, pp. 140–41, 753.

society. He has then to understand various societies of the past and present, or significant "parts" of those societies, exactly as they understand or understood themselves. Within the limits of this purely historical and hence merely preparatory or ancillary work, that kind of objectivity which implies the foregoing of evaluations is legitimate and even indispensable from every point of view. Particularly in regard to such a phenomenon as a doctrine, it is obvious that one cannot judge of its soundness or explain it in sociological or other terms before one has understood it, i.e., before one has understood it exactly as its originator understood it.

It is curious that Weber, who was so fond of that kind of objectivity which requires the forgoing of value judgments, was almost blind in regard to the sphere which may be said to be the home, and the only home, of nonevaluating objectivity. He realized clearly that the conceptual framework which he used was rooted in the social situation of his time. It is easy to see, for instance, that his distinction of three ideal types of legitimacy (traditional, rational, and charismatic) reflects the situation as it existed in Continental Europe after the French Revolution when the struggle between the residues of the pre-Revolutionary regimes and the Revolutionary regimes was understood as a contest between tradition and reason. The manifest inadequacy of this scheme, which perhaps fitted the situation in the nineteenth century but hardly any other situation, forced Weber to add the charismatic type of legitimacy to the two types imposed on him by his environment. But this addition did not remove, it merely concealed, the basic limitation inherent in his scheme. The addition created the impression that the scheme was now comprehensive, but, in fact, it could not be made comprehensive by any additions because of its parochial origin: not a comprehensive reflection on the nature of political society but merely the experience of two or three generations had supplied the basic orientation. Since

Weber believed that no conceptual scheme used by social science can be of more than ephemeral validity, he was not seriously disturbed by this state of affairs. In particular, he was not seriously disturbed by the danger that the imposition of his definitely "dated" scheme might prevent the unbiased understanding of earlier political situations. He did not wonder whether his scheme fitted the manner in which, say, the protagonists of the great political conflicts recorded in history had conceived of their causes, that is to say, the manner in which they had conceived of the principles of legitimacy. For fundamentally the same reason, he did not hesitate to describe Plato as an "intellectual," without for one moment considering the fact that the whole work of Plato may be described as a critique of the notion of "the intellectual." He did not hesitate to consider the dialogue between the Athenians and Melians in Thucydides' *History* as a sufficient basis for asserting that "in the Hellenic polis of the classical time, a most naked 'Machiavellianism' was regarded as a matter of course in every respect and as wholly unobjectionable from an ethical point of view." To say nothing of other considerations, he did not pause to wonder how Thucydides himself had conceived of that dialogue. He did not hesitate to write: "The fact that Egyptian sages praised obedience, silence, and absence of presumptuousness as godly virtues, had its source in bureaucratic subordination. In Israel, the source was the plebeian character of the clientele." Similarly, his sociological explanation of Hindu thought is based on the premise that natural right "of any kind" presupposes the natural equality of all men, if not even a blessed state at the beginning and at the end. Or, to take what is perhaps the most telling example, when discussing the question of what has to be regarded as the essence of a historical phenomenon like Calvinism, Weber said: By calling something the essence of a historical phenomenon, one either means that aspect of the phenomenon which one considers to be of permanent value, or else that aspect through which it exercised the greatest historical influence. He did not even allude to a third possibility, which is, in fact, the first and most obvious one, namely, that the essence of Calvinism, e.g., would have to be identified with what Calvin himself regarded as the essence, or as the chief characteristic, of his work.[21]

Weber's methodological principles were bound to affect his work in an adverse manner. We shall illustrate this by glancing at his most famous historical essay, his study on Protestant ethics and the spirit of capitalism. He contended that Calvinist theology was a major cause of the capitalist spirit. He stressed the fact that the effect was in no way intended by Calvin, that Calvin would have been shocked by it, and—what is more important—that the crucial link in the chain of causation (a peculiar interpretation of the dogma of predestination) was rejected by Calvin but emerged "quite naturally" among the epigones and, above all, among the broad stratum of the general run of Calvinists. Now, if one speaks about a teaching of the rank of Calvin's, the mere reference to "epigones" and the "general run" of men implies a value judgment on that interpretation of the dogma of predestination which these people adopted: epigones and the general run of men are very likely to miss the decisive point. Weber's implied value judgment is fully justified in the eyes of everyone who has understood the theological doctrine of Calvin; the peculiar interpretation of the dogma of predestination that allegedly led to the emergence of the capitalistic spirit is based on a radical misunderstanding of Calvin's doctrine. It is a corruption of that doctrine or, to use Calvin's own language, it is a carnal interpretation of a spiritual teaching. The maximum that Weber could reasonably have claimed to have proved is,

21. *Religionssoziologie*, I, 89; II, 136 n., 143–45; III, 232–33; *Wissenschaftslehre*, pp. 93–95, 170–73, 184, 199, 206–9, 214, 249–50.

then, that a corruption or degeneration of Calvin's theology
led to the emergence of the capitalist spirit. Only by means of
this decisive qualification can his thesis be brought into even
approximate harmony with the facts to which he refers. But
he was prevented from making this crucial qualification because he had imposed on himself the taboo regarding value
judgments. By avoiding an indispensable value judgment, he
was forced into giving a factually incorrect picture of what had
happened. For his fear of value judgments prompted him to
identify the essence of Calvinism with its historically most influential aspect. He instinctively avoided identifying the essence of Calvinism with what Calvin himself considered essential, because Calvin's self-interpretation would naturally act
as a standard by which to judge objectively the Calvinists who
claimed to follow Calvin.[22]

22. *Religionssoziologie*, I, 81–82, 103–4, 112. One can hardly say that the problem
stated by Weber in his study on the spirit of capitalism has been solved. To prepare a
solution, one would have to free Weber's formulation of the problem from the particular limitation which was due to his "Kantianism." He may be said to have rightly
identified the spirit of capitalism with the view that limitless accumulation of capital
and profitable investment of capital is a moral duty, and perhaps the highest moral
duty, and to have rightly contended that this spirit is characteristic of the modern
Western world. But he also said that the spirit of capitalism consists in regarding the
limitless accumulation of capital as an end in itself. He could not prove the latter contention except by referring to dubious or ambiguous impressions. He was forced to
make that contention because he assumed that "moral duty" and "end in itself" are
identical. His "Kantianism" also forced him to sever every connection between "moral
duty" and "the common good." He was forced to introduce into his analysis of earlier
moral thought a distinction, not warranted by the texts, between the "ethical" justification of the unlimited accumulation of capital and its "utilitarian" justification.
As a consequence of his peculiar notion of "ethics," every reference to the common
good in earlier literature tended to appear to him as a lapse into low utilitarianism.
One may venture to say that no writer outside mental institutions ever justified the
duty, or the moral right, to unlimited acquisition on any other ground than that of
service to the common good. The problem of the genesis of the capitalist spirit is then
identical with the problem of the emergence of the minor premise, "but the unlimited
accumulation of capital is most conducive to the common good." For the major
premise, "it is our duty to devote ourselves to the common good or to the love of our
neighbors," was not affected by the emergence of the capitalist spirit. That major

The rejection of value judgments endangers historical objectivity. In the first place, it prevents one from calling a spade a spade. In the second place, it endangers that kind of objectivity which legitimately requires the forgoing of evaluations, namely, the objectivity of interpretation. The historian who

---

premise was accepted by both the philosophic and the theological tradition. The question, then, is which transformation of the philosophic or of the theological tradition or of both caused the emergence of the minor premise mentioned. Weber took it for granted that the cause must be sought in the transformation of the theological tradition, i.e., in the Reformation. But he did not succeed in tracing the capitalist spirit to the Reformation or, in particular, to Calvinism except by the use of "historical dialectics" or by means of questionable psychological constructions. The utmost one could say is that he traced the capitalist spirit to the corruption of Calvinism. Tawney rightly pointed out that the capitalist Puritanism studied by Weber was late Puritanism or that it was the Puritanism that had already made its peace with "the world." This means that the Puritanism in question had made its peace with the capitalist world already in existence: the Puritanism in question was then not the cause of the capitalist world or of the capitalist spirit. If it is impossible to trace the capitalist spirit to the Reformation, one is forced to wonder whether the minor premise under consideration did not emerge through the transformation of the philosophic tradition, as distinguished from the transformation of the theological tradition. Weber considered the possibility that the origin of the capitalist spirit might have to be sought in the Renaissance, but, as he rightly observed, the Renaissance as such was an attempt to restore the spirit of classical antiquity, i.e., a spirit wholly different from the capitalist spirit. What he failed to consider was that in the course of the sixteenth century there was a conscious break with the whole philosophic tradition, a break that took place on the plane of purely philosophic or rational or secular thought. This break was originated by Machiavelli, and it led to the moral teachings of Bacon and Hobbes: thinkers whose writings preceded by decades those writings of their Puritan countrymen on which Weber's thesis is based. One can hardly say more than that Puritanism, having broken more radically with the "pagan" philosophic tradition (i.e., chiefly with Aristotelianism) than Roman Catholicism and Lutheranism had done, was more open to the new philosophy than were the latter. Puritanism thus could become a very important, and perhaps the most important, "carrier" of the new philosophy both natural and moral— of a philosophy which had been created by men of an entirely non-Puritan stamp. In brief, Weber overestimated the importance of the revolution that had taken place on the plane of theology, and he underestimated the importance of the revolution that had taken place on the plane of rational thought. By paying more careful attention than he did to the purely secular development, one would also be able to restore the connection, arbitrarily severed by him, between the emergence of the capitalist spirit and the emergence of the science of economics (cf. also Ernst Troeltsch, *The Social Teaching of the Christian Churches* [1949], pp. 624 and 894).

takes it for granted that objective value judgments are impossible cannot take very seriously that thought of the past which was based on the assumption that objective value judgments are possible, i.e., practically all thought of earlier generations. Knowing beforehand that that thought was based on a fundamental delusion, he lacks the necessary incentive for trying to understand the past as it understood itself.

Almost all that we have said up to this point was necessary in order to clear away the most important obstacles to an understanding of Weber's central thesis. Only now are we able to grasp its precise meaning. Let us reconsider our last example. What Weber should have said was that the corruption of Calvinist theology led to the emergence of the capitalist spirit. This would have implied an objective value judgment on vulgar Calvinism: the epigones unwittingly destroyed what they intended to preserve. Yet this implied value judgment is of very limited significance. It does not prejudge the real issue in any way. For, assuming that Calvinist theology were a bad thing, its corruption was a good thing. What Calvin would have considered a "carnal" understanding could, from another point of view, be approved as a "this-worldly" understanding, leading to such good things as secularist individualism and secularist democracy. Even from the latter point of view, vulgar Calvinism would appear as an impossible position, a halfway house, but preferable to Calvinism proper for the same reason that Sancho Panza may be said to be preferable to Don Quixote. The rejection of vulgar Calvinism is then inevitable from every point of view. But this merely means that only after having rejected vulgar Calvinism is one faced with the real issue: the issue of religion versus irreligion, i.e., of genuine religion versus noble irreligion, as distinguished from the issue of mere sorcery, or mechanical ritualism versus the irreligion of specialists without vision and voluptuaries without heart. It is this real issue which, according to Weber, cannot be settled by human reason, just as the conflict between different genuine religions of the highest rank (e.g., the conflict between Deutero-Isaiah, Jesus, and Buddha) cannot be settled by human reason. Thus, in spite of the fact that social science stands or falls by value judgments, social science or social philosophy cannot settle the decisive value conflicts. It is indeed true that one has already passed a value judgment when speaking of Gretchen and a prostitute. But this value judgment proves to be merely provisional the moment one comes face to face with a radically ascetic position which condemns all sexuality. From this point of view, the open degradation of sexuality through prostitution may appear to be a cleaner thing than the disguise of the true nature of sexuality through sentiment and poetry. It is indeed true that one cannot speak of human affairs without praising the intellectual and moral virtues and blaming the intellectual and moral vices. But this does not dispose of the possibility that all human virtues would ultimately have to be judged to be no more than splendid vices. It would be absurd to deny that there is an objective difference between a blundering general and a strategic genius. But if war is absolutely evil, the difference between the blundering general and the strategic genius will be on the same level as the difference between a blundering thief and a genius in thievery.

It seems, then, that what Weber really meant by his rejection of value judgments would have to be expressed as follows: The objects of the social sciences are constituted by reference to values. Reference to values presupposes appreciation of values. Such appreciation enables and forces the social scientist to evaluate the social phenomena, i.e., to distinguish between the genuine and the spurious and between the higher and the lower: between genuine religion and spurious religion, between genuine leaders and charlatans, between knowledge and mere lore or sophistry, between virtue and vice, between moral sensitivity and moral obtuseness, between art and trash, between vitality and degeneracy, etc. Reference to values is incompatible with neutrality; it can never be "purely theoretical." But nonneutrality does not necessarily mean approval; it may also mean rejection. In fact, since the various values are incompatible with one another, the approval of any one value necessarily implies the rejection of some other value or values. Only on the basis of such acceptance or rejection of values, of "ultimate values," do the objects of the social sciences come to sight. For all further work, for the causal analysis of these objects, it must be a matter of indifference whether the student has accepted or rejected the value in question.[23]

At any rate, Weber's whole notion of the scope and function of the social sciences rests on the allegedly demonstrable premise that the conflict between ultimate values cannot be resolved by human reason. The question is whether that premise has really been demonstrated, or whether it has merely been postulated under the impulse of a specific moral preference.

At the threshold of Weber's attempt to demonstrate his basic premise, we encounter two striking facts. The first is that Weber, who wrote thousands of pages, devoted hardly more than thirty of them to a thematic discussion of the basis of his whole position. Why was that basis so little in need of proof? Why was it self-evident to him? A provisional answer is supplied by the second observation we can make prior to any analysis of his arguments. As he indicated at the beginning of his discussion of the subject, his thesis was only the generalized version of an older and more common view, namely, that the conflict between ethics and politics is insoluble: political action is sometimes impossible without incurring moral guilt. It seems, then, that it was the spirit of "power politics" that begot Weber's position. Nothing is more revealing than the fact that, in a related context when speaking of conflict and

23. *Wissenschaftslehre*, pp. 90, 124–25, 175, 180–82, 199.

peace, Weber put "peace" in quotation marks, whereas he did
not take this precautionary measure when speaking of conflict.
Conflict was for Weber an unambiguous thing, but peace was
not: peace is phony, but war is real.[24]

Weber's thesis that there is no solution to the conflict between values was then a part, or a consequence, of the comprehensive view according to which human life is essentially an
inescapable conflict. For this reason, "peace and universal happiness" appeared to him to be an illegitimate or fantastic goal.
Even if that goal could be reached, he thought, it would not
be desirable; it would be the condition of "the last men who
have invented happiness," against whom Nietzsche had directed his "devastating criticism." If peace is incompatible
with human life or with a truly human life, the moral problem
would seem to allow of a clear solution: the nature of things
requires a warrior ethics as the basis of a "power politics"
that is guided exclusively by considerations of the national
interest; or "the most naked Machiavellianism [would have to
be] regarded as a matter of course in every respect, and as
wholly unobjectionable from an ethical point of view." But
we would then be confronted with the paradoxical situation
that the individual is at peace with himself while the world is
ruled by war. The strife-torn world demands a strife-torn individual. The strife would not go to the root of the individual, if
he were not forced to negate the very principle of war: he must
negate the war from which he cannot escape and to which he
must dedicate himself, as evil or sinful. Lest there be peace
anywhere, peace must not be simply rejected. It is not sufficient
to recognize peace as the necessary breathing time between
wars. There must be an absolute duty directing us toward universal peace or universal brotherhood, a duty conflicting with
the equally high duty that directs us to participate in "the
eternal struggle" for "elbow room" for our nation. Conflict

24. *Ibid.*, pp. 466, 479; *Politische Schriften*, pp. 17–18, 310.

would not be supreme if guilt could be escaped. The question of whether one can speak of guilt, if man is forced to become guilty, was no longer discussed by Weber: he needed the necessity of guilt. He had to combine the anguish bred by atheism (the absence of any redemption, of any solace) with the anguish bred by revealed religion (the oppressive sense of guilt). Without that combination, life would cease to be tragic and thus lose its depth.[25]

Weber assumed as a matter of course that there is no hierarchy of values: all values are of the same rank. Now, precisely if this is the case, a social scheme that satisfies the requirements of two values is preferable to one whose scope is more limited. The comprehensive scheme might demand that some of the requirements of each of the two values would have to be sacrificed. In this case the question would arise as to whether the extreme or one-sided schemes are not so good as, or are better than, the apparently more comprehensive schemes. To answer that question, one would have to know whether it is at all possible to adopt one of the two values, while unqualifiedly rejecting the other. If it is impossible, some sacrifice of the apparent requirements of the two component values would be a dictate of reason. The optimal scheme might not be realizable except under certain very favorable conditions, and the actual conditions here and now may be very unfavorable. This would not deprive the optimal scheme of its importance, because it would remain indispensable as the basis for rational judgment about the various imperfect schemes. In particular, its importance would be in no way affected by the fact that in given situations one can choose only between two equally imperfect schemes. Last but not least, in all reflections on such matters one must not be oblivious for one moment of the general significance for social

25. *Politische Schriften*, pp. 18, 20; *Wissenschaftslehre*, pp. 540, 550; *Religionssoziologie*, I, 568–69.

life of extremism, on the one hand, and moderation, on the other. Weber pushed all considerations of this character aside by declaring that "the middle line is no whit more scientifically correct than the most extreme party ideals of the right and the left" and that the middle line is even inferior to the extreme solutions, since it is less unambiguous.[26] The question, of course, is whether social science does not have to be concerned with sensible solutions to social problems and whether moderation is not more sensible than extremism. However sensible Weber may have been as a practical politician, however much he may have abhorred the spirit of narrow party fanaticism, as a social scientist he approached social problems in a spirit that had nothing in common with the spirit of statesmanship and that could serve no other practical end than to encourage narrow obstinacy. His unshakable faith in the supremacy of conflict forced him to have at least as high a regard for extremism as for moderate courses.

But we can no longer delay turning to Weber's attempts to prove his contention that the ultimate values are simply in conflict with one another. We shall have to limit ourselves to a discussion of two or three specimens of his proofs.[27] The first

26. *Wissenschaftslehre*, pp. 154, 461.

27. While Weber referred rather frequently in general terms to a considerable number of insoluble value conflicts, his attempt to prove his basic contention is limited, as far as I can see, to the discussion of three or four examples. The example which will not be discussed in the text concerns the conflict between eroticism and all impersonal or supra-personal values: a genuine erotic relation between a man and a woman can be regarded, "from a certain standpoint," "as the sole or at any rate as the most royal road" to a genuine life; if someone opposes all saintliness or all goodness, all ethical or aesthetic norms, everything that is valuable from the point of view of culture or of personality, in the name of genuine erotic passion, reason has to be absolutely silent. The particular standpoint which permits or fosters this attitude is not, as one might expect, that of Carmen but that of intellectuals who suffer from the specialization or "professionalization" of life. To such people "marriage-free sexual life could appear as the only link that still connects man (who by then had completely left the cycle of the old, simple, and organic peasant existence) with the natural source of all life." It is probably sufficient to say that appearances may be deceptive. But we feel compelled to

one is the example that he used in order to illustrate the character of most issues of social policy. Social policy is concerned with justice; but what justice in society requires cannot be decided, according to Weber, by any ethics. Two opposed views are equally legitimate or defensible. According to the first view, one owes much to him who achieves or contributes much; according to the second view, one should demand much from him who can achieve or contribute much. If one adopts the first view, one would have to grant great opportunities to great talent. If one adopts the second view, one would have to prevent the talented individual from exploiting his superior opportunities. We shall not complain about the loose way in which Weber stated what he considered, rather strangely, an insuperable difficulty. We merely note that he did not think it necessary to indicate any reason by which the first view can be supported. The second view, however, seemed to require an explicit argument. According to Weber, one may argue, as Babeuf did, in the following way: the injustice of the unequal distribution of mental gifts and the gratifying feeling of prestige which attends the mere possession of superior gifts have to be compensated by social measures destined to prevent the talented individual from exploiting his great opportunities. Before one could say that this view is tenable, one would have to know whether it makes sense to say that nature committed an injustice by distributing her gifts unequally, whether it is a duty of society to remedy that injustice, and whether envy has a right to be heard. But even if one would grant that Babeuf's

---

add that, according to Weber, this late return to the most natural in man is bound up with what he chose to call "die systematische Herauspräparierung der Sexualsphäre" (*Wissenschaftslehre*, pp. 468–69; *Religionssoziologie*, I, 560–62). He thus proved indeed that eroticism as he understood it conflicts with "all esthetic norms"; but he proved at the same time that the intellectuals' attempt to escape specialization through eroticism merely leads to specialization in eroticism (cf. *Wissenschaftslehre*, p. 540). He proved, in other words, that his erotic Weltanschauung is not defensible before the tribunal of human reason.

view, as stated by Weber, is as defensible as the first view, what would follow? That we have to make a blind choice? That we have to incite the adherents of the two opposed views to insist on their opinions with all the obstinacy that they can muster? If, as Weber contends, no solution is morally superior to the other, the reasonable consequence would be that the decision has to be transferred from the tribunal of ethics to that of convenience or expediency. Weber emphatically excluded considerations of expediency from the discussion of this issue. If demands are made in the name of justice, he declared, consideration of which solution would supply the best "incentives" is out of place. But is there no connection between justice and the good of society, and between the good of society and incentives to socially valuable activity? Precisely if Weber were right in asserting that the two opposite views are equally defensible, would social science as an objective science have to stigmatize as a crackpot any man who insisted that only one of the views is in accordance with justice.[28]

Our second example is Weber's alleged proof that there is an insoluble conflict between what he calls the "ethics of responsibility" and the "ethics of intention." According to the former, man's responsibility extends to the foreseeable consequences of his actions, whereas, according to the latter, man's responsibility is limited to the intrinsic rightness of his actions. Weber illustrated the ethics of intention by the example of syndicalism: the syndicalist is concerned not with the consequences or the success of his revolutionary activity but with his own integrity, with preserving in himself and awakening in others a certain moral attitude and nothing else. Even a conclusive proof that in a given situation his revolutionary activity would be destructive, for all the foreseeable future, of the very existence of revolutionary workers would not be a valid argument against a convinced syndicalist. Weber's convinced

28. *Wissenschaftslehre*, p. 467.

syndicalist is an *ad hoc* construction, as is shown by his remark that if the syndicalist is consistent, his kingdom is not of this world. In other words, if he were consistent, he would cease to be a syndicalist, i.e., a man who is concerned with the liberation of the working class in this world, and by means belonging to this world. The ethics of intention, which Weber imputed to syndicalism, is, in reality, an ethics alien to all this-worldly social or political movements. As he stated on another occasion, within the dimension of social action proper "the ethics of intention and the ethics of responsibility are not absolute opposites, but supplement each other: both united constitute the genuine human being." That ethics of intention that is incompatible with what Weber once called the ethics of a genuine human being is a certain interpretation of Christian ethics or, more generally expressed, a strictly otherworldly ethics. What Weber really meant when speaking of the insoluble conflict between the ethics of intention and the ethics of responsibility was, then, that the conflict between this-worldly ethics and otherworldly ethics is insoluble by human reason.[29]

Weber was convinced that, on the basis of a strictly this-worldly orientation, no objective norms are possible: there cannot be "absolutely valid" and, at the same time, specific norms except on the basis of revelation. Yet he never proved that the unassisted human mind is incapable of arriving at objective norms or that the conflict between different this-worldly ethical doctrines is insoluble by human reason. He merely proved that otherworldly ethics, or rather a certain

29. For a more adequate discussion of the problem of "responsibility" and "intention" compare Thomas Aquinas *Summa theologica* i. 2. qu. 20, *a.* 5; Burke, *Present Discontents* (*The Works of Edmund Burke* ["Bohn's Standard Library"], I, 375–77); Lord Charnwood, *Abraham Lincoln* (Pocket Books ed.), pp. 136–37, 164–65; Churchill, *Marlborough*, VI, 599–600. *Wissenschaftslehre*, pp. 467, 475, 476, 546; *Politische Schriften*, pp. 441–44, 448–49, 62–63; *Soziologie und Sozialpolitik*, pp. 512–14; *Religionssoziologie*, II, 193–94.

type of otherworldly ethics, is incompatible with those standards of human excellence or of human dignity which the unassisted human mind discerns. One could say, without in the
least becoming guilty of irreverence, that the conflict between
this-worldly and otherworldly ethics need not be of serious
concern to social science. As Weber himself pointed out, social
science attempts to understand social life from a this-worldly
point of view. Social science is human knowledge of human
life. Its light is the natural light. It tries to find rational or
reasonable solutions to social problems. The insights and solutions at which it arrives might be questioned on the basis of
superhuman knowledge or of divine revelation. But, as Weber
indicated, social science as such cannot take notice of such
questionings, because they are based on presuppositions which
can never be evident to unassisted human reason. By accepting
presuppositions of this character, social science would transform itself into either Jewish or Christian or Islamic or Bud-
dhistic or some other "denominational" social science. In addition, if genuine insights of social science can be questioned
on the basis of revelation, revelation is not merely above reason but against reason. Weber had no compunction in saying
that every belief in revelation is ultimately belief in the absurd. Whether this view of Weber, who, after all, was not a
theological authority, is compatible with an intelligent belief
in revelation need not concern us here.[30]

Once it is granted that social science, or this-worldly understanding of human life, is evidently legitimate, the difficulty
raised by Weber appears to be irrelevant. But he refused to
grant that premise. He contended that science or philosophy
rests, in the last analysis, not on evident premises that are at
the disposal of man as man but on faith. Granting that only
science or philosophy can lead to the truth which man can

30. *Wissenschaftslehre*, pp. 33, n. 2, 39, 154, 379, 466, 469, 471, 540, 542, 545–47,
550–54; *Politische Schriften*, pp. 62–63; *Religionssoziologie*, I, 566.

know, he raised the question of whether the search for knowable truth is good, and he decided that this question can no longer be answered by science or philosophy. Science or philosophy is unable to give a clear or certain account of its own basis. The goodness of science or philosophy was no problem as long as one could think that it is "the way to true being" or to "true nature" or to "true happiness." But these expectations have proved to be illusory. Henceforth, science or philosophy can have no other goal than to ascertain that very limited truth which is accessible to man. Yet, in spite of this amazing change in the character of science or philosophy, the quest for truth continues to be regarded as valuable in itself, and not merely with a view to its practical results—which, in their turn, are of questionable value: to increase man's power means to increase his power for evil as well as for good. By regarding the quest for truth as valuable in itself, one admits that one is making a preference which no longer has a good or sufficient reason. One recognizes therewith the principle that preferences do not need good or sufficient reasons. Accordingly, those who regard the quest for truth as valuable in itself may regard such activities as the understanding of the genesis of a doctrine, or the editing of a text—nay, the conjectural correction of any corrupt reading in any manuscript—as ends in themselves: the quest for truth has the same dignity as stamp collecting. Every pursuit, every whim, becomes as defensible or as legitimate as any other. But Weber did not always go so far. He also said that the goal of science is clarity, i.e., clarity about the great issues, and this means ultimately clarity not indeed about the whole but about the situation of man as man. Science or philosophy is then the way toward freedom from delusion; it is the foundation of a free life, of a life that refuses to bring the sacrifice of the intellect and dares to look reality in its stern face. It is concerned with the knowable truth, which is valid regardless of whether we like it or not. Weber went up to this point. But he refused to say that science or philosophy is concerned with the truth which is valid for all men regardless of whether they desire to know it or not. What stopped him? Why did he deny to the knowable truth its inescapable power?[31]

He was inclined to believe that twentieth-century man has eaten of the fruit of the tree of knowledge, or can be free from the delusions which blinded all earlier men: we see the situation of man without delusions; we are disenchanted. But under the influence of historicism, he became doubtful whether one can speak of the situation of man as man or, if one can, whether this situation is not seen differently in different ages in such a manner that, in principle, the view of any age is as legitimate or as illegitimate as that of any other. He wondered, therefore, whether what appeared to be the situation of man as man was more than the situation of present-day man, or "the inescapable datum of our historical situation." Hence what originally appeared as freedom from delusions presented itself eventually as hardly more than the questionable premise of our age or as an attitude that will be superseded, in due time, by an attitude that will be in conformity with the next epoch. The thought of the present age is characterized by disenchantment or unqualified "this-worldliness," or irreligion. What claims to be freedom from delusions is as much and as little delusion as the faiths which prevailed in the past and which may prevail in the future. We are irreligious because fate forces us to be irreligious and for no other reason. Weber refused to bring the sacrifice of the intellect; he did not wait for a religious revival or for prophets or saviors; and he was not at all certain whether a religious revival would follow the present age. But he was certain that all devotion to causes or ideals has its roots in religious faith and, therefore, that the

31. *Wissenschaftslehre*, pp. 60–61, 184, 213, 251, 469, 531, 540, 547, 549; *Politische Schriften*, pp. 128, 213; *Religionssoziologie*, I, 569–70.

decline of religious faith will ultimately lead to the extinction of all causes or ideals. He tended to see before him the alternative of either complete spiritual emptiness or religious revival. He despaired of the modern this-worldly irreligious experiment, and yet he remained attached to it because he was fated to believe in science as he understood it. The result of this conflict, which he could not resolve, was his belief that the conflict between values cannot be resolved by human reason.[32]

Yet the crisis of modern life and of modern science does not necessarily make doubtful the idea of science. We must therefore try to state in more precise terms what Weber had in mind when he said that science seemed to be unable to give a clear or certain account of itself.

Man cannot live without light, guidance, knowledge; only through knowledge of the good can he find the good that he needs. The fundamental question, therefore, is whether men can acquire that knowledge of the good without which they cannot guide their lives individually or collectively by the unaided efforts of their natural powers, or whether they are dependent for that knowledge on Divine Revelation. No alternative is more fundamental than this: human guidance or divine guidance. The first possibility is characteristic of philosophy or science in the original sense of the term, the second is presented in the Bible. The dilemma cannot be evaded by any harmonization or synthesis. For both philosophy and the Bible proclaim something as the one thing needful, as the only thing that ultimately counts, and the one thing needful proclaimed by the Bible is the opposite of that proclaimed by philosophy: a life of obedient love versus a life of free insight. In every attempt at harmonization, in every synthesis however impressive, one of the two opposed elements is sacrificed, more or less subtly but in any event surely, to the other: philosophy,

32. *Wissenschaftslehre*, pp. 546–47, 551–55; *Religionssoziologie*, I, 204, 523.

which means to be the queen, must be made the handmaid of revelation or vice versa.

If we take a bird's-eye view of the secular struggle between philosophy and theology, we can hardly avoid the impression that neither of the two antagonists has ever succeeded in really refuting the other. All arguments in favor of revelation seem to be valid only if belief in revelation is presupposed; and all arguments against revelation seem to be valid only if unbelief is presupposed. This state of things would appear to be but natural. Revelation is always so uncertain to unassisted reason that it can never compel the assent of unassisted reason, and man is so built that he can find his satisfaction, his bliss, in free investigation, in articulating the riddle of being. But, on the other hand, he yearns so much for a solution of that riddle and human knowledge is always so limited that the need for divine illumination cannot be denied and the possibility of revelation cannot be refuted. Now it is this state of things that seems to decide irrevocably against philosophy and in favor of revelation. Philosophy has to grant that revelation is possible. But to grant that revelation is possible means to grant that philosophy is perhaps not the one thing needful, that philosophy is perhaps something infinitely unimportant. To grant that revelation is possible means to grant that the philosophic life is not necessarily, not evidently, *the* right life. Philosophy, the life devoted to the quest for evident knowledge available to man as man, would itself rest on an unevident, arbitrary, or blind decision. This would merely confirm the thesis of faith, that there is no possibility of consistency, of a consistent and thoroughly sincere life, without belief in revelation. The mere fact that philosophy and revelation cannot refute each other would constitute the refutation of philosophy by revelation.

It was the conflict between revelation and philosophy or science in the full sense of the term and the implications of that conflict that led Weber to assert that the idea of science or philosophy suffers from a fatal weakness. He tried to remain faithful to the cause of autonomous insight, but he despaired when he felt that the sacrifice of the intellect, which is abhorred by science or philosophy, is at the bottom of science or philosophy.

But let us hasten back from these awful depths to a superficiality which, while not exactly gay, promises at least a quiet sleep. Having come up to the surface again, we are welcomed by about six hundred large pages covered with the smallest possible number of sentences, as well as with the largest possible number of footnotes, and devoted to the methodology of the social sciences. Yet we notice very soon that we have not escaped trouble. For Weber's methodology is something different from what methodology usually is. All intelligent students of Weber's methodology have felt that it is philosophic. It is possible to articulate that feeling. Methodology, as reflection on the correct procedure of science, is necessarily reflection on the limitations of science. If science is indeed the highest form of human knowledge, it is reflection on the limitations of human knowledge. And if it is knowledge that constitutes the specific character of man among all earthly beings, methodology is reflection on the limitations of humanity or on the situation of man as man. Weber's methodology comes very close to meeting this demand.

To remain somewhat nearer to what he himself thought of his methodology, we shall say that his notion of science, both natural and social, is based on a specific view of reality. For, according to him, scientific understanding consists in a peculiar transformation of reality. It is therefore impossible to clarify the meaning of science without a previous analysis of reality as it is in itself, i.e., prior to its transformation by science. Weber did not say much about this subject. He was less concerned with the character of reality than with the different ways in which reality is transformed by the different types of science. For his primary concern was with preserving the integrity of the historical or cultural sciences against two apparent dangers: against the attempt to shape these sciences on the pattern of the natural sciences and against the attempt to interpret the dualism of natural and historical-cultural sciences in terms of a metaphysical dualism ("body-mind" or "necessity-freedom"). But his methodological theses remain unintelligible, or at any rate irrelevant, if one does not translate them into theses regarding the character of reality. When he demanded, for example, that interpretive understanding be subservient to causal explanation, he was guided by the observation that the intelligible is frequently overpowered by what is no longer intelligible or that the lower is mostly stronger than the higher. In addition, his preoccupations left him time to indicate his view of what reality is prior to its transformation by science. According to him, reality is an infinite and meaningless sequence, or a chaos, of unique and infinitely divisible events, which in themselves are meaningless: all meaning, all articulation, originates in the activity of the knowing or evaluating subject. Very few people today will be satisfied with this view of reality, which Weber had taken over from neo-Kantianism and which he modified merely by adding one or two emotional touches. It is sufficient to remark that he himself was unable to adhere consistently to that view. He certainly could not deny that there is an articulation of reality that precedes all scientific articulation: that articulation, that wealth of meaning, which we have in mind when speaking of the world of common experience or of the natural understanding of the world.[33] But he did not even attempt a coherent analysis of the social world as it is known to "common sense," or of social reality as it is known in social life or in action. The place of such an analysis is occupied in his work by defini-

33. *Wissenschaftslehre*, pp. 5, 35, 50–51, 61, 67, 71, 126, 127 n., 132–34, 161–62, 166, 171, 173, 175, 177–78, 180, 208, 389, 503.

tions of ideal types, of artificial constructs which are not even meant to correspond to the intrinsic articulation of social reality and which, in addition, are meant to be of a strictly ephemeral character. Only a comprehensive analysis of social reality as we know it in actual life, and as men always have known it since there have been civil societies, would permit an adequate discussion of the possibility of an evaluating social science. Such an analysis would make intelligible the fundamental alternatives which essentially belong to social life and would therewith supply a basis for responsible judgment on whether the conflict between these alternatives is, in principle, susceptible of a solution.

In the spirit of a tradition of three centuries, Weber would have rejected the suggestion that social science must be based on an analysis of social reality as it is experienced in social life or known to "common sense." According to that tradition, "common sense" is a hybrid, begotten by the absolutely subjective world of the individual's sensations and the truly objective world progressively discovered by science. This view stems from the seventeenth century, when modern thought emerged by virtue of a break with classical philosophy. But the originators of modern thought still agreed with the classics in so far as they conceived of philosophy or science as the perfection of man's natural understanding of the natural world. They differed from the classics in so far as they opposed the new philosophy or science, as the truly natural understanding of the world, to the perverted understanding of the world had by classical and medieval philosophy or science, or by "the school."[34] The victory of the new philosophy or science was decided by the victory of its decisive part, namely, the new physics. That victory led eventually to the result that

34. Compare Jacob Klein, "Die griechische Logistik und die Entstehung der modernen Algebra," *Quellen und Studien zur Geschichte der Mathematik, Astronomie und Physik* (1936), III, 125.

the new physics and the new natural science in general became independent of the rump of philosophy which from then on came to be called "philosophy" in contradistinction to "science"; and, in fact, "science" became the authority for "philosophy." "Science," we may say, is the successful part of modern philosophy or science, whereas "philosophy" is its less successful part. Thus not modern philosophy but modern natural science came to be regarded as the perfection of man's natural understanding of the natural world. But in the nineteenth century it became more and more apparent that a drastic distinction must be made between what was then called the "scientific" understanding (or "the world of science") and the "natural" understanding (or "the world in which we live"). It became apparent that the scientific understanding of the world emerges by way of a radical modification, as distinguished from a perfection, of the natural understanding. Since the natural understanding is the presupposition of the scientific understanding, the analysis of science and of the world of science presupposes the analysis of the natural understanding, the natural world, or the world of common sense. The natural world, the world in which we live and act, is not the object or the product of a theoretical attitude; it is a world not of mere objects at which we detachedly look but of "things" or "affairs" which we handle. Yet as long as we identify the natural or prescientific world with the world in which we live, we are dealing with an abstraction. The world in which we live is already a product of science, or at any rate it is profoundly affected by the existence of science. To say nothing of technology, the world in which we live is free from ghosts, witches, and so on, with which, but for the existence of science, it would abound. To grasp the natural world as a world that is radically prescientific or prephilosophic, one has to go back behind the first emergence of science or philosophy. It is not necessary for this purpose to engage in extensive and necessarily hypothetical anthropological studies. The information that classical philosophy supplies about its origins suffices, especially if that information is supplemented by consideration of the most elementary premises of the Bible, for reconstructing the essential character of "the natural world." By using that information, so supplemented, one would be enabled to understand the origin of the idea of natural right.

III

THE ORIGIN OF THE IDEA OF NATURAL RIGHT

☼

TO UNDERSTAND the problem of natural right, one must start, not from the "scientific" understanding of political things but from their "natural" understanding, i.e., from the way in which they present themselves in political life, in action, when they are our business, when we have to make decisions. This does not mean that political life necessarily knows of natural right. Natural right had to be discovered, and there was political life prior to that discovery. It means merely that political life in all its forms necessarily points toward natural right as an inevitable problem. Awareness of this problem is not older than political science but coeval with it. Hence a political life that does not know of the idea of natural right is necessarily unaware of the possibility of political science and, indeed, of the possibility of science as such, just as a political life that is aware of the possibility of science necessarily knows natural right as a problem.

The idea of natural right must be unknown as long as the idea of nature is unknown. The discovery of nature is the work of philosophy. Where there is no philosophy, there is no knowledge of natural right as such. The Old Testament, whose basic premise may be said to be the implicit rejection of philosophy, does not know "nature": the Hebrew term for "nature" is unknown to the Hebrew Bible. It goes without saying that "heaven and earth," for example, is not the same thing as "nature." There is, then, no knowledge of natural right as such in the Old Testament. The discovery of nature necessarily precedes the discovery of natural right. Philosophy is older than political philosophy.

Philosophy is the quest for the "principles" of all things, and this means primarily the quest for the "beginnings" of all things or for "the first things." In this, philosophy is at one with myth. But the *philosophos* ("lover of wisdom") is not identical with the *philomythos* ("lover of myth"). Aristotle calls the first philosophers simply "men who discoursed on nature" and distinguishes them from the men who preceded them and "who discoursed on gods."[1] Philosophy as distinguished from myth came into being when nature was discovered, or the first philosopher was the first man who discovered nature. The whole history of philosophy is nothing but the record of the ever repeated attempts to grasp fully what was implied in that crucial discovery which was made by some Greek twenty-six hundred years ago or before. To understand the meaning of that discovery in however provisional a manner, one must return from the idea of nature to its prephilosophic equivalent.

The purport of the discovery of nature cannot be grasped if one understands by nature "the totality of phenomena." For the discovery of nature consists precisely in the splitting-up of that totality into phenomena which are natural and phenomena which are not natural: "nature" is a term of distinction. Prior to the discovery of nature, the characteristic behavior of any thing or any class of things was conceived of as its custom or its way. That is to say, no fundamental distinction was made between customs or ways which are always and everywhere the same and customs or ways which differ from tribe to tribe. Barking and wagging the tail is the way of dogs, menstruation is the way of women, the crazy things done by madmen are the way of madmen, just as not eating pork is the way

1. Aristotle *Metaphysics* 981^{b}27–29, 982^{b}18 (cf. *Nicomachean Ethics* 1117^{b}33–35), 983^{b}7 ff., 1071^{b}26–27; Plato *Laws* 891^c, 892^{c}2–7, 896^{a}5–^{b}3.

of Jews and not drinking wine is the way of Moslems. "Custom" or "way" is the prephilosophic equivalent of "nature."

While every thing or every class of things has its custom or way, there is a particular custom or way which is of paramount importance: "our" way, the way of "us" living "here," the way of life of the independent group to which a man belongs. We may call it the "paramount" custom or way. Not all members of the group remain always in that way, but they mostly return to it if they are properly reminded of it: the paramount way is the right path. Its rightness is guaranteed by its oldness: "There is a sort of presumption against novelty, drawn out of a deep consideration of human nature and human affairs; and the maxim of jurisprudence is well laid down, *Vetustas pro lege semper habetur*." But not everything old everywhere is right. "Our" way is the right way because it is both old and "our own" or because it is both "home-bred and prescriptive."[2] Just as "old and one's own" originally was identical with right or good, so "new and strange" originally stood for bad. The notion connecting "old" and "one's own" is "ancestral." Prephilosophic life is characterized by the primeval identification of the good with the ancestral. Therefore, the right way necessarily implies thoughts about the ancestors and hence about the first things simply.[3]

For one cannot reasonably identify the good with the ancestral if one does not assume that the ancestors were absolutely superior to "us," and this means that they were superior to

2. Burke, *Letters on a Regicide Peace*, i and iv; cf. Herodotus iii. 38 and i. 8.

3. "The right way" would seem to be the link between "way" (or "custom") in general and "the first things," i.e., between the roots of the two most important meanings of "nature": "nature" as essential character of a thing or a group of things and "nature" as "the first things." For the second meaning see Plato's *Laws* 891^{c}1–4 and 892^{c}2–7. For the first meaning, consider Aristotle's as well as the Stoic's reference to "way" in their definitions of nature (Aristotle *Physics* 193^{b}13–19, 194^{a}27–30, and 199^{a}9–10; Cicero *De natura deorum* ii. 57 and 81). When "nature" is denied, "custom" is restored to its original place. Compare Maimonides *Guide of the Perplexed* i. 71 and 73; and Pascal, *Pensées*, ed. Brunschvicg, Frags. 222, 233, 92.

all ordinary mortals; one is driven to believe that the ancestors, or those who established the ancestral way, were gods or sons of gods or at least "dwelling near the gods." The identification of the good with the ancestral leads to the view that the right way was established by gods or sons of gods or pupils of gods: the right way must be a divine law. Seeing that the ancestors are ancestors of a distinct group, one is led to believe that there is a variety of divine laws or codes, each of which is the work of a divine or semidivine being.[4]

Originally, the questions concerning the first things and the right way are answered before they are raised. They are answered by authority. For authority as the right of human beings to be obeyed is essentially derivative from law, and law is originally nothing other than the way of life of the community. The first things and the right way cannot become questionable or the object of a quest, or philosophy cannot emerge, or nature cannot be discovered, if authority as such is not doubted or as long as at least any general statement of any being whatsoever is accepted on trust.[5] The emergence of the idea of natural right presupposes, therefore, the doubt of authority.

Plato has indicated by the conversational settings of his *Republic* and his *Laws* rather than by explicit statements how indispensable doubt of authority or freedom from authority is for the discovery of natural right. In the *Republic* the discussion of natural right starts long after the aged Cephalus, *the* father, the head of the house, has left to take care of the sacred offerings to the gods: the absence of Cephalus, or of what he stands for, is indispensable for the quest for natural right. Or, if you wish, men like Cephalus do not need to know of natural right. Besides, the discussion makes the participants wholly

4. Plato *Laws* 624ᵃ1–6, 634ᵉ1–2, 662ᶜ7, ᵈ7–ᵉ7; *Minos* 318ᶜ1–3; Cicero *Laws* ii. 27; cf. Fustel de Coulanges, *La Cité antique*, Part III, chap. xi.

5. Cf. Plato *Charmides* 161ᵉ3–8 and *Phaedrus* 275ᵉ1–3 with *Apology of Socrates* 21ᵇ6–ᶜ2; cf. also Xenophon *Apology of Socrates* 14–15 with *Cyropaedia* vii. 2. 15–17.

oblivious of a torch race in honor of a goddess which they were supposed to watch—the quest for natural right replaces that torch race. The discussion recorded in the *Laws* takes place while the participants, treading in the footsteps of Minos, who, being the son and pupil of Zeus, had brought the Cretans their divine laws, are walking from a Cretan city to the cave of Zeus. Whereas their conversation is recorded in its entirety, nothing is said of whether they arrived at their initial goal. The end of the *Laws* is devoted to the central theme of the *Republic:* natural right, or political philosophy and the culmination of political philosophy, replace the cave of Zeus. If we take Socrates as the representative of the quest for natural right, we may illustrate the relation of that quest to authority as follows: in a community governed by divine laws, it is strictly forbidden to subject these laws to genuine discussion, i.e., to critical examination, in the presence of young men; Socrates, however, discusses natural right—a subject whose discovery presupposes doubt of the ancestral or divine code—not only in the presence of young men but in conversation with them. Some time before Plato, Herodotus had indicated this state of things by the place of the only debate which he recorded concerning the principles of politics: he tells us that that free discussion took place in truth-loving Persia after the slaughter of the Magi.[6] This is not to deny that, once the idea of natural right has emerged and become a matter of course, it can easily be adjusted to the belief in the existence of divinely revealed law. We merely contend that the predominance of that belief prevents the emergence of the idea of natural right or makes the quest for natural right infinitely unimportant: if man knows by divine revelation what the right path is, he does not have to discover that path by his unassisted efforts.

6. Plato *Laws* 634^{d}7–635^{a}5; cf. *Apology of Socrates* 23^{c}2 ff. with *Republic* 538^{o}5–^{e}6; Herodotus iii. 76 (cf. i. 132).

The original form of the doubt of authority and therefore the direction which philosophy originally took or the perspective in which nature was discovered were determined by the original character of authority. The assumption that there is a variety of divine codes leads to difficulties, since the various codes contradict one another. One code absolutely praises actions which another code absolutely condemns. One code demands the sacrifice of one's first-born son, whereas another code forbids all human sacrifices as an abomination. The burial rites of one tribe provoke the horror of another. But what is decisive is the fact that the various codes contradict one another in what they suggest regarding the first things. The view that the gods were born of the earth cannot be reconciled with the view that the earth was made by the gods. Thus the question arises as to which code is the right code and which account of the first things is the true account. The right way is now no longer guaranteed by authority; it becomes a question or the object of a quest. The primeval identification of the good with the ancestral is replaced by the fundamental distinction between the good and the ancestral; the quest for the right way or for the first things is the quest for the good as distinguished from the ancestral.[7] It will prove to be the quest for what is good by nature as distinguished from what is good merely by convention.

The quest for the first things is guided by two fundamental distinctions which antedate the distinction between the good and the ancestral. Men must always have distinguished (e.g., in judicial matters) between hearsay and seeing with one's own eyes and have preferred what one has seen to what he has merely heard from others. But the use of this distinction was originally limited to particular or subordinate matters. As regards the most weighty matters—the first things and the right

7. Plato *Republic* 538^{d}3-4 and ^{e}5-6; *Statesman* 296^{e}8-9; *Laws* 702^{e}5-8; Xenophon *Cyropaedia* ii. 2. 26; Aristotle *Politics* 1269^{a}3-8, 1271^{b}23-24.

way—the only source of knowledge was hearsay. Confronted with the contradiction between the many sacred codes, some-one—a traveler, a man who had seen the cities of many men and recognized the diversity of their thoughts and customs—suggested that one apply the distinction between seeing with one's own eyes and hearsay to all matters, and especially to the most weighty matters. Judgment on, or assent to, the divine or venerable character of any code or account is suspended until the facts upon which the claims are based have been made manifest or demonstrated. They must be made manifest—manifest to all, in broad daylight. Thus man becomes alive to the crucial difference between what his group considers unquestionable and what he himself observes; it is thus that the I is enabled to oppose itself to the We without any sense of guilt. But it is not the I as I that acquires that right. Dreams and visions had been of decisive importance for establishing the claims of the divine code or of the sacred account of the first things. By virtue of the universal application of the distinction between hearsay and seeing with one's own eyes, a distinction is now made between the one true and common world perceived in waking and the many untrue and private worlds of dreams and visions. Thus it appears that neither the We of any particular group nor a unique I, but man as man, is the measure of truth and untruth, of the being or nonbeing of all things. Finally, man thus learns to distinguish between the names of things which he knows through hearsay and which differ from group to group and the things themselves which he, as well as any other human being, can see with his own eyes. He thus can start to replace the arbitrary distinctions of things which differ from group to group by their "natural" distinctions.

The divine codes and the sacred accounts of the first things were said to be known not from hearsay but by way of super-human information. When it was demanded that the distinction between hearsay and seeing with one's own eyes be applied to the most weighty matters, it was demanded that the superhuman origin of all alleged superhuman information must be proved by examination in the light, not, for example, of traditional criteria used for distinguishing between true and false oracles, but of such criteria as ultimately derive in an evident manner from the rules which guide us in matters fully accessible to human knowledge. The highest kind of human knowledge that existed prior to the emergence of philosophy or science was the arts. The second prephilosophic distinction that originally guided the quest for the first things was the distinction between artificial or man-made things and things that are not man-made. Nature was discovered when man embarked on the quest for the first things in the light of the fundamental distinctions between hearsay and seeing with one's own eyes, on the one hand, and between things made by man and things not made by man, on the other. The first of these two distinctions motivated the demand that the first things must be brought to light by starting from what all men can see now. But not all visible things are an equally adequate starting point for the discovery of the first things. The manmade things lead to no other first things than man, who certainly is not the first thing simply. The artificial things are seen to be inferior in every respect to, or to be later than, the things that are not made but found or discovered by man. The artificial things are seen to owe their being to human contrivance or to forethought. If one suspends one's judgment regarding the truth of the sacred accounts of the first things, one does not know whether the things that are not manmade owe their being to forethought of any kind, i.e., whether the first things originate all other things by way of forethought, or otherwise. Thus one realizes the possibility that the first things originate all other things in a manner fundamentally different from all origination by way of forethought. The assertion that all visible things have been produced by thinking beings or that there are any superhuman thinking beings requires henceforth a demonstration: a demonstration that starts from what all can see now.[8]

In brief, then, it can be said that the discovery of nature is identical with the actualization of a human possibility which, at least according to its own interpretation, is trans-historical, trans-social, trans-moral, and trans-religious.[9]

The philosophic quest for the first things presupposes not merely that there are first things but that the first things are always and that things which are always or are imperishable are more truly beings than the things which are not always. These presuppositions follow from the fundamental premise that no being emerges without a cause or that it is impossible that "at first Chaos came to be," i.e., that the first things jumped into being out of nothing and through nothing. In other words, the manifest changes would be impossible if there did not exist something permanent or eternal, or the manifest contingent beings require the existence of something necessary and therefore eternal. Beings that are always are of higher dignity than beings that are not always, because only the former can be the ultimate cause of the latter, of the being of the latter, or because what is not always finds its place within the order constituted by what is always. Beings that are not always, are less truly beings than beings that are al-

---

8. Plato Laws 888ᶜ–889ᶜ, 891ᶜ1–9, 892ᶜ2–7, 966ᵈ6–967ᵉ1. Aristotle Metaphysics 989ᵇ29–990ᵃ5, 1000ᵃ9–20, 1042ᵃ3 ff.; De caelo 298ᵇ13–24. Thomas Aquinas Summa theologica i. qu. 2, a. 3.

9. This view is still immediately intelligible, as can be seen, to a certain extent, from the following remark of A. N. Whitehead: "After Aristotle, ethical and religious interests began to influence metaphysical conclusions. . . . It may be doubted whether any properly general metaphysics can ever, without the illicit introduction of other considerations, get much further than Aristotle" (Science and the Modern World [Mentor Books ed.], pp. 173–74). Cf. Thomas Aquinas Summa theologica i. 2. qu. 58, a. 4–5, and qu. 104, a. 1; ii. 2, qu. 19, a. 7, and qu. 45, a. 3 (on the relation of philosophy to morality and religion).

ways, because to be perishable means to be in between being and not-being. One may express the same fundamental premise also by saying that "omnipotence" means power limited by knowledge of "natures,"[10] that is to say, of unchangeable and knowable necessity; all freedom and indeterminacy presuppose a more fundamental necessity.

Once nature is discovered, it becomes impossible to understand equally as customs or ways the characteristic or normal behavior of natural groups and of the different human tribes; the "customs" of natural beings are recognized as their natures, and the "customs" of the different human tribes are recognized as their conventions. The primeval notion of "custom" or "way" is split up into the notions of "nature," on the one hand, and "convention," on the other. The distinction between nature and convention, between *physis* and *nomos*, is therefore coeval with the discovery of nature and hence with philosophy.[11]

Nature would not have to be discovered if it were not hidden. Hence "nature" is necessarily understood in contradistinction to something else, namely, to that which hides nature in so far as it hides nature. There are scholars who refuse to take "nature" as a term of distinction, because they believe that everything which is, is natural. But they tacitly assume that man knows by nature that there is such a thing as nature or that "nature" is as unproblematic or as obvious as, say, "red." Besides, they are forced to distinguish between natural or existent things and illusory things or things which pretend to exist without existing; but they leave unarticulated the manner of being of the most important things which pretend to exist without existing. The distinction between nature and

10. Consider *Odyssey* x. 303–6.

11. As regards the earliest records of the distinction between nature and convention, see Karl Reinhardt, *Parmenides und die Geschichte der griechischen Philosophie* (Bonn, 1916), pp. 82–88.

convention implies that nature is essentially hidden by authoritative decisions. Man cannot live without having thoughts about the first things, and, it was presumed, he cannot live well without being united with his fellows by identical thoughts about the first things, i.e., without being subject to authoritative decisions concerning the first things: it is the law that claims to make manifest the first things or "what is." The law, in its turn, appeared to be a rule that derives its binding force from the agreement or the convention of the members of the group. The law or the convention has the tendency, or the function, to hide nature; it succeeds to such an extent that nature is, to begin with, experienced or "given" only as "custom." Hence the philosophic quest for the first things is guided by that understanding of "being" or "to be" according to which the most fundamental distinction of manners of. being is that between "to be in truth" and "to be by virtue of law or convention"—a distinction that survived in a barely recognizable form in the scholastic distinction between *ens reale* and *ens fictum*.[12]

The emergence of philosophy radically affects man's attitude toward political things in general and toward laws in particular, because it radically affects his understanding of these things. Originally, the authority par excellence or the root of all authority was the ancestral. Through the discovery of nature, the claim of the ancestral is uprooted; philosophy appeals from the ancestral to the good, to that which is good intrinsically, to that which is good by nature. Yet philosophy uproots the claim of the ancestral in such a manner as to preserve an essential element of it. For, when speaking of nature, the first philosophers meant the first things, i.e., the oldest things; philosophy appeals from the ancestral to something

12. Plato *Minos* 315ª1–b2 and 319c3; *Laws* 889e3–5, 890ª6–7, 891e1–2, 904ª9–b1; *Timaeus* 40d–41ª; cf. also Parmenides, Frag. 6 [Diels]; see P. Bayle, *Pensées diverses*, § 49.

older than the ancestral. Nature is the ancestor of all ancestors or the mother of all mothers. Nature is older than any tradition; hence it is more venerable than any tradition. The view that natural things have a higher dignity than things produced by men is based not on any surreptitious or unconscious borrowings from myth, or on residues of myth, but on the discovery of nature itself. Art presupposes nature, whereas nature does not presuppose art. Man's "creative" abilities, which are more admirable than any of his products, are not themselves produced by man: the genius of Shakespeare was not the work of Shakespeare. Nature supplies not only the materials but also the models for all arts; "the greatest and fairest things" are the work of nature as distinguished from art. By uprooting the authority of the ancestral, philosophy recognizes that nature is *the* authority.[13]

It would be less misleading, however, to say that, by uprooting authority, philosophy recognizes nature as *the* standard. For the human faculty that, with the help of sense-perception, discovers nature is reason or understanding, and the relation of reason or understanding to its objects is fundamentally different from that obedience without reasoning why that corresponds to authority proper. By calling nature the highest authority, one would blur the distinction by which philosophy stands or falls, the distinction between reason and authority. By submitting to authority, philosophy, in particular political philosophy, would lose its character; it would degenerate into ideology, i.e., apologetics for a given or emerging social order, or it would undergo a transformation into theology or legal learning. With regard to the situation in the eighteenth century, Charles Beard has said: "The clergy and the monarchists claimed special rights as divine right. The revolutionists resorted to nature."[14] What is true of the

13. Cicero *Laws* ii. 13 and 40; *De finibus* iv. 72; v. 17.
14. *The Republic* (New York, 1943), p. 38.

eighteenth-century revolutionists is true, *mutatis mutandis*, of all philosophers qua philosophers. The classical philosophers did full justice to the great truth underlying the identification of the good with the ancestral. Yet they could not have laid bare the underlying truth if they had not rejected that identification itself in the first place. Socrates, in particular, was a very conservative man as far as the ultimate practical conclusions of his political philosophy were concerned. Yet Aristophanes pointed to the truth by suggesting that Socrates' fundamental premise could induce a son to beat up his own father, i.e., to repudiate in practice the most natural authority.

The discovery of nature or of the fundamental distinction between nature and convention is the necessary condition for the emergence of the idea of natural right. But it is not its sufficient condition: all right might be conventional. This precisely is the theme of the basic controversy in political philosophy: Is there any natural right? It seems that the answer which prevailed prior to Socrates was the negative one, i.e., the view which we have called "conventionalism."[15] It is not surprising that philosophers should first have inclined toward conventionalism. Right presents itself, to begin with, as identical with law or custom or as a character of it; and custom or convention comes to sight, with the emergence of philosophy, as that which hides nature.

The crucial pre-Socratic text is a saying of Heraclitus: "In God's view, all things are fair [noble] and good and just, but men have made the supposition that some things are just and others are unjust." The very distinction between just and unjust is merely a human supposition or a human convention.[16] God, or whatever one may call the first cause, is beyond good

15. Cf. Plato *Laws* 889^{d}7–890^{a}2 with 891^{c}1–5 and 967^{a}7 ff.; Aristotle *Metaphysics* 990^{a}3–5 and *De caelo* 298^{b}13–24; Thomas Aquinas, *Summa theologica* i. qu. 44, *a.* 2.

16. Frag. 102; cf. Frags. 58, 67, 80.

and evil and even beyond good and bad. God is not concerned with justice in any sense that is relevant to human life as such: God does not reward justice and punish injustice. Justice has no superhuman support. That justice is good and injustice is bad is due exclusively to human agencies and ultimately to human decisions. "No traces of divine justice are found except where just men reign; otherwise there is one event, as we see, to the righteous and to the wicked." The denial of natural right thus appears to be the consequence of the denial of particular providence.[17] But the example of Aristotle alone would suffice to show that it is possible to admit natural right without believing in particular providence or in divine justice proper.[18]

For, however indifferent to moral distinctions the cosmic order may be thought to be, human nature, as distinguished from nature in general, may very well be the basis of such distinctions. To illustrate the point by the example of the best-known pre-Socratic doctrine, namely, of atomism, the fact that the atoms are beyond good and bad does not justify the inference that there is nothing by nature good or bad for any compounds of atoms, and especially for those compounds which we call "men." In fact, no one can say that all distinctions between good and bad which men make or all human preferences are merely conventional. We must therefore distinguish between those human desires and inclinations which

17. Spinoza, *Tractatus theologico-politicus*, chap. xix (§ 20, Bruder ed.). Victor Cathrein (*Recht, Naturrecht und positives Recht* [Freiburg im Breisgau, 1901], p. 139) says: ". . . lehnt man das Dasein eines persönlichen Schöpfers und Weltregierers ab, so ist das Naturrecht nicht mehr festzuhalten."

18. *Nicomachean Ethics* 1178b7–22; F. Socinus, *Praelectiones theologicae*, cap. 2; Grotius, *De jure belli ac pacis*, Prolegomena § 11; Leibniz, *Nouveaux essais*, Book I, chap. ii; § 2. Consider the following passages from Rousseau's *Contrat social:* "On voit encore que les parties contractantes seraient entre elles sous la seule loi de nature et sans aucun garant de leurs engagements réciproques . . ." (III, chap. 16) and "À considérer humainement les choses, faute de sanction naturelle, les lois de la justice sont vaines parmi les hommes" (II, chap. 6).

are natural and those which originate in conventions. Further-more, we must distinguish between those human desires and inclinations which are in accordance with human nature and therefore good for man, and those which are destructive of his nature or his humanity and therefore bad. We are thus led to the notion of a life, a human life, that is good because it is in accordance with nature.[19] Both parties to the controversy admit that there is such a life, or, more generally expressed, they admit the primacy of the good as distinguished from the just.[20] The controversial issue is whether the just is good (by nature good) or whether the life in accordance with human nature requires justice or morality.

In order to arrive at a clear distinction between the natural and the conventional, we have to go back to the period in the life of the individual[21] or of the race which antedates convention. We have to go back to the origins. With a view to the connection between right and civil society, the question of the origin of right transforms itself into the question of the origin of civil society or of society in general. This question leads to the question of the origin of the human race. It further leads to the question of what man's original condition was like: whether it was perfect or imperfect and, if it was imperfect, whether the imperfection had the character of gentleness (good-naturedness or innocence) or of savagery.

If we examine the record of the age-old discussion of these questions, we can easily receive the impression that almost

19. This notion was accepted by "almost all" classical philosophers, as Cicero emphasizes (*De finibus* v. 17). It was rejected, above all, by the Skeptics (see Sextus Empiricus *Pyrrhonica* iii. 235).

20. Plato *Republic* 493ᵉ1–5, 504ᵈ4–505ᵃ4; *Symposium* 206ᵉ2–207ᵃ2; *Theaetetus* 177ᶜ6–ᵈ7; Aristotle *Nicomachean Ethics* 1094ᵃ1–3 and ᵇ14–18.

21. As regards reflections on how man is "immediately from the moment of his birth," see, e.g., Aristotle *Politics* 1254ᵃ23 and *Nicomachean Ethics* 1144ᵇ4–6; Cicero *De finibus* ii. 31–32; iii. 16; v. 17, 43, and 55; Diogenes Laertius x. 137; Grotius, *op. cit.*, Prolegomena § 7; Hobbes, *De cive*, i, 2, annot. 1.

any answer to the questions regarding the origins is compatible with the acceptance or the rejection of natural right.[22] These difficulties have contributed to the depreciation, not to say the complete disregard, of the questions concerning the origin of civil society and of the condition of "the first men." What is important, we have been told, is "the idea of the state" and in no way "the historical origin of the state."[23] This modern view is a consequence of the rejection of nature as the standard. Nature and Freedom, Reality and Norm, the Is and the Ought, appeared to be wholly independent of one another; hence it seemed that we cannot learn anything important about civil society and about right by studying the origins. From the point of view of the ancients, however, the question of the origins is of decisive importance because the correct answer to it clarifies the status, the dignity, of civil society and of right. One inquires into the origins or the genesis of civil society, or of right and wrong, in order to find out whether civil society and right or wrong are based on nature or merely on convention.[24] And the question of the "essential" origin of civil society and of right or wrong cannot be answered without consideration of what is known about the beginnings or the "historical" origins.

As for the question of whether man's actual condition in the beginning was perfect or imperfect, the answer to it decides whether the human race is fully responsible for its actual imperfection or whether that imperfection is "excused" by the original imperfection of the race. In other words, the view

22. As for the combination of the assumption of savage beginnings with the acceptance of natural right, cf. Cicero *Pro Sestio* 91–92 with *Tusc. Disp.* v. 5–6, *Republic* i. 2, and *Offices* ii. 15. See also Polybius vi. 4. 7, 5. 7–6. 7, 7. 1. Consider the implication of Plato *Laws* 680ᵈ4–7 and of Aristotle *Politics* 1253ᵃ35–38.

23. Hegel, *Philosophy of Right*, § 258; cf. Kant, *Metaphysik der Sitten*, ed. Vorlaender, pp. 142 and 206–7.

24. Cf. Aristotle *Politics* 1252ᵃ18 ff. and 24 ff. with 1257ᵃ4 ff. Consider Plato *Republic* 369ᵇ5–7, *Laws* 676ᵃ1–3; also Cicero *Republic* i. 39–41.

that man's beginning was perfect is in accordance with the equation of the good with the ancestral, as well as with theology rather than philosophy. For man remembered and admitted at all times that the arts were invented by man or that the first age of the world did not know the arts; but philosophy necessarily presupposes the arts; therefore, if the philosophic life is indeed the right life or the life according to nature, man's beginnings were necessarily imperfect.[25]

For our present purpose it is sufficient to give an analysis of the standard argument used by conventionalism. That argument is to the effect that there cannot be natural right because "the just things" differ from society to society. This argument has shown an amazing vitality throughout the ages, a vitality which seems to contrast with its intrinsic worth. As usually presented, the argument consists of a simple enumeration of the different notions of justice that prevail or prevailed in different nations or at different times within the same nation. As we have indicated before, the mere fact of variety or mutability of "the just things" or of the notions of justice does not warrant the rejection of natural right except if one makes certain assumptions, and these assumptions are in most cases not even stated. We are therefore compelled to reconstruct the conventionalist argument out of scattered and fragmentary remarks.

It is granted on all sides that there cannot be natural right if the principles of right are not unchangeable.[26] But the facts to which conventionalism refers do not seem to prove that the principles of right are changeable. They merely seem to prove that different societies have different notions of justice or of the principles of justice. As little as man's varying notions of

25. Plato *Laws* 677^{b}5–678^{b}3, 679^c; Aristotle *Metaphysics* 981^{b}13–25.

26. Aristotle *Nicomachean Ethics* 1094^{b}14–16 and 1134^{b}18–27; Cicero *Republic* iii. 13–18 and 20; Sextus Empiricus *Pyrrhonica* iii. 218 and 222. Cf. Plato *Laws* 889^{e}6–8 and Xenophon *Memorabilia* iv. 4. 19.

the universe prove that there is no universe or that there cannot be *the* true account of the universe or that man can never arrive at true and final knowledge of the universe, so little seem man's varying notions of justice to prove that there is no natural right or that natural right is unknowable. The variety of notions of justice can be understood as the variety of errors, which variety does not contradict, but presupposes, the existence of the one truth regarding justice. This objection to conventionalism would hold if the existence of natural right were compatible with the fact that all men or most men were or are ignorant of natural right. But when speaking of natural right, one implies that justice is of vital importance to man or that man cannot live or live well without justice; and life in accordance with justice requires knowledge of the principles of justice. If man has such a nature that he cannot live, or live well, without justice, he must have by nature knowledge of the principles of justice. But if this were the case, all men would agree as regards the principles of justice, just as they agree as regards the sensible qualities.[27]

Yet this demand seems to be unreasonable; there is not even universal agreement as regards the sensible qualities. Not all men, but only all normal men, agree as regards sounds, colors, and the like. Accordingly, the existence of natural right requires merely that all normal men should agree as regards the principles of justice. The lack of universal agreement can be explained by a corruption of human nature in those who ignore the true principles, a corruption which, for obvious reasons, is more frequent and more effective than the corresponding corruption in regard to the perception of sensible qualities.[28] But if it is true that the notions of justice differ from society to society or from age to age, this view of natural right will lead to the hard consequence that the members of one par-

27. Cicero *Republic* iii. 13 and *Laws* i. 47; Plato *Laws* 889e.
28. Cicero *Laws* i. 33 and 47.

ticular society or perhaps even only one generation in one particular society or, at the most, the members of some particular
societies must be regarded as the only normal human beings in
existence. For all practical purposes, this means that the natural right teacher will identify natural right with those notions of justice that are cherished by his own society or by his
own "civilization." By speaking of natural right, he will do
nothing else than claim universal validity for the prejudices of
his group. If it is asserted that, as a matter of fact, many societies agree in regard to the principles of justice, it is at least
as plausible to rejoin that this agreement is due to accidental
causes (such as similarity of conditions of life or mutual influence) than to say that these particular societies alone have
preserved human nature intact. If it is asserted that all civilized nations agree in regard to the principles of justice, one
would first have to know what is meant by "civilization." If
the natural right teacher identifies civilization with recognition of natural right or an equivalent, he says, in effect, that
all men who accept the principles of natural right accept the
principles of natural right. If he understands by "civilization"
a high development of the arts or sciences, his contention is
refuted by the fact that conventionalists are frequently civilized men; and believers in natural right or in the principles
which are said to constitute the essence of natural right are
frequently very little civilized.[29]

This argument against natural right presupposes that all
knowledge which men need in order to live well is natural in
the sense in which the perception of sensible qualities and
other kinds of effortless perception are natural. It loses its
force, therefore, once one assumes that knowledge of natural
right must be acquired by human effort or that knowledge of
natural right has the character of science. This would explain
why knowledge of natural right is not always available. It

29. Cf. Locke, *An Essay Concerning Human Understanding*, Book I, chap. iii, sec. 20.

would lead to the consequence that there is no possibility of a good or just life or no possibility of "the cessation of evil" before such knowledge has become available. But science has as its object what is always or what is unchangeable or what is truly. Therefore, natural right, or justice, must truly exist, and therefore it must "have everywhere the same power."[30] Thus it seems that it must have an effect that is always the same and that never ceases at least on human thought on justice. Yet, in fact, we see that human thoughts on justice are in a state of disagreement and fluctuation.

But this very fluctuation and disagreement would seem to prove the effectiveness of natural right. As regards such things as are unquestionably conventional—weights, measures money, and the like—one can hardly speak of disagreement between the various societies. Different societies make different arrangements in regard to weights, measures, and money; these arrangements do not contradict one another. But if different societies hold different views regarding the principles of justice, their views contradict one another. Differences regarding things which are unquestionably conventional do not arouse serious perplexities, whereas differences regarding the principles of right and wrong necessarily do. The disagreement regarding the principles of justice thus seems to reveal a genuine perplexity aroused by a divination or insufficient grasp of natural right—a perplexity caused by something self-subsistent or natural that eludes human grasp. This suspicion could be thought to be confirmed by a fact which, at first glance, seems to speak decisively in favor of conventionalism. Everywhere it is said that it is just to do what the law commands or that the just is identical with the legal, i.e., with what human beings establish as legal or agree to regard as legal. Yet does this not imply that there is a measure of universal agreement in regard to justice? It is true that, on reflec-

30. Aristotle *Nicomachean Ethics* 1134[b]19.

tion, people deny that the just is simply identical with the legal, for they speak of "unjust" laws. But does not the unreflective universal agreement point to the workings of nature? And does not the untenable character of the universal belief in the identity of the just with the legal indicate that the legal, while not being identical with the just, reflects natural right more or less dimly? The evidence adduced by conventionalism is perfectly compatible with the possibility that natural right exists and, as it were, solicits the indefinite variety of notions of justice or the indefinite variety of laws, or is at the bottom of all laws.[31]

The decision depends now on the result of the analysis of law. Law reveals itself as something self-contradictory. On the one hand, it claims to be something essentially good or noble: it is the law that saves the cities and everything else. On the other hand, the law presents itself as the common opinion or decision of the city, i.e., of the multitude of citizens. As such, it is by no means essentially good or noble. It may very well be the work of folly and baseness. There is certainly no reason to assume that the makers of laws are as a rule wiser than "you and I"; why, then, should "you and I" submit to their decision? The mere fact that the same laws which were solemnly enacted by the city are repealed by the same city with equal solemnity would seem to show the doubtful character of the wisdom that went into their making.[32] The question, then, is whether the claim of the law to be something good or noble can be simply dismissed as altogether unfounded or whether it contains an element of truth.

The law claims that it saves the cities and everything else. It claims to secure the common good. But the common good is

31. Plato *Republic* 340ª7–8 and 338ᵈ10–ᵉ2; Xenophon *Memorabilia* iv. 6. 6; Aristotle *Nicomachean Ethics* 1129ᵇ12; Heraclitus, Frag. 114.

32. Plato *Hippias maior* 284ᵈ⁻ᵉ; *Laws* 644ᵈ2–3 and 780ᵈ4–5; *Minos* 314ᶜ1–ᵉ5; Xenophon *Memorabilia* i. 2. 42 and iv. 4. 14; Aeschylus *Seven* 1071–72; Aristophanes *Clouds* 1421–22.

exactly what we mean by "the just." Laws are just to the extent that they are conducive to the common good. But if the just is identical with the common good, the just or right cannot be conventional: the conventions of a city cannot make good for the city what is, in fact, fatal for it and vice versa. The nature of things and not convention then determines in each case what is just. This implies that what is just may very well differ from city to city and from period to period: the variety of just things is not only compatible with, but a consequence of, the principle of justice, namely, that the just is identical with the common good. Knowledge of what is just here and now, which is knowledge of what is by nature, or intrinsically, good for this city now, cannot be scientific knowledge. Still less can it be knowledge of the type of sense-perception. To establish what is just in each case is the function of the political art or skill. That art or skill is comparable to the art of the physician, who establishes what is in each case healthy or good for the human body.[33]

Conventionalism avoids this consequence by denying that there is in truth a common good. What is called the "common good" is, in fact, in each case the good, not of the whole, but of a part. The laws which claim to be directed toward the common good claim indeed to be the decision of the city. But the city owes such unity as it possesses, and therewith its being, to its "constitution" or to its regime: the city is always either a democracy or an oligarchy or a monarchy and so on. The difference of regimes has its root in the difference of the parts or sections out of which the city is composed. Therefore, every regime is the rule of a section of the city. Hence the laws are, in fact, the work not of the city but of that section of the city which happens to be in control. It is needless to say that democracy, which claims to be the rule of all, is, in fact, the

33. Cf. Aristotle *Nicomachean Ethics* 1129^{b}17–19 and *Politics* 1282^{b}15–17 with Plato *Theaetetus* 167^{c}2–8, 172^{a}1–^{b}6, and 177^{c}6–178^{b}1.

rule of a part; for democracy is at the most the rule of the majority of all adults who inhabit the territory of the city; but the majority are the poor; and the poor are a section, however numerous, which has an interest distinct from the interests of the other sections. The ruling section is, of course, concerned exclusively with its own interest. But it pretends for an obvious reason that the laws which it lays down with a view to its own interest are good for the city as a whole.[34]

Yet may there not be mixed regimes, i.e., regimes which more or less successfully try to establish a fair balance between the conflicting interests of the essential sections of the city? Or is it not possible that the true interest of one particular section (of the poor or of the gentlemen, for example) coincides with the common interest? Objections of this kind presuppose that the city is a genuine whole or, more precisely, that the city exists by nature. But the city would seem to be a conventional or fictitious unity. For what is natural comes into being and exists without violence. All violence applied to a being makes that being do something which goes against its grain, i.e., against its nature. But the city stands or falls by violence, compulsion, or coercion. There is, then, no essential difference between political rule and the rule of a master over his slaves. But the unnatural character of slavery seems to be obvious: it goes against any man's grain to be made a slave or to be treated as a slave.[35]

Furthermore, the city is a multitude of citizens. A citizen appears to be the offspring, the natural product, of born citizens, of a citizen father and a citizen mother. Yet he is a citizen only if the citizen father and the citizen mother who generated

34. Plato *Laws* 889^{d}4–890^{a}2 and 714^{b}3–^{d}10; *Republic* 338^{d}7–339^{a}4 and 340^{a}7–8; Cicero *Republic* iii. 23.

35. Aristotle *Politics* 1252^{a}7–17, 1253^{b}20–23, 1255^{a}8–11 (cf. *Nicomachean Ethics* 1096^{a}5–6, 1109^{b}35–1110^{a}4, 1110^{b}15–17, 1179^{b}28–29, 1180^{a}4–5, 18–21; *Metaphysics* 1015^{a}26–33). Plato *Protagoras* 337^{c}7–^{d}3; *Laws* 642^{c}6–^{d}1; Cicero *Republic* iii. 23; *De finibus* v. 56; Fortescue, *De laudibus legum Angliae* chap. xlii (ed. Chrimes, p. 104).

him are lawfully wedded to each other, or rather if his presumed father is the husband of his mother. Otherwise, he is only a "natural" child and not a "legitimate" child. And what a legitimate child is depends not on nature but on law or convention. For the family in general, and the monogamous family in particular, is not a natural group, as even Plato was forced to admit. There is also the fact called "naturalization," by virtue of which a "natural" foreigner is artificially transformed into a "natural" citizen. In a word, who is or who is not a citizen depends on the law, and on the law alone. The difference between citizens and noncitizens is not natural but conventional. Therefore, all citizens are, in fact, "made" and not "born." It is convention that arbitrarily cuts off one segment of the human race and sets it off against the rest. One might think for a moment that the civil society which is truly natural, or the genuine civil society, would coincide with the group that embraces all those, and only those, who speak the same language. But languages are admittedly conventional. Accordingly, the distinction between Greeks and barbarians is merely conventional. It is as arbitrary as the division of all numbers into two groups, one consisting of the number 10,000 and the other consisting of all other numbers. The same applies to the distinction between free men and slaves. This distinction is based on the convention that people taken prisoner in war and not ransomed are to be made slaves; not nature but convention makes slaves, and therewith freemen as distinguished from slaves. To conclude, the city is a multitude of human beings who are united not by nature but solely by convention. They have united or banded together in order to take care of their common interest—over against other human beings who are not by nature distinguished from them: over against foreigners and slaves. Hence what claims to be the common good is, in fact, the interest of a part which claims to be a whole, or a part which forms a unity only by virtue of this claim, this pretense, this convention. If the city is conventional, the common good is conventional, and therewith it is proved that right or justice is conventional.[36]

How adequate this account of justice is, is said to appear from the fact that it "saves the phenomena" of justice; it is said to make intelligible those simple experiences regarding right and wrong which are at the bottom of the natural right doctrines. In those experiences, justice is understood as the habit of refraining from hurting others or as the habit of helping others or as the habit of subordinating the good of a part (the good of the individual or of a section) to the good of the whole. Justice thus understood is indeed necessary for the preservation of the city. But it is unfortunate for the defenders of justice that it is also required for the preservation of a gang of robbers: the gang could not last a single day if its members did not refrain from hurting one another, if they did not help one another, or if each member did not subordinate his own good to the good of the gang. To this the objection is made that the justice practiced by robbers is not genuine justice or that it is precisely justice which distinguishes the city from a gang of robbers. The so-called "justice" of robbers is in the service of manifest injustice. But is not exactly the same true of the city? If the city is not a genuine whole, what is called the "good of the whole," or the just, in opposition to the unjust or selfish, is, in fact, merely the demand of collective selfishness; and there is no reason why collective selfishness should claim to be more respectable than the selfishness of the individual. In other words, the robbers are said to practice justice only among themselves, whereas the city is said to practice justice also toward those who do not belong to the city or

36. Antiphon, in Diels, *Vorsokratiker* (5th ed.), B44 (A7, B2). Plato *Protagoras* 337^{c}7–^{d}3; *Republic* 456^{b}12–^{c}3 (and context); *Statesman* 262^{c}10–^{e}5; Xenophon *Hiero* 4. 3–4; Aristotle *Politics* 1275^{a}1–2, ^{b}21–31, 1278^{a}30–35; Cicero *Republic* iii. 16–17 and *Laws* ii. 5. Consider the implication of the comparison of civil societies to "herds" (see Xenophon *Cyropaedia* i. 1. 2; cf. Plato *Minos* 318^{a}1–3).

toward other cities. But is this true? Are the maxims of foreign policy essentially different from the maxims on which gangs of robbers act? Can they be different? Are cities not compelled to use force and fraud or to take away from other cities what belong to the latter, if they are to prosper? Do they not come into being by usurping a part of the earth's surface which by nature belongs equally to all others?[37]

It is, of course, possible for the city to refrain from hurting other cities or to be resigned to poverty, just as the individual can live justly if he wants to. But the question is whether in acting thus men would live according to nature or merely follow convention. Experience shows that only few individuals and hardly any cities act justly except when they are compelled to do so. Experience shows that justice by itself is ineffectual. This merely confirms what was shown before, that justice has no basis in nature. The common good proved to be the selfish interest of a collective. The selfish interest of the collective is derived from the selfish interest of the only natural elements of the collective, namely, of the individuals. By nature everyone seeks his own good and nothing but his own good. Justice, however, tells us to seek other men's good. What justice demands from us is then against nature. The natural good, the good which does not depend on the whims and follies of man, this substantial good appears to be the very opposite of that shadowy good called "right" or "justice." It is the natural good which is one's own good toward which everyone is drawn by nature, whereas right or justice becomes attractive only through compulsion and ultimately through convention. Even those who assert that right is natural have to admit that justice consists in a kind of reciprocity; men are bidden to do to others what they desire to have done to themselves. Men are compelled to benefit others because they desire

<hr>

37. Plato *Republic* 335[d]11–12 and 351[c]7–[d]13; Xenophon *Memorabilia* iv. 4. 12 and 8. 11; Aristotle *Nicomachean Ethics* 1129[b]11–19, 1130[a]3–5 and 1134[b]2–6; Cicero *Offices* i. 28–29; *Republic* iii. 11–31.

to be benefited by others: in order to receive kindness, one must show kindness. Justice appears to be derivative from selfishness and subservient to it. This amounts to an admission that by nature everyone seeks only his own good. To be good at seeking one's own good is prudence or wisdom. Prudence or wisdom is therefore incompatible with justice proper. The man who is truly just is unwise or a fool—a man duped by convention.[38]

Conventionalism claims, then, to be perfectly compatible with the admission that the city and right are useful for the individual: the individual is too weak to live, or to live well, without the assistance of others. Everyone is better off in civil society than in a condition of solitude and savagery. Yet the fact that something is useful does not prove that it is natural. Crutches are useful for a man who has lost a leg; is wearing crutches according to nature? Or, to express this more adequately, can things that exist exclusively because calculation has found out that they would be useful be said to be natural to man? Can one say of things which are desired exclusively on the basis of calculation or which are not desired spontaneously or for their own sake that they are natural to man? The city and right are no doubt advantageous; but are they free from great disadvantages? Therefore, the conflict between the self-interest of the individual and the demands of the city or of right is inevitable. The city cannot settle this conflict except by declaring that the city or right is of higher dignity than the self-interest of the individual or that it is sacred. But this claim, which is of the essence of the city and of right, is essentially fictitious.[39]

The nerve of the conventionalist argument, then, is this:

38. Thrasymachus, in Diels, *Vorsokratiker* (5th ed.), B8; Plato *Republic* 343^{c}3, 6-7, ^{d}2, 348^{c}11-12, 360^{d}5; *Protagoras* 333^{d}4-^{e}1; Xenophon *Memorabilia* ii. 2. 11-12; Aristotle *Nicomachean Ethics* 1130^{a}3-5, 1132^{b}33-1133^{a}5, 1134^{b}5-6; Cicero *Republic* iii. 16, 20, 21, 23, 24, 29-30.

39. Plato *Protagoras* 322^{b}6, 327^{c}4-^{e}1; Cicero *Republic* i. 39-40, iii. 23, 26; *De finibus* ii. 59; cf. also Rousseau, *Discours sur l'origine de l'inégalité* (Flammarion ed.), p. 173.

right is conventional because right belongs essentially to the city[40] and the city is conventional. Contrary to our first impression, conventionalism does not assert that the meaning of right or justice is altogether arbitrary or that there is no universal agreement of any kind in regard to right or justice. On the contrary, conventionalism presupposes that all men understand by justice fundamentally the same thing: to be just means not to hurt others, or it means to help others or to be concerned with the common good. Conventionalism rejects natural right on these grounds: (1) justice stands in an inescapable tension with everyone's natural desire, which is directed solely toward his own good; (2) as far as justice has a foundation in nature—as far as it is, generally speaking, advantageous to the individual—its demands are limited to the members of the city, i.e., of a conventional unit; what is called "natural right" consists of certain rough rules of social expediency which are valid only for the members of the particular group and which, in addition, lack universal validity even in intra-group relations; (3) what is universally meant by "right" or "justice" leaves wholly undetermined the precise meaning of "helping" or "hurting" or "the common good"; it is only through specification that these terms become truly meaningful, and every specification is conventional. The variety of notions of justice confirms rather than proves the conventional character of justice.

When Plato attempts to establish the existence of natural right, he reduces the conventionalist thesis to the premise that the good is identical with the pleasant. Conversely, we see that classical hedonism led to the most uncompromising depreciation of the whole political sphere. It would not be surprising if the primeval equation of the good with the ancestral had been replaced, first of all, by the equation of the good with the pleasant. For when the primeval equation is

40. Aristotle *Politics* 1253^{a}37–38.

rejected on the basis of the distinction between nature and convention, the things forbidden by ancestral custom or the divine law present themselves as emphatically natural and hence intrinsically good. The things forbidden by ancestral custom are forbidden because they are desired; and the fact that they are forbidden by convention shows that they are not desired on the basis of convention; they are then desired by nature. Now what induces man to deviate from the narrow path of ancestral custom or divine law appears to be the desire for pleasure and the aversion to pain. The natural good thus appears to be pleasure. Orientation by pleasure becomes the first substitute for the orientation by the ancestral.[41]

The most developed form of classical hedonism is Epicureanism. Epicureanism is certainly that form of conventionalism which has exercised the greatest influence throughout the ages. Epicureanism is unambiguously materialistic. And it was in materialism that Plato found the root of conventionalism.[42] The Epicurean argument runs as follows: To find what is by nature good, we have to see what kind of thing it is whose goodness is guaranteed by nature or whose goodness is felt independently of any opinion, and hence, in particular, independently of any convention. What is good by nature shows itself in what we seek from the moment of birth, prior to all reasoning, calculation, discipline, restraint, or compulsion. Good, in this sense, is only the pleasant. Pleasure is the only good that is immediately felt or sensibly perceived as good. Therefore, the primary pleasure is the pleasure of the body, and this means, of course, the pleasure of one's own body; everyone seeks by nature only his own good; all concern with other people's good is derivative. Opinion, which comprises

41. Antiphon, in Diels, *Vorsokratiker* (5th ed.), B44, A5; Thucydides v. 105; Plato *Republic* 364ª2–4 and 538ᶜ6–539ª4; *Laws* 662ᵈ, 875ᵇ1–ᶜ3, 886ª8–ᵇ2, 888ª3; *Protagoras* 352ᵈ6 ff.; *Clitophon* 407ᵈ4–6; *Eighth Letter* 354ᵉ5–355ª1 (cf. also *Gorgias* 495ᵈ1–5); Xenophon *Memorabilia* ii. 1; Cicero *Laws* i. 36 and 38–39.

42. *Laws* 889ᵇ–890ª.

both right and wrong reasoning, leads men toward three kinds of objects of choice: toward the greatest pleasure, toward the useful, and toward the noble. As for the first, since we observe that various kinds of pleasure are connected with pain, we are induced to distinguish between more or less preferable pleasures. Thus we notice the difference between those natural pleasures which are necessary and those which are not necessary. Furthermore, we realize that there are pleasures which are free of any admixture of pain, and others which are not. Finally, we are led to see that there is a term of pleasure, a complete pleasure, and this pleasure proves to be the end toward which we are tending by nature and to be accessible only through philosophy. As for the useful, it is not in itself pleasant, but is conducive to pleasure, to genuine pleasure. The noble, on the other hand, is neither genuinely pleasant nor conducive to genuine pleasure. The noble is that which is praised, which is pleasant only because it is praised or because it is regarded as honorable; the noble is good only because people call it good or say that it is good; it is good only by convention. The noble reflects in a distorted manner the substantial good for the sake of which men made the fundamental convention or the social compact. Virtue belongs to the class of the useful things. Virtue is, indeed, desirable, but it is not desirable for its own sake. It becomes desirable only on the basis of calculation, and it contains an element of compulsion and therefore of pain. It is, however, productive of pleasure.[43] Yet there is a crucial difference between justice and the other virtues. Prudence, temperance, and courage bring about pleasure through their

43. Epicurus *Ratae sententiae* 7; Diogenes Laertius x 137; Cicero *De finibus* i. 30, 32, 33, 35, 37, 38, 42, 45, 54, 55, 61, 63; ii. 48, 49, 107, 115; iii. 3; iv. 51; *Offices* iii. 116–17; *Tusc. Disp.* v. 73; *Acad. Pr.* ii. 140; *Republic* iii. 26. Cf. the formulation of the Epicurean principle by Philip Melanchthon (*Philosophiae moralis epitome*, Part I: *Corpus Reformatorum*, Vol. XVI, col. 32): "Illa actio est finis, ad quam natura ultro fertur, et non coacta. Ad voluptatem ultro rapiuntur homines maximo impetu, ad virtutem vix cogi possunt. Ergo voluptas est finis hominis, non virtus." Cf. also Hobbes, *De cive*, i, 2.

natural consequences, whereas justice produces the pleasure which is expected from it—a sense of security—only on the basis of convention. The other virtues have a salutary effect regardless of whether or not other people know of one's being prudent, temperate, or courageous. But one's justice has a salutary effect only if one is thought to be just. The other vices are evils independently of whether they are detected or detectable by others or not. But injustice is an evil only with a view to the hardly avoidable danger of detection. The tension between justice and what is by nature good comes out most clearly if one compares justice with friendship. Both justice and friendship originate in calculation, but friendship comes to be intrinsically pleasant or desirable for its own sake. Friendship is at any rate incompatible with compulsion. But justice and the association that is concerned with justice—the city—stand or fall by compulsion. And compulsion is unpleasant.[44]

The greatest document of philosophic conventionalism and, in fact, its only document available to us that is both authentic

44. Epicurus *Ratae sententiae* 34; *Gnomologium Vaticanum* 23; Cicero *De finibus* i. 51 (cf. 41), 65–70; ii. 28 and 82; *Offices* iii. 118. In *Ratae sententiae* 31, Epicurus says: "The right [or the just] of nature is a *symbolon* of the advantage deriving from men's not harming each other and not being harmed." As is shown by *Ratae sententiae* 32 ff., this cannot mean that there is a natural right in the strict sense, i.e., a right independent of, or prior to, all covenants or compacts: the *symbolon* is identical with a compact of some kind. What Epicurus suggests is that, in spite of the infinite variety of just things, justice or right is everywhere designed primarily to fulfil one and the same function: right understood in the light of its universal or primary function is, in a sense, "the right of nature." It is opposed to the fabulous or superstitious accounts of justice which are generally accepted in the cities. "The right of nature" is that principle of right which is admitted by the conventionalist doctrine. "The right of nature" thus becomes equivalent to "the nature of right" (*Ratae sententiae* 37) as opposed to the false opinions about right. The expression "the nature of right" is used by Glaucon in his summary of the conventionalist doctrine in the *Republic* (359^{b}4–5): the nature of right consists in a certain convention that is against nature. Gassendi, the famous restorer of Epicureanism, had stronger incentives than the ancient Epicureans for asserting the existence of natural right. In addition, Hobbes had taught him how Epicureanism could be combined with the assertion of natural right. Yet Gassendi did not avail himself of this novel opportunity. See his paraphrase of *Ratae sententiae* 31 (*Animadversiones* [Lyon, 1649], pp. 1748–49).

and comprehensive is the poem *On the Nature of Things* by the Epicurean Lucretius. According to Lucretius, men roamed originally in forests, without social bonds of any kind or without any conventional restraint. Their weakness and their fear of the dangers threatening them from wild beasts induced them to unite for the sake of protection or for the sake of the pleasure deriving from security. After they entered society, the savage life of the beginning gave way to habits of kindness and fidelity. This early society, the society antedating by far the foundation of cities, was the best and most happy society that ever was. Right would be natural if the life of the early society were the life according to nature. But the life according to nature is the life of the philosopher. And philosophy is impossible in early society. Philosophy has its home in cities, and the destruction, or at least the impairment, of the way of life characteristic of early society is characteristic of the life in cities. The happiness of the philosopher, the only true happiness, belongs to an entirely different epoch than the happiness of society. There is, then, a disproportion between the requirements of philosophy or of the life according to nature and the requirements of society as society. It is owing to this necessary disproportion that right cannot be natural. The disproportion is necessary for the following reason. The happiness of early, noncoercive society was ultimately due to the reign of a salutary delusion. The members of early society lived within a finite world or a closed horizon; they trusted in the eternity of the visible universe or in the protection afforded to them by "the walls of the world." It was this trust which made them innocent, kind, and willing to devote themselves to the good of others; for it is fear which makes men savage. The trust in the firmness of "the walls of the world" was not yet shaken by reasoning about natural catastrophes. Once this trust was shaken, men lost their innocence, they became savage; and thus the need for coercive society arose. Once this trust was shaken, men had no choice but to seek support and consolation in the belief in active gods; the free will of the gods should guarantee the firmness of "the walls of the world" which had been seen to lack intrinsic or natural firmness; the goodness of the gods should be a substitute for the lack of intrinsic firmness of "the walls of the world." The belief in active gods then grows out of fear for our world and attachment to our world—the world of sun and moon and stars, and the earth covering itself with fresh green every spring, the world of life as distinguished from the lifeless but eternal elements (the atoms and the void) out of which our world has come into being and into which it will perish again. Yet, however comforting the belief in active gods may be, it has engendered unspeakable evils. The only remedy lies in breaking through "the walls of the world" at which religion stops and in becoming reconciled to the fact that we live in every respect in an unwalled city, in an infinite universe in which nothing that man can love can be eternal. The only remedy lies in philosophizing, which alone affords the most solid pleasure. Yet philosophy is repulsive to the people because philosophy requires freedom from attachment to "our world." On the other hand, the people cannot return to the happy simplicity of early society. They must therefore continue the wholly unnatural life that is characterized by the co-operation of coercive society and religion. The good life, the life according to nature, is the retired life of the philosopher who lives at the fringes of civil society. The life devoted to civil society and to the service of others is not the life according to nature.[45]

45. In reading Lucretius' poem, one must constantly keep in mind the fact that what strikes the reader first, and what is meant to strike the reader first, is "the sweet" (or what is comforting to unphilosophic man) and not "the bitter" or "the sad." The poem's opening with the praise of Venus and its ending with the somber description of the plague are only the most obvious and by no means the most important examples of the principle stated in i. 935 ff. and iv. 10 ff. For the understanding of the section dealing with human society (v. 925–1456), one has to consider, in addition, the plan of this

We must make a distinction between philosophic conventionalism and vulgar conventionalism. Vulgar conventionalism is presented most clearly in "the unjust speech" which Plato intrusted to Thrasymachus and to Glaucon and Adeimantus. According to it, the greatest good, or the most pleasant thing, is to have more than the others or to rule others. But the city and right necessarily impose some restraint on the desire for the greatest pleasure; they are incompatible with the greatest pleasure or with what is the greatest good by nature; they are against nature; they originate in convention. Hobbes would say that the city and right originate in the desire for life and that the desire for life is at least as natural as the desire for ruling others. To this objection the representative of vulgar conventionalism would reply that mere life is misery and that a miserable life is not a life which our nature seeks. The city and right are against nature because they sacrifice the greater good to the lesser good. It is true that the desire for superiority to others can come into its own only within the city. But this merely means that the life according to nature consists in cleverly exploiting the opportunities created by convention or in taking advantage of the good-natured trust which the many put in convention. Such exploitation requires that one be not hampered by sincere respect for city and right. The life according to nature requires such perfect inner freedom from the power of convention as is combined with the appearance of conventional behavior. The appearance of justice combined with actual injustice will lead one to the summit of happiness. One must indeed be clever to hide one's in-

---

particular section: (*a*) prepolitical life (925–1027), (*b*) the inventions belonging to prepolitical life (1028–1104), (*c*) political society (1105–60), (*d*) the inventions belonging to political society (1161–1456). Cf. the reference to fire in 1011 with 1091 ff., and the references to *facies viresque* as well as to gold in 1111–13 with 1170–71 and 1241 ff. Cf. from this point of view 977–81 with 1211 ff.; cf. also 1156 with 1161 and 1222–25 (see ii. 620–23, and Cicero *De finibus* i. 51). See also i. 72–74, 943–45; iii. 16–17, 59–86; v. 91–109, 114–21, 1392–1435; vi. 1–6, 596–607.

justice successfully while practicing it on a large scale; but this merely means that the life according to nature is the preserve of a small minority, of the natural elite, of those who are truly men and not born to be slaves. To be more precise, the summit of happiness is the life of the tyrant, of the man who has successfully committed the greatest crime by subordinating the city as a whole to his private good and who can afford to drop the appearance of justice or legality.[46]

Vulgar conventionalism is the vulgarized version of philosophic conventionalism. Philosophic and vulgar conventionalism agree as to this: that by nature everyone seeks only his own good or that it is according to nature that one does not pay any regard to other people's good or that the regard for others arises only out of convention. Yet philosophic conventionalism denies that to pay no regard to others means to desire to have more than others or to be superior to others. Philosophic conventionalism is so far from regarding the desire for superiority as natural that it regards it as vain or opinion-bred. Philosophers, who as such have tasted more solid pleasures than those deriving from wealth, power, and the like, could not possibly identify the life according to nature with the life of the tyrant. Vulgar conventionalism owes its origin to a corruption of philosophic conventionalism. It makes sense to trace that corruption to "the sophists." The sophists may be said to have "published" and therewith debased the conventionalist teaching of pre-Socratic philosophers.

"Sophist" is a term which has many meanings. Among other things it may mean a philosopher, or a philosopher who holds unpopular views, or a man who shows his lack of good taste by teaching noble subjects for pay. At least since Plato, "sophist" is normally used in contradistinction to "philosopher" and therewith in a derogatory sense. "The Sophists" in

46. Plato *Republic* 344ᵃ⁻ᶜ, 348ᵈ, 358ᵉ3–362ᶜ, 364ᵃ1–4, 365ᶜ6–ᵈ2; *Laws* 890ᵃ7–9.

the historical sense are certain fifth-century Greeks who are presented by Plato and other philosophers as sophists in the precise sense, i.e., as nonphilosophers of a certain type. The sophist in the precise sense is a teacher of sham wisdom. Sham wisdom is not identical with untrue doctrine. Otherwise Plato would have been a sophist in the eyes of Aristotle, and vice versa. An erring philosopher is something entirely different from a sophist. Nothing prevents a sophist from occasionally and perhaps habitually teaching the truth. What is characteristic of the sophist is unconcern with the truth, i.e., with the truth about the whole. The sophist, in contradistinction to the philosopher, is not set in motion and kept in motion by the sting of the awareness of the fundamental difference between conviction or belief and genuine insight. But this is clearly too general, for unconcern with the truth about the whole is not a preserve of the sophist. The sophist is a man who is unconcerned with the truth, or does not love wisdom, although he knows better than most other men that wisdom or science is the highest excellence of man. Being aware of the unique character of wisdom, he knows that the honor deriving from wisdom is the highest honor. He is concerned with wisdom, not for its own sake, not because he hates the lie in the soul more than anything else, but for the sake of the honor or the prestige that attends wisdom. He lives or acts on the principle that prestige or superiority to others or having more than others is the highest good. He acts on the principle of vulgar conventionalism. Since he accepts the teaching of philosophic conventionalism and thus is more articulate than the many who act on the same principle on which he acts, he can be regarded as the most fitting representative of vulgar conventionalism. There arises, however, this difficulty. The sophist's highest good is the prestige deriving from wisdom. To achieve his highest good, he must display his wisdom. Displaying his wisdom means teaching the view that the life according to nature or the life of the wise man consists in combining actual injustice with the appearance of justice. Yet admitting that one is, in fact, unjust is incompatible with successfully preserving the appearance of justice. It is incompatible with wisdom, and it therefore makes impossible the honor deriving from wisdom. Sooner or later the sophist is therefore forced to conceal his wisdom or to bow to views which he regards as merely conventional. He must become resigned to deriving his prestige from propagating more or less respectable views. It is for this reason that one cannot speak of *the* teaching, i.e., of the explicit teaching, of the sophists.

As regards the most famous sophist, Protagoras, Plato imputes to him a myth which adumbrates the conventionalist thesis. The myth of the *Protagoras* is based on the distinction between nature, art, and convention. Nature is represented by the subterraneous work of certain gods and by the work of Epimetheus. Epimetheus, the being in whom thought follows production, represents nature in the sense of materialism, according to which thought comes later than thoughtless bodies and their thoughtless motions. The subterraneous work of the gods is work without light, without understanding, and has therefore fundamentally the same meaning as the work of Epimetheus. Art is represented by Prometheus, by Prometheus' theft, by his rebellion against the will of the gods above. Convention is represented by Zeus's gift of justice to "all": that "gift" becomes effective only through the punitive activity of civil society, and its requirements are perfectly fulfilled by the mere semblance of justice.[47]

---

47. *Protagoras* 322^{b}6–8, 323^{b}2–^{c}2, 324^{a}3–^{c}5, 325^{a}6–^{d}7, 327^{d}1–2. There seems to be a contradiction between the myth of the *Protagoras* and the *Theaetetus*, where the conventionalist thesis is presented as an improved version of Protagoras' thesis, which in its denials of ordinarily held views goes much beyond conventionalism (167^{c}2–7, 172^{a}1–^{b}6, 177^{c}6–^{d}6). But, as the context shows, what Protagoras says in the myth of the *Protagoras* is likewise an improved version of his real thesis. In the *Protagoras* the improvement is effected under the pressure of the situation (the presence of a prospective pupil) by Protagoras himself, whereas in the *Theaetetus* it is effected on his behalf by Socrates.

I conclude this chapter with a brief remark about pre-Socratic natural right. I shall not speak of those types of natural right doctrine which were fully developed by Socrates and his followers. I shall limit myself to a sketch of that type which was rejected by the classics: egalitarian natural right.

The doubt of the natural character of both slavery and the division of the human race into distinct political or ethnic groups finds its most simple expression in the thesis that all men are by nature free and equal. Natural freedom and natural equality are inseparable from each other. If all men are by nature free, no one is by nature the superior of any other, and hence by nature all men are equal to each other. If all men are by nature free and equal, it is against nature to treat any man as unfree or unequal; the preservation or restoration of natural freedom or equality is required by natural right. Thus the city appears to be against natural right, for the city stands or falls by inequality or subordination and by the restriction of freedom. The effective denial of natural freedom and equality by the city must be traced to violence and ultimately to wrong opinion or the corruption of nature. This means that natural freedom and equality will be thought to have been fully effective at the beginning, when nature was not yet corrupted by opinion. The doctrine of natural freedom and equality thus allies itself with the doctrine of a golden age. Yet one may assume that original innocence is not irretrievably lost and that, in spite of the natural character of freedom and equality, civil society is indispensable. In that case one must look for a way in which civil society can be brought into some degree of harmony with natural freedom and equality. The only way in which this can be done is to assume that civil society, to the extent to which it is in agreement with natural right, is based on the consent or, more precisely, on the contract of the free and equal individuals.

It is doubtful whether the doctrines of natural freedom and equality, as well as of the social compact, were originally meant as political theses and not rather as theoretical theses setting forth the questionable character of civil society as such. As long as nature was regarded as the standard, the contractualist doctrine, regardless of whether it was based on the egalitarian or the nonegalitarian premise, necessarily implied a depreciation of civil society, because it implied that civil society is not natural but conventional.[48] This must be borne in mind if one wants to understand the specific character and the tremendous political effect of the contractualist doctrines of the seventeenth and eighteenth centuries. For in the modern era the notion that nature is the standard was abandoned, and therewith the stigma on whatever is conventional or contractual was taken away. As for premodern times, it is safe to assume that all contractualist doctrines implied the depreciation of whatever owed its origin to contract.

In a passage of Plato's *Crito*, Socrates is presented as deriving his duty of obedience to the city of Athens and her laws from a tacit contract. To understand this passage, one has to compare it with its parallel in the *Republic*. In the *Republic* the philosopher's duty of obedience to the city is not derived from any contract. The reason is obvious. The city of the *Republic* is the best city, the city according to nature. But the city of Athens, that democracy, was from Plato's point of view a most imperfect city.[49] Only the allegiance to an inferior community can be derivative from contract, for an honest man keeps his promises to everyone regardless of the worth of him to whom he made the promise.

48. Aristotle *Politics* 1280^{b}10–13; Xenophon *Memorabilia* iv. 4. 13–14 (Cf. *Resp. Laced.* 8. 5).

49. *Crito* 50^{c}4–52^{e}5 (cf. 52^{e}5–6); *Republic* 519^{e}8–520^{e}1.

IV

CLASSIC NATURAL RIGHT

❊

SOCRATES is said to have been the first who called philosophy down from heaven and forced it to make inquiries about life and manners and good and bad things. In other words, he is said to have been the founder of political philosophy.[1] To the extent to which this is true, he was the originator of the whole tradition of natural right teachings. The particular natural right doctrine which was originated by Socrates and developed by Plato, Aristotle, the Stoics, and the Christian thinkers (especially Thomas Aquinas) may be called the classic natural right doctrine. It must be distinguished from the modern natural right doctrine that emerged in the seventeenth century.

The full understanding of the classic natural right doctrine would require a full understanding of the change in thought that was effected by Socrates. Such an understanding is not at our disposal. From a cursory reading of the pertinent texts which at first glance seem to supply the most authentic information, the modern reader almost inevitably arrives at the following view: Socrates turned away from the study of nature and limited his investigations to human things. Being unconcerned with nature, he refused to look at human things in the light of the subversive distinction between nature and law (convention). He rather identified law with nature. He cer-

---

1. Cicero *Tusc. Disp.* v. 10; Hobbes, *De cive*, Preface, near the beginning. As for the alleged Pythagorean origins of political philosophy, consider Plato *Republic* 600^{a}9–^{b}5 as well as Cicero *Tusc. Disp.* v. 8–10 and *Republic* i. 16.

tainly identified the just with the legal.[2] He thus restored the ancestral morality, although in the element of reflection. This view mistakes Socrates' ambiguous starting point or the ambiguous result of his inquiries for the substance of his thought. To mention for the moment only one point, the distinction between nature and law (convention) retains its full significance for Socrates and for classic natural right in general. The classics presuppose the validity of that distinction when demanding that the law should follow the order established by nature, or when speaking of the co-operation between nature and law. They oppose to the denial of natural right and natural morality the distinction between natural right and legal right as well as the distinction between natural and (merely) human morality. They preserve the same distinction by distinguishing between genuine virtue and political or vulgar virtue. The characteristic institutions of Plato's best polity are "in accordance with nature," and they are "against the habits or custom," whereas the opposite institutions, which are customary practically everywhere, are "against nature." Aristotle could not explain what money is except by distinguishing between natural wealth and conventional wealth. He could not explain what slavery is except by distinguishing between natural slavery and legal slavery.[3]

Let us then see what is implied by Socrates' turning to the study of human things. His study of human things consisted in raising the question "What is?" in regard to those things— for instance, the question "What is courage?" or "What is the city?" But it was not limited to raising the question "What is?" in regard to specific human things, such as the various

2. Plato *Apology of Socrates* 19ᵃ8–ᵈ7; Xenophon *Memorabilia* i. 1. 11–16; iv. 3. 14; 4. 12 ff., 7, 8. 4; Aristotle *Metaphysics* 987ᵇ1–2; *De part. anim.* 642ᵃ28–30; Cicero *Republic* i. 15–16.

3. Plato *Republic* 456ᵇ12–ᶜ2, 452ᵃ7, ᶜ6–7, 484ᶜ7–ᵈ3, 500ᵈ4–8, 501ᵇ1–ᶜ2; *Laws* 794ᵈ4–795ᵈ5; Xenophon *Oeconomicus* 7. 16 and *Hiero* 3. 9; Aristotle *Nicomachean Ethics* 1133ᵃ29–31 and 1134ᵇ18–1135ᵃ5; *Politics* 1255ᵃ1–ᵇ15, 1257ᵇ10 ff.

virtues. Socrates was forced to raise the question as to what the human things as such are, or what the *ratio rerum humanarum* is.[4] But it is impossible to grasp the distinctive character of human things as such without grasping the essential difference between human things and the things which are not human, i.e., the divine or natural things. This, in turn, presupposes some understanding of the divine or natural things as such. Socrates' study of the human things was then based on the comprehensive study of "all things." Like every other philosopher, he identified wisdom, or the goal of philosophy, with the science of all the beings: he never ceased considering "what each of the beings is."[5]

Contrary to appearances, Socrates' turn to the study of human things was based, not upon disregard of the divine or natural things, but upon a new approach to the understanding of all things. That approach was indeed of such a character that it permitted, and favored, the study of human things as such, i.e., of the human things in so far as they are not reducible to the divine or natural things. Socrates deviated from his predecessors by identifying the science of the whole, or of everything that is, with the understanding of "what each of the beings is." For "to be" means "to be something" and hence to be different from things which are "something else"; "to be" means therefore "to be a part." Hence the whole cannot "be" in the same sense in which everything that is "something" "is"; the whole must be "beyond being." And yet the whole is the totality of the parts. To understand the whole then means to understand all the parts of the whole or the articulation of the whole. If "to be" is "to be something," the being of a thing, or the nature of a thing, is primarily its

4. Compare Cicero *Republic* ii. 52, where the understanding of the *ratio rerum civilium*, as distinguished from the setting-up of a model for political action, is said to be the purpose of Plato's *Republic*.

5. Xenophon *Memorabilia* i. 1. 16; iv. 6. 1, 7; 7. 3–5.

What, its "shape" or "form" or "character," as distinguished in particular from that out of which it has come into being. The thing itself, the completed thing, cannot be understood as a product of the process leading up to it, but, on the contrary, the process cannot be understood except in the light of the completed thing or of the end of the process. The What is, as such, the character of a class of things or of a "tribe" of things—of things which by nature belong together or form a natural group. The whole has a natural articulation. To understand the whole, therefore, means no longer primarily to discover the roots out of which the completed whole, the articulated whole, the whole consisting of distinct groups of things, the intelligible whole, the *cosmos*, has grown, or to discover the cause which has transformed the *chaos* into a *cosmos*, or to perceive the unity which is hidden behind the variety of things or appearances, but to understand the unity that is revealed in the manifest articulation of the completed whole. This view supplies the basis for the distinction between the various sciences: the distinction between the various sciences corresponds to the natural articulation of the whole. This view makes possible, and it favors in particular, the study of the human things as such.

Socrates seems to have regarded the change which he brought about as a return to "sobriety" and "moderation" from the "madness" of his predecessors. In contradistinction to his predecessors, he did not separate wisdom from moderation. In present-day parlance one can describe the change in question as a return to "common sense" or to "the world of common sense." That to which the question "What is?" points is the *eidos* of a thing, the shape or form or character or "idea" of a thing. It is no accident that the term *eidos* signifies primarily that which is visible to all without any particular effort or what one might call the "surface" of the things. Socrates started not from what is first in itself or first by nature but from what is first for us, from what comes to sight first, from the phenomena. But the being of things, their What, comes first to sight, not in what we see of them, but in what is said about them or in opinions about them. Accordingly, Socrates started in his understanding of the natures of things from the opinions about their natures. For every opinion is based on some awareness, on some perception with the mind's eye, of something. Socrates implied that disregarding the opinions about the natures of things would amount to abandoning the most important access to reality which we have, or the most important vestiges of the truth which are within our reach. He implied that "the universal doubt" of all opinions would lead us, not into the heart of the truth, but into a void. Philosophy consists, therefore, in the ascent from opinions to knowledge or to the truth, in an ascent that may be said to be guided by opinions. It is this ascent which Socrates had primarily in mind when he called philosophy "dialectics." Dialectics is the art of conversation or of friendly dispute. The friendly dispute which leads toward the truth is made possible or necessary by the fact that opinions about what things are, or what some very important groups of things are, contradict one another. Recognizing the contradiction, one is forced to go beyond opinions toward the consistent view of the nature of the thing concerned. That consistent view makes visible the relative truth of the contradictory opinions; the consistent view proves to be the comprehensive or total view. The opinions are thus seen to be fragments of the truth, soiled fragments of the pure truth. In other words, the opinions prove to be solicited by the self-subsisting truth, and the ascent to the truth proves to be guided by the self-subsistent truth which all men always divine.

On this basis it becomes possible to understand why the variety of opinions about right or justice not only is compatible with the existence of natural right or the idea of justice but is required by it. The variety of notions of justice could be said to refute the contention that there is natural right, if the existence of natural right required actual consent of all men in regard to the principles of right. But we learn from Socrates, or from Plato, that what is required is not more than potential consent. Plato, as it were, says: Take any opinion about right, however fantastic or "primitive," that you please; you can be certain prior to having investigated it that it points beyond itself, that the people who cherish the opinion in question contradict that very opinion somehow and thus are forced to go beyond it in the direction of the one true view of justice, provided that a philosopher arises among them.

Let us try to express this in more general terms. All knowledge, however limited or "scientific," presupposes a horizon, a comprehensive view within which knowledge is possible. All understanding presupposes a fundamental awareness of the whole: prior to any perception of particular things, the human soul must have had a vision of the ideas, a vision of the articulated whole. However much the comprehensive visions which animate the various societies may differ, they all are visions of the same—of the whole. Therefore, they do not merely differ from, but contradict, one another. This very fact forces man to realize that each of those visions, taken by itself, is merely an opinion about the whole or an inadequate articulation of the fundamental awareness of the whole and thus points beyond itself toward an adequate articulation. There is no guaranty that the quest for adequate articulation will ever lead beyond an understanding of the fundamental alternatives or that philosophy will ever legitimately go beyond the stage of discussion or disputation and will ever reach the stage of decision. The unfinishable character of the quest for adequate articulation of the whole does not entitle one, however, to limit philosophy to the understanding of a part, however important.

For the meaning of a part depends on the meaning of the whole. In particular, such interpretation of a part as is based on fundamental experiences alone, without recourse to hypothetical assumptions about the whole, is ultimately not superior to other interpretations of that part which are frankly based on such hypothetical assumptions.

Conventionalism disregards the understanding embodied in opinion and appeals from opinion to nature. For this reason, to say nothing of others, Socrates and his successors were forced to prove the existence of natural right on the ground chosen by conventionalism. They had to prove it by appeal to the "facts" as distinguished from the "speeches."[6] As will appear presently, this seemingly more direct appeal to being merely confirms the fundamental Socratic thesis.

The basic premise of conventionalism appeared to be the identification of the good with the pleasant. Accordingly, the basic part of the classic natural right teaching is the critique of hedonism. The thesis of the classics is that the good is essentially different from the pleasant, that the good is more fundamental than the pleasant. The most common pleasures are connected with the satisfaction of wants; the wants precede the pleasures; the wants supply, as it were, the channels within which pleasure can move; they determine what can possibly be pleasant. The primary fact is not pleasure, or the desire for pleasure, but rather the wants and the striving for their satisfaction. It is the variety of wants that accounts for the variety of pleasures; the difference of kinds of pleasures cannot be understood in terms of pleasure but only by reference to the wants which make possible the various kinds of pleasures. The different kinds of wants are not a bundle of urges; there is a natural order of the wants. Different kinds of beings seek or enjoy different kinds of pleasure: the pleasures of an ass differ from the pleasures of a human being. The order of the wants of a being points back to the natural constitution, to the What, of the

6. See Plato _Republic_ 358e3, 367b2–5, e2, 369a5–6, c9–10, 370a8–b1.

being concerned; it is that constitution which determines the order, the hierarchy, of the various wants or of the various inclinations of a being. To the specific constitution there corresponds a specific operation, a specific work. A being is good, it is "in order," if it does its proper work well. Hence man will be good if he does well the proper work of man, the work corresponding to the nature of man and required by it. To determine what is by nature good for man or the natural human good, one must determine what the nature of man, or man's natural constitution, is. It is the hierarchic order of man's natural constitution which supplies the basis for natural right as the classics understood it. In one way or another everyone distinguishes between the body and the soul; and everyone can be forced to admit that he cannot, without contradicting himself, deny that the soul stands higher than the body. That which distinguishes the human soul from the souls of the brutes, that which distinguishes man from the brutes, is speech or reason or understanding. Therefore, the proper work of man consists in living thoughtfully, in understanding, and in thoughtful action. The good life is the life that is in accordance with the natural order of man's being, the life that flows from a well-ordered or healthy soul. The good life simply, is the life in which the requirements of man's natural inclinations are fulfilled in the proper order to the highest possible degree, the life of a man who is awake to the highest possible degree, the life of a man in whose soul nothing lies waste. The good life is the perfection of man's nature. It is the life according to nature. One may therefore call the rules circumscribing the general character of the good life "the natural law." The life according to nature is the life of human excellence or virtue, the life of a "high-class person," and not the life of pleasure as pleasure.[7]

7. Plato *Gorgias* 499e6–500a3; *Republic* 369e10 ff.; compare *Republic* 352d6–353e6, 433a1–b4, 441d12 ff., and 444d13–445b4 with Aristotle *Nicomachean Ethics* 1098a8–17; Cicero *De finibus* ii. 33–34, 40; iv. 16, 25, 34, 37; v. 26; *Laws* i. 17, 22, 25, 27, 45, 58–62.

The thesis that the life according to nature is the life of human excellence can be defended on hedonistic grounds. Yet the classics protested against this manner of understanding the good life. For, from the point of view of hedonism, nobility of character is good because it is conducive to a life of pleasure or even indispensable for it: nobility of character is the handmaid of pleasure; it is not good for its own sake. According to the classics, this interpretation distorts the phenomena as they are known from experience to every unbiased and competent, i.e., not morally obtuse, man. We admire excellence without any regard to our pleasures or to our benefits. No one understands by a good man or man of excellence a man who leads a pleasant life. We distinguish between better and worse men. The difference between them is indeed reflected in the difference in the kinds of pleasure which they prefer. But one cannot understand this difference in the level of pleasures in terms of pleasure; for that level is determined not by pleasure but by the rank of human beings. We know that it is a vulgar error to identify the man of excellence with one's benefactor. We admire, for example, a strategic genius at the head of the victorious army of our enemies. There are things which are admirable, or noble, by nature, intrinsically. It is characteristic of all or most of them that they contain no reference to one's selfish interests or that they imply a freedom from calculation. The various human things which are by nature noble or admirable are essentially the parts of human nobility in its completion, or are related to it; they all point toward the well-ordered soul, incomparably the most admirable human phenomenon. The phenomenon of admiration of human excellence cannot be explained on hedonistic or utilitarian grounds, except by means of *ad hoc* hypotheses. These hypotheses lead to the assertion that all admiration is, at best, a kind of telescoped calculation of benefits for ourselves. They are the outcome of a materialistic or crypto-materialistic view, which forces its holders to understand the higher as nothing but the effect of the lower, or which prevents them from considering the possibility that there are phenomena which are simply irreducible to their conditions, that there are phenomena that form a class by themselves. The hypotheses in question are not conceived in the spirit of an empirical science of man.[8]

Man is by nature a social being. He is so constituted that he cannot live, or live well, except by living with others. Since it is reason or speech that distinguishes him from the other animals, and speech is communication, man is social in a more radical sense than any other social animal: humanity itself is sociality. Man refers himself to others, or rather he is referred to others, in every human act, regardless of whether that act is "social" or "antisocial." His sociality does not proceed, then, from a calculation of the pleasures which he expects from association, but he derives pleasure from association because he is by nature social. Love, affection, friendship, pity, are as natural to him as concern with his own good and calculation of what is conducive to his own good. It is man's natural sociality that is the basis of natural right in the narrow or strict sense of right. Because man is by nature social, the perfection of his nature includes the social virtue par excellence, justice; justice and right are natural. All members of the same species are akin to one another. This natural kinship is deepened and transfigured in the case of man as a consequence of his radical sociality. In the case of man the individual's concern with procreation is only a part of his concern with the preservation of the species. There is no relation of man to man in which man is absolutely free to act as he pleases or as it suits him. And all men are somehow aware of this fact. Every ideology is an attempt to justify before one's self or

8. Plato *Gorgias* 497ᵈ8 ff.; *Republic* 402ᵈ1–9; Xenophon *Hellenica* vii. 3. 12; Aristotle *Nicomachean Ethics* 1174ᵃ1–8; *Rhetoric* 1366ᵇ36 ff.; Cicero *De finibus* ii. 45, 64–65, 69; v. 47, 61; *Laws* i. 37, 41, 48, 51, 55, 59.

others such courses of action as are somehow felt to be in need of justification, i.e., as are not obviously right. Why did the Athenians believe in their autochthony, except because they knew that robbing others of their land is not just and because they felt that a self-respecting society cannot become reconciled to the notion that its foundation was laid in crime?[9] Why do the Hindus believe in their *karma* doctrine if not because they know that otherwise their caste system would be indefensible? By virtue of his rationality, man has a latitude of alternatives such as no other earthly being has. The sense of this latitude, of this freedom, is accompanied by a sense that the full and unrestrained exercise of that freedom is not right. Man's freedom is accompanied by a sacred awe, by a kind of divination that not everything is permitted.[10] We may call this awe-inspired fear "man's natural conscience." Restraint is therefore as natural or as primeval as freedom. As long as man has not cultivated his reason properly, he will have all sorts of fantastic notions as to the limits set to his freedom; he will elaborate absurd taboos. But what prompts the savages in their savage doings is not savagery but the divination of right.

Man cannot reach his perfection except in society or, more precisely, in civil society. Civil society, or the city as the classics conceived of it, is a closed society and is, in addition, what today would be called a "small society." A city, one may say, is a community in which everyone knows, not indeed every other member, but at least an acquaintance of every other member. A society meant to make man's perfection pos-

9. Plato *Republic* 369^b5–370^b2; *Symposium* 207^a6–^c1; *Laws* 776^d5–778^a6; Aristotle *Politics* 1253^a7–18, 1278^b18–25; *Nicomachean Ethics* 1161^b1–8 (cf. Plato *Republic* 395^e5) and 1170^b10–14; *Rhetoric* 1373^b6–9; Isocrates *Panegyricus* 23–24; Cicero *Republic* i. 1, 38–41; iii. 1–3, 25; iv. 3; *Laws* i. 30, 33–35, 43; *De finibus* ii. 45, 78, 109–10; iii. 62–71; iv. 17–18; Grotius *De jure belli*, Prolegomena, §§ 6–8.

10. Cicero *Republic* v. 6; *Laws* i. 24, 40; *De finibus* iv. 18.

sible must be kept together by mutual trust, and trust presupposes acquaintance. Without such trust, the classics thought, there cannot be freedom; the alternative to the city, or a federation of cities, was the despotically ruled empire (headed, if possible, by a deified ruler) or a condition approaching anarchy. A city is a community commensurate with man's natural powers of firsthand or direct knowledge. It is a community which can be taken in in one view, or in which a mature man can find his bearings through his own observation, without having to rely habitually on indirect information in matters of vital importance. For direct knowledge of men can safely be replaced by indirect knowledge only so far as the individuals who make up the political multitude are uniform or "mass-men." Only a society small enough to permit mutual trust is small enough to permit mutual responsibility or supervision—the supervision of actions or manners which is indispensable for a society concerned with the perfection of its members; in a very large city, in "Babylon," everyone can live more or less as he lists. Just as man's natural power of firsthand knowledge, so his power of love or of active concern, is by nature limited; the limits of the city coincide with the range of man's active concern for nonanonymous individuals. Furthermore, political freedom, and especially that political freedom that justifies itself by the pursuit of human excellence, is not a gift of heaven; it becomes actual only through the efforts of many generations, and its preservation always requires the highest degree of vigilance. The probability that all human societies should be capable of genuine freedom at the same time is exceedingly small. For all precious things are exceedingly rare. An open or all-comprehensive society would consist of many societies which are on vastly different levels of political maturity, and the chances are overwhelming that the lower societies would drag down the higher ones. An open or all-comprehensive society will exist on a lower level of humanity than a closed society, which, through generations, has made a supreme effort toward human perfection. The prospects for the existence of a good society are therefore greater if there is a multitude of independent societies than if there is only one independent society. If the society in which man can reach the perfection of his nature is necessarily a closed society, the distinction of the human race into a number of independent groups is according to nature. This distinction is not natural in the sense that the members of one civil society are by nature different from the members of others. Cities do not grow like plants. They are not simply based on comment descent. They come into being through human actions. There is an element of choice and even of arbitrariness involved in the "settling together" of these particular human beings to the exclusion of others. This would be unjust only if the condition of those excluded were impaired by their exclusion. But the condition of people who have not yet made any serious effort toward the perfection of human nature is, of necessity, bad in the decisive respect; it cannot possibly be impaired by the mere fact that those among them whose souls have been stirred by the call to perfection do make such efforts. Besides, there is no necessary reason why those excluded should not form a civil society of their own. Civil society as a closed society is possible and necessary in accordance with justice, because it is in accordance with nature.[11]

If restraint is as natural to man as is freedom, and restraint must in many cases be forcible restraint in order to be effective, one cannot say that the city is conventional or against nature because it is coercive society. Man is so built that he cannot achieve the perfection of his humanity except by keeping

11. Plato *Republic* 423ᵃ5–ᵉ5; *Laws* 681ᶜ4–ᵈ5, 708ᵇ1–ᵈ7, 738ᵈ6–ᵉ5, 949ᵉ3 ff.; Aristotle *Nicomachean Ethics* 1158ᵃ10–18, 1170ᵇ20–1171ᵃ20; *Politics* 1253ᵃ30–31, 1276ᵃ27–34 (cf. Thomas Aquinas, *ad loc.*), 1326ᵃ9–ᵇ26; Isocrates *Antidosis* 171–72; Cicero *Laws* ii. 5; cf. Thomas, *Summa theologica* i. qu. 65, *a.* 2, ad 3.

down his lower impulses. He cannot rule his body by persuasion. This fact alone shows that even despotic rule is not per se against nature. What is true of self-restraint, self-coercion, and power over one's self applies in principle to the restraint and coercion of others and to power over others. To take the extreme case, despotic rule is unjust only if it is applied to beings who can be ruled by persuasion or whose understanding is sufficient: Prospero's rule over Caliban is by nature just. Justice and coercion are not mutually exclusive; in fact, it is not altogether wrong to describe justice as a kind of benevolent coercion. Justice and virtue in general are necessarily a kind of power. To say that power as such is evil or corrupting would therefore amount to saying that virtue is evil or corrupting. While some men are corrupted by wielding power, others are improved by it: "power will show a man."[12]

The full actualization of humanity would then seem to consist, not in some sort of passive membership in civil society, but in the properly directed activity of the statesman, the legislator, or the founder. Serious concern for the perfection of a community requires a higher degree of virtue than serious concern for the perfection of an individual. The judge and ruler has larger and nobler opportunities to act justly than the ordinary man. The good man is not identical simply with the good citizen but with the good citizen who exercises the function of a ruler in a good society. It is then something more solid than the dazzling splendor and clamor that attends high office and something more noble than the concern with the well-being of their bodies which induces men to pay homage to political greatness. Being sensitive to mankind's great objects, freedom and empire, they sense somehow that politics is the field on which human excellence can show itself in its full growth and on whose proper cultivation every form of excel-

12. Plato *Republic* 372^{b}7–8 and 607^{a}4, 519^{e}4–520^{a}5, 561^{d}5–7; *Laws* 689^e ff.; Aristotle *Nicomachean Ethics* 1130^{a}1–2, 1180^{a}14–22; *Politics* 1254^{a}18–20, ^{b}5–6, 1255^{a}3–22, 1325^{b}7 ff.

lence is in a way dependent. Freedom and empire are desired as elements or conditions of happiness. But the feelings which are stirred by the very words "freedom" and "empire" point to a more adequate understanding of happiness than that which underlies the identification of happiness with the well-being of the body or the gratification of vanity; they point to the view that happiness or the core of happiness consists in human excellence. Political activity is then properly directed if it is directed toward human perfection or virtue. The city has therefore ultimately no other end than the individual. The morality of civil society or of the state is the same as the morality of the individual. The city is essentially different from a gang of robbers because it is not merely an organ, or an expression, of collective selfishness. Since the ultimate end of the city is the same as that of the individual, the end of the city is peaceful activity in accordance with the dignity of man, and not war and conquest.[13]

Since the classics viewed moral and political matters in the light of man's perfection, they were not egalitarians. Not all men are equally equipped by nature for progress toward perfection, or not all "natures" are "good natures." While all men, i.e., all normal men, have the capacity for virtue, some need guidance by others, whereas others do not at all or to a much lesser degree. Besides, regardless of differences of natural capacity, not all men strive for virtue with equal earnestness. However great an influence must be ascribed to the way in which men are brought up, the difference between good and bad upbringing is partly due to the difference between a favorable and an unfavorable natural "environment." Since men

---

13. Thucydides iii. 45. 6; Plato *Gorgias* 464^{b}3–^{c}3, 478^{a}1–^{b}5, 521^{d}6–^{e}1; *Clitopho* 408^{b}2–5; *Laws* 628^{b}6–^{e}1, 645^{b}1–8; Xenophon *Memorabilia* ii. 1. 17; iii. 2. 4; iv. 2. 11; Aristotle *Nicomachean Ethics* 1094^{b}7–10, 1129^{b}25–1130^{a}8; *Politics* 1278^{b}1–5, 1324^{b}23–41, 1333^{b}39 ff.; Cicero *Republic* i. 1; iii. 10–11, 34–41; vi. 13, 16; Thomas Aquinas, *De regimine principum* i. 9.

are then unequal in regard to human perfection, i.e., in the decisive respect, equal rights for all appeared to the classics as most unjust. They contended that some men are by nature superior to others and therefore, according to natural right, the rulers of others. It is sometimes suggested that the view of the classics was rejected by the Stoics and especially by Cicero and that this change marks an epoch in the development of natural right doctrine or a radical break with the natural right doctrine of Socrates, Plato, and Aristotle. But Cicero himself, who must be supposed to have known what he was talking about, was wholly unaware of a radical difference between Plato's teaching and his own. The crucial passage in Cicero's *Laws*, which according to a common view is meant to establish egalitarian natural right, is, in fact, meant to prove man's natural sociality. In order to prove man's natural sociality, Cicero speaks of all men being similar to one another, i.e., akin to one another. He presents the similarity in question as the natural basis of man's benevolence to man: *simile simili gaudet*. It is a comparatively unimportant question whether an expression used by Cicero in this context might not be indicative of a slight bias in favor of egalitarian conceptions. It suffices to remark that Cicero's writings abound with statements which reaffirm the classical view that men are unequal in the decisive respect and which reaffirm the political implications of that view.[14]

In order to reach his highest stature, man must live in the best kind of society, in the kind of society that is most conducive to human excellence. The classics called the best society the best *politeia*. By this expression they indicated, first of all, that, in order to be good, society must be civil or politi-

<hr />

14. Plato *Republic* 374e4–376c6, 431c5–7, 485a4–487a5; Xenophon *Memorabilia* iv. 1. 2; *Hiero* 7. 3; Aristotle *Nicomachean Ethics* 1099b18–20, 1095b10–13, 1179b7–1180a10, 1114a31–b25; *Politics* 1254a29–31, 1267b7, 1327b18–39; Cicero *Laws* i. 28–35; *Republic* i. 49, 52; iii. 4, 37–38; *De finibus* iv. 21, 56; v. 69; *Tusc. Disp.* ii. 11, 13; iv. 31–32; v. 68; *Offices* i. 105, 107. Thomas Aquinas, *Summa theologica* i. qu. 96, *a.* 3 and 4.

cal society, a society in which there exists government of men and not merely administration of things. *Politeia* is ordinarily translated by "constitution." But when using the term "constitution" in a political context, modern men almost inevitably mean a legal phenomenon, something like the fundamental law of the land, and not something like the constitution of the body or of the soul. Yet *politeia* is not a legal phenomenon. The classics used *politeia* in contradistinction to "laws." The *politeia* is more fundamental than any laws; it is the source of all laws. The *politeia* is rather the factual distribution of power within the community than what constitutional law stipulates in regard to political power. The *politeia* may be defined by laws, but it need not be. The laws regarding a *politeia* may be deceptive, unintentionally and even intentionally, as to the true character of the *politeia*. No law, and hence no constitution, can be the fundamental political fact, because all laws depend on human beings. Laws have to be adopted, preserved, and administered by men. The human beings making up a political community may be "arranged" in greatly different ways in regard to the control of communal affairs. It is primarily the factual "arrangement" of human beings in regard to political power that is meant by *politeia*.

The American Constitution is not the same thing as the American way of life. *Politeia* means the way of life of a society rather than its constitution. Yet it is no accident that the unsatisfactory translation "constitution" is generally preferred to the translation "way of life of a society." When speaking of constitution, we think of government; we do not necessarily think of government when speaking of the way of life of a community. When speaking of *politeia*, the classics thought of the way of life of a community as essentially determined by its "form of government." We shall translate *politeia* by "regime," taking regime in the broad sense in which we sometimes take it when speaking, e.g., of the Ancien

Régime of France. The thought connecting "way of life of a society" and "form of government" can provisionally be stated as follows: The character, or tone, of a society depends on what the society regards as most respectable or most worthy of admiration. But by regarding certain habits or attitudes as most respectable, a society admits the superiority, the superior dignity, of those human beings who most perfectly embody the habits or attitudes in question. That is to say, every society regards a specific human type (or a specific mixture of human types) as authoritative. When the authoritative type is the common man, everything has to justify itself before the tribunal of the common man; everything which cannot be justified before that tribunal becomes, at best, merely tolerated, if not despised or suspect. And even those who do not recognize that tribunal are, willy-nilly, molded by its verdicts. What is true of the society ruled by the common man applies also to societies ruled by the priest, the wealthy merchant, the war lord, the gentleman, and so on. In order to be truly authoritative, the human beings who embody the admired habits or attitudes must have the decisive say within the community in broad daylight: they must form the regime. When the classics were chiefly concerned with the different regimes, and especially with the best regime, they implied that the paramount social phenomenon, or that social phenomenon than which only the natural phenomena are more fundamental, is the regime.[15]

15. Plato *Republic* 497ª3–5, 544ᵈ6–7; *Laws* 711ᵉ5–8. Xenophon *Ways and Means* 1.1; *Cyropaedia* i. 2. 15; Isocrates *To Nicocles* 31; *Nicocles* 37; *Areopagiticus* 14; Aristotle *Nicomachean Ethics* 1181ᵇ12–23; *Politics* 1273ª40 ff., 1278ᵇ11–13, 1288ª23–24, 1289ª12–20, 1292ᵇ11–18, 1295ᵇ1, 1297ª14 ff.; Cicero *Republic* i. 47; v. 5–7; *Laws* i. 14–15, 17, 19; iii. 2. Cicero has indicated the higher dignity of "regime" as distinguished from "laws" by the contrast between the settings of his *Republic* and his *Laws*. The *Laws* are meant as a sequel to the *Republic*. In the *Republic* the younger Scipio, a philosopher-king, has a three-day conversation with some of his contemporaries about the best regime; in the *Laws* Cicero has a one-day conversation with some of his contemporaries about the laws appropriate to the best regime. The discussion of the *Republic* takes

The central significance of the phenomena called "regimes" has become somewhat blurred. The reasons for this change are the same as those responsible for the fact that political history has ceded its former pre-eminence to social, cultural, economic, etc., history. The emergence of these new branches of history finds its culmination—and its legitimation—in the concept of "civilizations" (or "cultures"). We are in the habit of speaking of "civilizations," where the classics spoke of "regimes." "Civilization" is the modern substitute for "regime." It is difficult to find out what a civilization is. A civilization is said to be a large society, but we are not told clearly what kind of society it is. If we inquire how one can tell one civilization from another, we are informed that the most obvious and least misleading mark is the difference in artistic styles. This means that civilizations are societies which are characterized by something which is never in the focus of interest of large societies as such: societies do not go to war with one another on account of differences of artistic styles. Our orientation by civilizations, instead of by regimes, would seem to be due to a peculiar estrangement from those life-and-death issues which move and animate societies and keep them together.

The best regime would today be called an "ideal regime" or simply an "ideal." The modern term "ideal" carries with it a host of connotations which obviate the understanding of what the classics meant by the best regime. Modern translators sometimes use "ideal" for rendering what the classics call "according to wish" or "according to prayer." The best regime is that for which one would wish or pray. Closer ex-

---

place in winter: the participants seek the sun; in addition, the discussion takes place in the year of Scipio's death: political things are viewed in the light of eternity. The discussion of the *Laws* takes place in summer: the participants seek shade (*Republic* i. 18; vi. 8, 12; *Laws* i. 14, 15; ii. 7, 69; iii. 30; *Offices* iii. 1). For illustrations compare, *inter alia*, Machiavelli, *Discorsi*, III, 29; Burke, *Conciliation with America*, toward the end; John Stuart Mill, *Autobiography* ("Oxford World's Classics" ed.), pp. 294 and 137.

amination would show that the best regime is the object of the wish or prayer of all good men or of all gentlemen: the best regime, as presented by classical political philosophy, is the object of the wish or prayer of gentlemen as that object is interpreted by the philosopher. But the best regime, as the classics understand it, is not only most desirable; it is also meant to be feasible or possible, i.e., possible on earth. It is both desirable and possible because it is according to nature. Since it is according to nature, no miraculous or nonmiraculous change in human nature is required for its actualization; it does not require the abolition or extirpation of that evil or imperfection which is essential to man and to human life; it is therefore possible. And, since it is in accordance with the requirements of the excellence or perfection of human nature, it. is most desirable. Yet, while the best regime is possible, its actualization is by no means necessary. Its actualization is very difficult, hence improbable, even extremely improbable. For man does not control the conditions under which it could become actual. Its actualization depends on chance. The best regime, which is according to nature, was perhaps never actual; there is no reason to assume that it is actual at present; and it may never become actual. It is of its essence to exist in speech as distinguished from deed. In a word, the best regime is, in itself—to use a term coined by one of the profoundest students of Plato's *Republic*—a "utopia."[16]

The best regime is possible only under the most favorable conditions. It is therefore just or legitimate only under the most favorable conditions. Under more or less unfavorable conditions, only more or less imperfect regimes are possible and therefore legitimate. There is only one best regime, but

16. Plato *Republic* 457ª3–4, ᶜ2, ᵈ4–9, 473ª5–ᵇ1, 499ᵇ2–ᶜ3, 502ᶜ5–7, 540ᵈ1–3, 592ª11; *Laws* 709ᵈ, 710ᶜ7–8, 736ᶜ5–ᵈ4, 740ᵉ8–741ª4, 742ᵉ1–4, 780ᵇ4–6, ᵉ1–2, 841ᶜ6–8, 960ᵈ5–ᵉ2; Aristotle *Politics* 1265ª18–19, 1270ᵇ20, 1295ª25–30, 1296ª37–38, 1328ª20–21, 1329ª15 ff., 1331ᵇ18–23, 1332ª28–ᵇ10, 1336ᵇ40 ff.

there is a variety of legitimate regimes. The variety of legitimate regimes corresponds to the variety of types of relevant circumstances. Whereas the best regime is possible only under the most favorable conditions, legitimate or just regimes are possible and morally necessary at all times and in all places. The distinction between the best regime and legitimate regimes has its root in the distinction between the noble and the just. Everything noble is just, but not everything just is noble. To pay one's debts is just, but not noble. Deserved punishment is just, but not noble. The farmers and artisans in Plato's best polity lead just lives, but they do not lead noble lives: they lack the opportunity for acting nobly. What a man does under duress is just in the sense that he cannot be blamed for it; but it can never be noble. Noble actions require, as Aristotle says, a certain equipment; without such equipment they are not possible. But we are obliged to act justly under all circumstances. A very imperfect regime may supply the only just solution to the problem of a given community; but, since such a regime cannot be effectively directed toward man's full perfection, it can never be noble.[17]

To avoid misunderstandings, it is necessary to say a few words about the answer, characteristic of the classics, to the question of the best regime. The best regime is that in which the best men habitually rule, or aristocracy. Goodness is, if not identical with wisdom, at any rate dependent on wisdom: the best regime would seem to be the rule of the wise. In fact, wisdom appeared to the classics as that title to rule which is highest according to nature. It would be absurd to hamper the free flow of wisdom by any regulations; hence the rule of the wise must be absolute rule. It would be equally absurd to ham-

17. Plato *Republic* 431^{b}9–433^{d}5, 434^{c}7–10; Xenophon *Cyropaedia* viii. 2. 23; *Agesilaus* 11. 8; Aristotle *Nicomachean Ethics* 1120^{a}11–20, 1135^{a}5; *Politics* 1288^{b}10 ff., 1293^{b}22–27, 1296^{b}25–35 (cf. [Thomas Aquinas] *ad loc.*), 1332^{a}10 ff.; *Rhetoric* 1366^{b}31–34; Polybius vi. 6. 6–9.

per the free flow of wisdom by consideration of the unwise wishes of the unwise; hence the wise rulers ought not to be responsible to their unwise subjects. To make the rule of the wise dependent on election by the unwise or consent of the unwise would mean to subject what is by nature higher to control by what is by nature lower, i.e., to act against nature. Yet this solution, which at first glance seems to be the only just solution for a society in which there are wise men, is, as a rule, impracticable. The few wise cannot rule the many unwise by force. The unwise multitude must recognize the wise as wise and obey them freely because of their wisdom. But the ability of the wise to persuade the unwise is extremely limited: Socrates, who lived what he taught, failed in his attempt to govern Xanthippe. Therefore, it is extremely unlikely that the conditions required for the rule of the wise will ever be met. What is more likely to happen is that an unwise man, appealing to the natural right of wisdom and catering to the lowest desires of the many, will persuade the multitude of his right: the prospects for tyranny are brighter than those for rule of the wise. This being the case, the natural right of the wise must be questioned, and the indispensable requirement for wisdom must be qualified by the requirement for consent. The political problem consists in reconciling the requirement for wisdom with the requirement for consent. But whereas, from the point of view of egalitarian natural right, consent takes precedence over wisdom, from the point of view of classic natural right, wisdom takes precedence over consent. According to the classics, the best way of meeting these two entirely different requirements—that for wisdom and that for consent or for freedom—would be that a wise legislator frame a code which the citizen body, duly persuaded, freely adopts. That code, which is, as it were, the embodiment of wisdom, must be as little subject to alteration as possible; the rule of law is to take the place of the rule of men, however wise. The administration of the law must be intrusted to a type of man who is most likely to administer it equitably, i.e., in the spirit of the wise legislator, or to "complete" the law according to the requirements of circumstances which the legislator could not have foreseen. The classics held that this type of man is the gentleman. The gentleman is not identical with the wise man. He is the political reflection, or imitation, of the wise man. Gentlemen have this in common with the wise man, that they "look down" on many things which are highly esteemed by the vulgar or that they are experienced in things noble and beautiful. They differ from the wise because they have a noble contempt for precision, because they refuse to take cognizance of certain aspects of life, and because, in order to live as gentlemen, they must be well off. The gentleman will be a man of not too great inherited wealth, chiefly landed, but whose way of life is urban. He will be an urban patrician who derives his income from agriculture. The best regime will then be a republic in which the landed gentry, which is at the same time the urban patriciate, well-bred and public spirited, obeying the laws and completing them, ruling and being ruled in turn, predominates and gives society its character. The classics devised or recommended various institutions which appeared to be conducive to the rule of the best. Probably the most influential suggestion was the mixed regime, mixed of kingship, aristocracy, and democracy. In the mixed regime the aristocratic element— the gravity of the senate—occupies the intermediate, i.e., the central or key position. The mixed regime is, in fact—and it is meant to be—an aristocracy which is strengthened and protected by the admixture of monarchic and democratic institutions. To summarize, one may say that it is characteristic of the classic natural right teaching to culminate in a twofold answer to the question of the best regime: the simply best regime would be the absolute rule of the wise; the practically best regime is the rule, under law, of gentlemen, or the mixed regime.[18]

According to a view which today is rather common and which may be described as Marxist or crypto-Marxist, the classics preferred the rule of the urban patriciate because they themselves belonged to the urban patriciate or were hangers-on of the urban patriciate. We need not take issue with the contention that, in studying a political doctrine, we must consider the bias, and even the class bias, of its originator. It suffices to demand that the class to which the thinker in question belongs be correctly identified. In the common view the fact is overlooked that there is a class interest of the philosophers qua philosophers, and this oversight is ultimately due to the denial of the possibility of philosophy. Philosophers as philosophers do not go with their families. The selfish or class interest of the philosophers consists in being left alone, in being allowed to live the life of the blessed on earth by devoting themselves to investigation of the most important subjects. Now it is an experience of many centuries in greatly different natural and moral climates that there was one and only one class which was habitually sympathetic to philosophy, and not intermittently, like kings; and this was the urban patriciate. The common people had no sympathy for philosophy and philosophers. As Cicero put it, philosophy was suspect to the many. Only in the nineteenth century did this state of things profoundly and manifestly change, and the change was ultimately due to a complete change in the meaning of philosophy.

18. Plato *Statesman* 293[e]7 ff.; *Laws* 680[e]1–4, 684[c]1–6, 690[b]8–[c]3, 691[d]7–692[b]1, 693[b]1–[e]8, 701[e], 744[b]1–[d]1, 756[e]9–10, 806[d]7 ff., 846[d]1–7; Xenophon *Memorabilia* iii. 9. 10–13; iv. 6. 12; *Oeconomicus* 4. 2 ff., 6. 5–10, 11. 1 ff.; *Anabasis* v. 8. 26; Aristotle *Nicomachean Ethics* 1160[a]32–1161[a]30; *Eudemian Ethics* 1242[b]27–31; *Politics* 1261[a]38–[b]3, 1265[b]33–1266[a]6, 1270[b]8–27, 1277[b]35–1278[a]22, 1278[a]37–1279[a]17, 1284[a]4–[b]34, 1289[a]39 ff.; Polybius vi. 51. 5–8; Cicero *Republic* i. 52, 55 (cf. 41), 56–63, 69; ii. 37–40, 55–56, 59; iv. 8; Diogenes Laertius vii. 131; Thomas Aquinas *Summa theologica* ii. 1. qu. 95, *a*. 1 ad 2 and *a*. 4; qu. 105, *a*. 1.

The classic natural right doctrine in its original form, if fully developed, is identical with the doctrine of the best regime. For the question as to what is by nature right or as to what is justice finds its complete answer only through the construction, in speech, of the best regime. The essentially political character of the classic natural right doctrine appears most clearly in Plato's *Republic*. Hardly less revealing is the fact that Aristotle's discussion of natural right is a part of his discussion of political right, especially if one contrasts the opening of Aristotle's statement with the statement of Ulpian in which natural right is introduced as a part of private right.[19] The political character of natural right became blurred, or ceased to be essential, under the influence of both ancient egalitarian natural right and the biblical faith. On the basis of the biblical faith, the best regime simply is the City of God; therefore, the best regime is coeval with Creation and hence always actual; and the cessation of evil, or Redemption, is brought about by God's supernatural action. The question of the best regime thus loses its crucial significance. The best regime as the classics understood it ceases to be identical with the perfect moral order. The end of civil society is no longer "virtuous life as such" but only a certain segment of the virtuous life. The notion of God as lawgiver takes on a certainty and definiteness which it never possessed in classical philosophy. Therefore natural right or, rather, natural law becomes independent of the best regime and takes precedence over it. The Second Table of the Decalogue and the principles embodied in it are of infinitely higher dignity than the best regime.[20] It is classic natural right in this profoundly modified form that has exercised

---

19. Aristotle *Nicomachean Ethics* 1134^{b}18–19; *Politics* 1253^{a}38; *Digest* i. 1. 1–4.

20. Compare Thomas Aquinas *Summa theologica* ii. 1. qu. 105, *a*. 1 with qu. 104, *a*. 3, qu. 100, *a*. 8, and 99, *a*. 4; also ii. 2. qu. 58, *a*. 6 and *a*. 12. See also Heinrich A. Rommen, *The State in Catholic Thought* (St. Louis, Mo.: B. Herder Book Co., 1945), pp. 309, 330–31, 477, 479. Milton, *Of Reformation Touching Church-Discipline in England* (*Milton's Prose* ["Oxford World's Classics" ed.], p. 55): " 'Tis not the common law, nor the civil, but piety, and justice, that are our foundresses; they stoop not, neither change

the most powerful influence on Western thought almost since the beginnings of the Christian Era. Still, even this crucial modification of the classical teaching was in a way anticipated by the classics. According to the classics, political life as such is essentially inferior in dignity to the philosophic life.

This observation leads to a new difficulty, or rather it leads us back to the same difficulty with which we have been confronted throughout—e.g., when we used terms like "gentlemen." If man's ultimate end is trans-political, natural right would seem to have a trans-political root. Yet can natural right be adequately understood if it is directly referred to this root? Can natural right be deduced from man's natural end? Can it be deduced from anything?

Human nature is one thing, virtue or the perfection of human nature is another. The definite character of the virtues and, in particular, of justice cannot be deduced from human nature. In the language of Plato, the idea of man is indeed compatible with the idea of justice, but it is a different idea. The idea of justice even seems to belong to a different kind of ideas than the idea of man, since the idea of man is not in the same way problematic as the idea of justice; there is hardly any disagreement as to whether a given being is a man, whereas there is habitual disagreement in regard to things just and noble. In the language of Aristotle, one could say that the relation of virtue to human nature is comparable to that of act and potency, and the act cannot be determined by starting from the potency, but, on the contrary, the potency becomes known by looking back to it from the act.[21] Human nature

---

colour for Aristocracy, Democracy, or Monarchy, nor yet at all interrupt their just courses, but *far above the taking notice of these inferior niceties* with perfect sympathy, wherever they meet, kiss each other." Italics are not in the original.

21. Plato *Republic* 523ª1–524ᵈ6; *Statesman* 285ᵈ8–286ª7; *Phaedrus* 250ᵇ1–5, 263ª1–ᵇ5; *Alcibiades* i. 111ᵇ11–112ᶜ7; Aristotle *Nicomachean Ethics* 1097ᵇ24–1098ª18; 1103ª23–26; 1106ª15–24; *De anima* 415ª16–22; Cicero *De finibus* iii. 20–23, 38; v. 46; Thomas Aquinas *Summa theologica* ii. 1. qu. 54, *a.* 1, and 55, *a.* 1.

"is" in a different manner than its perfection or virtue. Virtue exists in most cases, if not in all cases, as an object of aspiration and not as fulfilment. Therefore, it exists in speech rather than in deed. Whatever may be the proper starting point for studying human nature, the proper starting point for studying the perfection of human nature, and hence, in particular, natural right, is what is said about these subjects or the opinions about them.

Very roughly speaking, we may distinguish three types of classic natural right teachings, or three different manners in which the classics understood natural right. These three types are the Socratic-Platonic, the Aristotelian, and the Thomistic. As regards the Stoics, it seems to me that their natural right teaching belongs to the Socratic-Platonic type. According to a view which today is fairly common, the Stoics originated an entirely new type of natural right teaching. But, to say nothing here of other considerations, this opinion is based on neglect of the close connection between stoicism and cynicism,[22] and cynicism was originated by a Socratic.

To describe, then, as concisely as we can the character of what we shall venture to call the "Socratic-Platonic-Stoic natural right teaching," we start from the conflict between the two most common opinions regarding justice: that justice is good and that justice consists in giving to everyone what is due to him. What is due to a man is defined by law, i.e., by the law of the city. But the law of the city may be foolish and hence harmful or bad. Therefore, the justice that consists in giving to everyone what is due to him may be bad. If justice is to remain good, we must conceive of it as essentially independent of law. We shall then define justice as the habit of giving

22. Cicero *De finibus* iii. 68; Diogenes Laertius vi. 14–15; vii. 3, 121; Sextus Empiricus *Pyrrhonica* iii. 200, 205. Montaigne opposes "[la] secte Stoïque, plus franche" to "la secte Peripatétique, plus civile" (*Essais*, II, 12 ["Chronique des lettres françaises," Vol. IV], p. 40).

to everyone what is due to him according to nature. A hint as to what is due to others according to nature is supplied by the generally accepted opinion according to which it is unjust to return a dangerous weapon to its lawful owner if he is insane or bent on the destruction of the city. This implies that nothing can be just which is harmful to others, or that justice is the habit of not harming others. This definition fails, however, to account for the frequent cases where we blame as unjust such men who, indeed, never harm another but scrupulously refrain from ever helping another by deed or by speech. Justice will then be the habit of benefiting others. The just man is he who gives to everyone, not what a possibly foolish law prescribes, but what is good for the other, i.e., what is by nature good for the other. Yet not everyone knows what is good for man in general, and for every individual in particular. Just as only the physician truly knows what is in each case good for the body, only the wise man truly knows what is good in each case for the soul. This being the case, there cannot be justice, i.e., giving to everyone what is by nature good for him, except in a society in which wise men are in absolute control.

Let us take the example of the big boy who has a small coat and the small boy who has a big coat. The big boy is the lawful owner of the small coat because he, or his father, has bought it. But it is not good for him; it does not fit him. The wise ruler will therefore take the big coat away from the small boy and give it to the big boy without any regard to legal ownership. The least we have to say is that just ownership is something entirely different from legal ownership. If there is to be justice, the wise rulers must assign to everyone what is truly due to him or what is by nature good for him. They will give to everyone only what he can use well, and they will take away from everyone what he cannot use well. Justice is then incompatible with what is generally understood by private ownership. All using is ultimately for the sake of action or doing; justice requires, therefore, above all, that everyone be assigned such a function or such a job as he can perform well. But everyone does best that for which he is best fitted by nature. Justice exists, then, only in a society in which everyone does what he can do well and in which everyone has what he can use well. Justice is identical with membership in such a society and devotion to such a society—a society according to nature.[23]

We must go further. The justice of the city may be said to consist in acting according to the principle "from everyone according to his capacity and to everyone according to his merits." A society is just if its living principle is "equality of opportunity," i.e., if every human being belonging to it has the opportunity, corresponding to his capacities, of deserving well of the whole and receiving the proper reward for his deserts. Since there is no good reason for assuming that the capacity for meritorious action is bound up with sex, beauty, and so on, "discrimination" on account of sex, ugliness, and so on is unjust. The only proper reward for service is honor, and therefore the only proper reward for outstanding service is great authority. In a just society the social hierarchy will correspond strictly to the hierarchy of merit and of merit alone. Now, as a rule, civil society regards as an indispensable condition for holding high office that the individual concerned be a born citizen, a son of a citizen father and a citizen mother. That is to say, civil society in one way or another qualifies the principle of merit, i.e., the principle par excellence of justice, by the wholly unconnected principle of indigenousness. In order to be truly just, civil society would have to drop this

23. Plato *Republic* 331ᶜ1–332ᶜ4, 335ᵈ11–12, 421ᵉ7–422ᵈ7 (cf. *Laws* 739ᵇ8–ᵉ3 and Aristotle *Politics* 1264ᵃ13–17), 433ᵉ3–434ᵃ1; *Crito* 49ᶜ; *Clitopho* 407ᵉ8–408ᵇ5, 410ᵇ1–3; Xenophon *Memorabilia* iv. 4. 12–13, 8. 11; *Oeconomicus* 1. 5–14; *Cyropaedia* i. 3. 16–17; Cicero *Republic* i. 27–28; iii. 11; *Laws* i. 18–19; *Offices* i. 28, 29, 31; iii. 27; *De finibus* iii. 71, 75; *Lucullus* 136–37; cf. Aristotle *Magna moralia* 1199ᵇ10–35.

qualification; civil society must be transformed into the "world-state." That this is necessary is said to appear also from the following consideration: Civil society as closed society necessarily implies that there is more than one civil society, and therewith that war is possible. Civil society must therefore foster warlike habits. But these habits are at variance with the requirements of justice. If people are engaged in war, they are concerned with victory and not with assigning to the enemy what an impartial and discerning judge would consider beneficial to the enemy. They are concerned with harming others, and the just man appeared to be a man who does not harm anyone. Civil society is therefore forced to make a distinction: the just man is he who does not harm, but loves, his friends or neighbors, i.e., his fellow-citizens, but who does harm or who hates his enemies, i.e., the foreigners who as such are at least potential enemies of his city. We may call this type of justice "citizen-morality," and we shall say that the city necessarily requires citizen-morality in this sense. But citizen-morality suffers from an inevitable self-contradiction. It asserts that different rules of conduct apply in war than in peace, but it cannot help regarding at least some relevant rules, which are said to apply to peace only, as universally valid. The city cannot leave it at saying, for instance, that deception, and especially deception to the detriment of others, is bad in peace but praiseworthy in war. It cannot help viewing with suspicion the man who is good at deceiving, or it cannot help regarding the devious or disingenuous ways which are required for any successful deception as simply mean or distasteful. Yet the city must command, and even praise, such ways if they are used against the enemy. To avoid this self-contradiction, the city must transform itself into the "world-state." But no human being and no group of human beings can rule the whole human race justly. Therefore, what is divined in speaking of the "world-state" as an all-comprehensive human society subject to one human government is in truth the cosmos ruled by God, which is then the only true city, or the city that is simply according to nature because it is the only city which is simply just. Men are citizens of this city, or freemen in it, only if they are wise; their obedience to the law which orders the natural city, to the natural law, is the same thing as prudence.[24]

24. Plato *Statesman* 271ᵈ3–272ᵃ1; *Laws* 713ᵃ2–ᵉ6; Xenophon *Cyropaedia* i. 6. 27–34; ii. 2. 26; Cicero *Republic* iii. 33; *Laws* i. 18–19, 22–23, 32, 61; ii. 8–11; Frag. 2; *De finibus* iv. 74; v. 65, 67; *Lucullus* 136–37. J. von Arnim, *Stoicorum veterum fragmenta* iii, Frags. 327 and 334. The problem discussed in this paragraph is adumbrated in Plato's *Republic* by the following feature, among others: Polemarchus' definition according to which justice consists in helping the friends and hurting the enemies is preserved in the requirement regarding the guardians according to which the guardians must be similar to dogs, namely, meek to friends or acquaintances and the opposite of meek to enemies or strangers (375ᵃ2–376ᵇ1; cf. 378ᶜ7, 537ᵃ4–7; and Aristotle *Politics* 1328ᵃ7–11). It should be noted that it is Socrates, and not Polemarchus, who first brings up the subject "enemies" (332ᵇ5; cf. also 335ᵃ6–7) and that Polemarchus appears as witness for Socrates in the latter's discussion with Thrasymachus in which Clitopho appears as witness for Thrasymachus (340ᵃ1–ᶜ1; cf. *Phaedrus* 257ᵇ3–4). If one considers these things, one is no longer bewildered by the information supplied by the *Clitopho* (410ᵃ7–ᵇ1), according to which the only definition of justice which Socrates himself suggested to Clitopho is the one which in the *Republic* Polemarchus suggests with the assistance of Socrates. Many interpreters of Plato do not sufficiently consider the possibility that his Socrates was as much concerned with understanding what justice is, i.e., with understanding the whole complexity of the problem of justice, as with preaching justice. For if one is concerned with understanding the problem of justice, one must go through the stage in which justice presents itself as identical with citizen-morality, and one must not merely rush through that stage. One may express the conclusion of the argument sketched in this paragraph by saying that there cannot be true justice if there is no divine rule or providence. One would not reasonably expect much virtue or much justice of men who live habitually in a condition of extreme scarcity so that they have to fight with one another constantly for the sake of mere survival. If there is to be justice among men, care must be taken that they are not compelled to think constantly of mere self-preservation and to act toward their fellows in the way in which men mostly act under such conditions. But such care cannot be human providence. The cause of justice is infinitely strengthened if the condition of man as man, and hence especially the condition of man in the beginning (when he could not yet have been corrupted by false opinions), was one of nonscarcity. There is then a profound kinship between the notion of natural law and the notion of a perfect beginning: the golden age or the Garden of Eden. Cf. Plato *Laws* 713ᵃ2–ᵉ2, as well as *Statesman* 271ᵈ3–272ᵇ1 and 272ᵈ6–273ᵃ1: the rule of God was accompanied by plenty and peace; scarcity leads to war. Cf. *Statesman* 274ᵇ5 ff. with *Protagoras* 322ᵃ8 ff.

This solution to the problem of justice obviously transcends the limits of political life.[25] It implies that the justice which is possible within the city, can be only imperfect or cannot be unquestionably good. There are still other reasons which force men to seek beyond the political sphere for perfect justice or, more generally, for the life that is truly according to nature. It is not possible here to do more than barely to indicate these reasons. In the first place, the wise do not desire to rule; they must therefore be compelled to rule. They must be compelled because their whole life is devoted to the pursuit of something which is absolutely higher in dignity than any human things—the unchangeable truth. And it appears to be against nature that the lower should be preferred to the higher. If striving for knowledge of the eternal truth is the ultimate end of man, justice and moral virtue in general can be fully legitimated only by the fact that they are required for the sake of that ultimate end or that they are conditions of the philosophic life. From this point of view the man who is merely just or moral without being a philosopher appears as a mutilated human being. It thus becomes a question whether the moral or just man who is not a philosopher is simply superior to the nonphilosophic "erotic" man. It likewise becomes a question whether justice and morality in general, in so far as they are required for the sake of the philosophic life, are identical, as regards both their meaning and their extension, with justice and morality as they are commonly understood, or whether morality does not have two entirely different roots, or whether what Aristotle calls moral virtue is not, in fact, merely political or vulgar virtue. The latter question can also be expressed by asking whether, by transforming opinion about morality into knowledge of morality, one does not

25. Cicero *Laws* i. 61–62; iii. 13–14; *De finibus* iv. 7, 22, 74; *Lucullus* 136–37; Seneca *Ep.* 68. 2.

transcend the dimension of morality in the politically relevant sense of the term.[26]

However this may be, both the obvious dependence of the philosophic life on the city and the natural affection which men have for men, and especially for their kin, regardless of whether or not these men have "good natures" or are potential philosophers, make it necessary for the philosopher to descend again into the cave, i.e., to take care of the affairs of the city, whether in a direct or more remote manner. In descending into the cave, the philosopher admits that what is intrinsically or by nature the highest is not the most urgent for man, who is essentially an "in-between" being—between the brutes and the gods. When attempting to guide the city, he knows then in advance that, in order to be useful or good for the city, the requirements of wisdom must be qualified or diluted. If these requirements are identical with natural right or with natural law, natural right or natural law must be diluted in order to become compatible with the requirements of the city. The city requires that wisdom be reconciled with consent. But to admit the necessity of consent, i.e., of the consent of the unwise, amounts to admitting a right of unwisdom, i.e., an irrational, if inevitable, right. Civil life requires a fundamental compromise between wisdom and folly, and this means a compromise between the natural right that is discerned by reason or understanding and the right that is based on opinion alone. Civil life requires the dilution of nat-

26. Plato *Republic* 486^{b}6–13, 519^{b}7–^{c}7, 520^{e}4–521^{b}11, 619^{b}7–^{d}1; *Phaedo* 82^{a}10–^{e}1; *Theaetetus* 174^{a}4–^{b}6; *Laws* 804^{b}5–^{e}1. As for the problem of the relation between justice and *eros*, one has to compare the *Gorgias* as a whole with the *Phaedrus* as a whole. An attempt in this direction was made by David Grene, *Man in His Pride: A Study in the Political Philosophy of Thucydides and Plato* (Chicago: University of Chicago Press, 1950), pp. 137–46 (cf. *Social Research*, 1951, pp. 394–97). Aristotle *Nicomachean Ethics* 1177^{a}25–34, ^{b}16–18, 1178^{a}9–^{b}21; *Eudemian Ethics* 1248^{b}10–1249^{b}25. Compare *Politics* 1325^{b}24–30 with the parallelism between the justice of the individual and the justice of the city in the *Republic*. Cicero *Offices* i. 28; iii. 13–17; *Republic* i. 28; *De finibus* iii. 48; iv. 22; cf. also *Republic* vi. 29 with iii. 11; Thomas Aquinas *Summa theologica* ii. 1. qu. 58, *a*. 4–5.

ural right by merely conventional right. Natural right would act as dynamite for civil society. In other words, the simply good, which is what is good by nature and which is radically distinct from the ancestral, must be transformed into the politically good, which is, as it were, the quotient of the simply good and the ancestral: the politically good is what "removes a vast mass of evil without shocking a vast mass of prejudice." It is in this necessity that the need for inexactness in political or moral matters is partly founded.[27]

The notion that natural right must be diluted in order to become compatible with civil society is the philosophic root of the later distinction between the primeval natural right and the secondary natural right.[28] This distinction was linked with the view that the primeval natural right, which excludes private property and other characteristic features of civil society, belonged to man's original state of innocence, whereas the secondary natural right is needed after man has become corrupted, as a remedy for his corruption. We must not overlook, however, the difference between the notion that natural right must be diluted and the notion of a secondary natural right. If the principles valid in civil society are diluted natural right, they are much less venerable than if they are regarded as secondary natural right, i.e., as divinely established and involving an absolute duty for fallen man. Only in the latter case is justice, as it is commonly understood, unquestionably good. Only in the latter case does natural right in the strict sense or the primary natural right cease to be dynamite for civil society.

Cicero has embodied in his writings, especially in the third book of his *Republic* and in the first two books of his *Laws*, a

27. Plato *Republic* 414^{b}8–415^{d}5 (cf. 331^{c}1–3), 501^{a}9–^{c}2 (cf. 500^{c}2–^{d}8 and 484^{c}8–^{d}3); *Laws* 739, 757^{a}5–758^{a}2; Cicero *Republic* ii. 57.

28. Cf. R. Stintzing, *Geschichte der deutschen Rechtswissenschaft*, I (Munich and Leipzig, 1880), pp. 302 ff., 307, 371; see also, e.g., Hooker, *Laws of Ecclesiastical Polity*, Book I, chap. x, sec. 13.

mitigated version of the original Stoic natural law teaching. Hardly any trace of the connection between stoicism and cynicism is left in his presentation. Natural law as presented by him does not seem to have to be diluted in order to become compatible with civil society; it seems to be in natural harmony with civil society. Accordingly, what one is tempted to call the "Ciceronian natural-law teaching" comes closer to what is regarded at present by some scholars as the typical premodern natural law teaching than any earlier doctrine of which we have more than fragments. It is therefore of some importance that Cicero's attitude toward the teaching in question be not misunderstood.[29]

In the *Laws*, in which Cicero and his companions seek the shade and in which Cicero himself presents the Stoic natural law teaching, he indicates that he is not certain of the truth of that doctrine. This is not surprising. The Stoic natural law teaching is based on the doctrine of divine providence and on an anthropocentric teleology. In his *On the Nature of the Gods* Cicero subjects that theological-teleological doctrine to severe criticism, with the result that he cannot admit it as more than approaching the semblance of truth. Similarly, he accepts in the *Laws* the Stoic doctrine of divination (which is a branch of the Stoic doctrine of providence), while he attacks it in the second book of his *On Divination*. One of the interlocutors in the *Laws* is Cicero's friend Atticus, who assents to the Stoic natural law doctrine but who, being an Epicurean, cannot have assented to it because he regarded it as true or in his capacity as thinker; he rather assented to it in his capacity as Roman citizen and more particularly as an adherent of aristocracy, because he regarded it as politically salutary. It is reasonable to assume that Cicero's seemingly unqualified acceptance of the Stoic natural law teaching has the same motivation as Atticus'. Cicero himself says that he wrote dialogues in order

29. See, e.g., *De finibus* iii. 64–67.

not to present his real views too openly. After all, he was an Academic skeptic and not a Stoic. And the thinker whom he claims to follow, and whom he admires most, is Plato himself, the founder of the Academy. The least that must be said is that Cicero did not regard the Stoic natural law teaching, in so far as it goes beyond Plato's teaching of natural right, as evidently true.[30]

In the *Republic*, in which the interlocutors seek the sun and which is admittedly a free imitation of Plato's *Republic*, the Stoic natural law teaching, or the defense of justice (i.e., the proof that justice is by nature good), is not presented by the chief character. Scipio, who occupies in Cicero's work the position which Socrates occupies in the Platonic model, is fully convinced of the smallness of all human things and therefore longs for the contemplative life to be enjoyed after death. That version of the Stoic natural law teaching—the exoteric version—which is in perfect harmony with the claims of civil society, is intrusted to Laelius, who is distrustful of philosophy in the full and strict sense of the term and who is absolutely at home on earth, in Rome; he is sitting in the center, imitating the earth. Laelius goes so far as to find no difficulty in reconciling natural law with the claims of the Roman Empire in particular. Scipio, however, indicates the original and unmitigated Stoic natural law teaching, which is incompatible with the claims of civil society. He likewise indicates how much of force and fraud was required for making Rome great: the Roman regime, which is the best regime in existence, is not simply just. He thus seems to indicate that "the natural law" on which civil society can act is, in truth, natural law diluted by a lower principle. The case against the natural character of right is made by Philus, who is an Academic skeptic, like

30. *Laws* i. 15, 18, 19, 21, 22, 25, 32, 35, 37–39, 54, 56; ii. 14, 32–34, 38–39; iii.1, 26, 37; *Republic* ii. 28; iv. 4; *De natura deorum* ii. 133 ff.; iii. 66 ff., 95; *De divinatione* ii. 70 ff.; *Offices* i. 22; *De finibus* ii. 45; *Tusc. Disp.* v. 11. Compare n. 24 above with chap. iii, n. 22.

Cicero himself.[31] It is then misleading to call Cicero an adherent of the Stoic natural law teaching.

To turn now to the Aristotelian natural right teaching, we have to note first that the only thematic treatment of natural right which is certainly by Aristotle and which certainly expresses Aristotle's own view covers barely one page of the *Nicomachean Ethics*. In addition, the passage is singularly elusive; it is not illumined by a single example of what is by nature right. This much, however, can safely be said: according to Aristotle, there is no fundamental disproportion between natural right and the requirements of political society, or there is no essential need for the dilution of natural right. In this, as well as in many other respects, Aristotle opposes the divine madness of Plato and, by anticipation, the paradoxes of the Stoics, in the spirit of his unrivaled sobriety. A right which necessarily transcends political society, he gives us to understand, cannot be the right natural to man, who is by nature a political animal. Plato never discusses any subject—be it the city or the heavens or numbers—without keeping in view the elementary Socratic question, "What is the right way of life?" And the simply right way of life proves to be the philosophic life. Plato eventually defines natural right with direct reference to the fact that the only life which is simply just is the life of the philosopher. Aristotle, on the other hand, treats each of the various levels of beings, and hence especially every level of human life, on its own terms. When he discusses justice, he discusses justice as everyone knows it and as it is understood in political life, and he refuses to be drawn into the dialectical whirlpool that carries us far beyond justice in the ordinary sense of the term toward the philosophic life. Not that he denies the ultimate right of that dialectical process or the tension between the requirements of philosophy and those

31. *Republic* i. 18, 19, 26–28, 30, 56–57; iii. 8–9; iv. 4; vi. 17–18; cf. *ibid.* ii. 4, 12, 15, 20, 22, 26–27, 31, 53, with i. 62; iii. 20–22, 24, 31, 35–36; cf. also *De finibus* ii. 59.

of the city; he knows that the simply best regime belongs to an entirely different epoch than fully developed philosophy. But he implies that the intermediate stages of that process, while not absolutely consistent, are sufficiently consistent for all practical purposes. It is true that those stages can exist only in a twilight, but this is a sufficient reason for the analyst—and especially for the analyst whose primary concern is with guiding human actions—to leave them in that twilight. In the twilight which is essential to human life as merely human, the justice which may be available in the cities appears to be perfect justice and unquestionably good; there is no need for the dilution of natural right. Aristotle says, then, simply that natural right is a part of political right. This does not mean that there is no natural right outside the city or prior to the city. To say nothing of the relations between parents and children, the relation of justice that obtains between two complete strangers who meet on a desert island is not one of political justice and is nevertheless determined by nature. What Aristotle suggests is that the most fully developed form of natural right is that which obtains among fellow-citizens; only among fellow-citizens do the relations which are the subject matter of right or justice reach their greatest density and, indeed, their full growth.

The second assertion regarding natural right which Aristotle makes—an assertion much more surprising than the first—is that all natural right is changeable. According to Thomas Aquinas, this statement must be understood with a qualification: the principles of natural right, the axioms from which the more specific rules of natural right are derived, are universally valid and immutable; what are mutable are only the more specific rules (e.g., the rule to return deposits). The Thomistic interpretation is connected with the view that there is a *habitus* of practical principles, a *habitus* which he calls "conscience" or, more precisely, *synderesis*. The very terms show that this view is alien to Aristotle; it is of Patristic origin. In addition, Aristotle says explicitly that all right—hence also all natural right—is changeable; he does not qualify that statement in any way. There exists an alternative medieval interpretation of Aristotle's doctrine, namely, the Averroistic view or, more adequately stated, the view characteristic of the *falāsifa* (i.e., of the Islamic Aristotelians) as well as of the Jewish Aristotelians. This view was set forth within the Christian world by Marsilius of Padua and presumably by other Christian or Latin Averroists. According to Averroës, Aristotle understands by natural right "legal natural right." Or, as Marsilius puts it, natural right is only quasi-natural; actually, it depends on human institution or convention; but it is distinguished from merely positive right by the fact that it is based on ubiquitous convention. In all civil societies the same broad rules of what constitutes justice necessarily grow up. They specify the minimum requirements of society; they correspond roughly to the Second Table of the Decalogue but include the command of divine worship. In spite of the fact that they seem to be evidently necessary and are universally recognized, they are conventional for this reason: Civil society is incompatible with any immutable rules, however basic; for in certain conditions the disregard of these rules may be needed for the preservation of society; but, for pedagogic reasons, society must present as universally valid certain rules which are generally valid. Since the rules in question obtain normally, all social teachings proclaim these rules and not the rare exceptions. The effectiveness of the general rules depends on their being taught without qualifications, without ifs and buts. But the omission of the qualifications which makes the rules more effective, makes them at the same time untrue. The unqualified rules are not natural right but conventional right.[32]

32. See L. Strauss, *Persecution and the Art of Writing* (Glencoe, Ill.: Free Press, 1952), pp. 95–141.

This view of natural right agrees with Aristotle in so far as it admits the mutability of all rules of justice. But it differs from Aristotle's view in so far as it implies the denial of natural right proper. How, then, can we find a safe middle road between these formidable opponents, Averroës and Thomas?

One is tempted to make the following suggestion: When speaking of natural right, Aristotle does not primarily think of any general propositions but rather of concrete decisions. All action is concerned with particular situations. Hence justice and natural right reside, as it were, in concrete decisions rather than in general rules. It is much easier to see clearly, in most cases, that this particular act of killing was just than to state clearly the specific difference between just killings as such and unjust killings as such. A law which solves justly a problem peculiar to a given country at a given time may be said to be just to a higher degree than any general rule of natural law which, because of its generality, may prevent a just decision in a given case. In every human conflict there exists the possibility of a just decision based on full consideration of all the circumstances, a decision demanded by the situation. Natural right consists of such decisions. Natural right thus understood is obviously mutable. Yet one can hardly deny that in all concrete decisions general principles are implied and presupposed. Aristotle recognized the existence of such principles, e.g., of those principles which he stated when speaking of "commutative" and "distributive" justice. Similarly, his discussion of the natural character of the city (a discussion which deals with the questions of principle raised by anarchism and pacifism), to say nothing of his discussion of slavery, is an attempt to establish principles of right. These principles would seem to be universally valid or unchangeable. What, then, does Aristotle mean by saying that all natural right is changeable? Or why does natural right ultimately reside in concrete decisions rather than in general rules?

There is a meaning of justice which is not exhausted by the principles of commutative and distributive justice in particular. Prior to being the commutatively and distributively just, the just is the common good. The common good consists normally in what is required by commutative and distributive justice or by other moral principles of this kind or in what is compatible with these requirements. But the common good also comprises, of course, the mere existence, the mere survival, the mere independence, of the political community in question. Let us call an extreme situation a situation in which the very existence or independence of a society is at stake. In extreme situations there may be conflicts between what the self-preservation of society requires and the requirements of commutative and distributive justice. In such situations, and only in such situations, it can justly be said that the public safety is the highest law. A decent society will not go to war except for a just cause. But what it will do during a war will depend to a certain extent on what the enemy—possibly an absolutely unscrupulous and savage enemy—forces it to do. There are no limits which can be defined in advance, there are no assignable limits to what might become just reprisals. But war casts its shadow on peace. The most just society cannot survive without "intelligence," i.e., espionage. Espionage is impossible without a suspension of certain rules of natural right. But societies are not only threatened from without. Considerations which apply to foreign enemies may well apply to subversive elements within society. Let us leave these sad exigencies covered with the veil with which they are justly covered. It suffices to repeat that in extreme situations the normally valid rules of natural right are justly changed, or changed in accordance with natural right; the exceptions are as just as the rules. And Aristotle seems to suggest that there is not a single rule, however basic, which is not subject to exception. One could say that in all cases the common good must be preferred to the private good and that this rule suffers no exception. But this rule does not say more than that justice must be observed, and we are anxious to know what it is that is required by justice or the common good. By saying that in extreme situations the public safety is the highest law, one implies that the public safety is not the highest law in normal situations; in normal situations the highest laws are the common rules of justice. Justice has two different principles or sets of principles: the requirements of public safety, or what is necessary in extreme situations to preserve the mere existence or independence of society, on the one hand, and the rules of justice in the more precise sense, on the other. And there is no principle which defines clearly in what type of cases the public safety, and in what type of cases the precise rules of justice, have priority. For it is not possible to define precisely what constitutes an extreme situation in contradistinction to a normal situation. Every dangerous external or internal enemy is inventive to the extent that he is capable of transforming what, on the basis of previous experience, could reasonably be regarded as a normal situation into an extreme situation. Natural right must be mutable in order to be able to cope with the inventiveness of wickedness. What cannot be decided in advance by universal rules, what can be decided in the critical moment by the most competent and most conscientious statesman on the spot, can be made visible as just, in retrospect, to all; the objective discrimination between extreme actions which were just and extreme actions which were unjust is one of the noblest duties of the historian.[33]

It is important that the difference between the Aristotelian view of natural right and Machiavellianism be clearly under-

33. As for the other principles of right which Aristotle recognized, it must suffice here to note that, according to him, a man who is not capable of being a member of civil society is not necessarily a defective human being; on the contrary, he may be a superior human being.

stood. Machiavelli denies natural right, because he takes his bearings by the extreme situations in which the demands of justice are reduced to the requirements of necessity, and not by the normal situations in which the demands of justice in the strict sense are the highest law. Furthermore, he does not have to overcome a reluctance as regards the deviations from what is normally right. On the contrary, he seems to derive no small enjoyment from contemplating these deviations, and he is not concerned with the punctilious investigation of whether any particular deviation is really necessary or not. The true statesman in the Aristotelian sense, on the other hand, takes his bearings by the normal situation and by what is normally right, and he reluctantly deviates from what is normally right only in order to save the cause of justice and humanity itself. No legal expression of this difference can be found. Its political importance is obvious. The two opposite extremes, which at present are called "cynicism" and "idealism," combine in order to blur this difference. And, as everyone can see, they have not been unsuccessful.

The variability of the demands of that justice which men can practice was recognized not only by Aristotle but by Plato as well. Both avoided the Scylla of "absolutism" and the Charybdis of "relativism" by holding a view which one may venture to express as follows: There is a universally valid hierarchy of ends, but there are no universally valid rules of action. Not to repeat what has been indicated before, when deciding what ought to be done, i.e., what ought to be done by this individual (or this individual group) here and now, one has to consider not only which of the various competing objectives is higher in rank but also which is most urgent in the circumstances. What is most urgent is legitimately preferred to what is less urgent, and the most urgent is in many cases lower in rank than the less urgent. But one cannot make a universal rule that urgency is a higher consideration than rank. For it is our duty to make the highest activity, as much as we can, the most urgent or the most needful thing. And the maximum of effort which can be expected necessarily varies from individual to individual. The only universally valid standard is the hierarchy of ends. This standard is sufficient for passing judgment on the level of nobility of individuals and groups and of actions and institutions. But it is insufficient for guiding our actions.

The Thomistic doctrine of natural right or, more generally expressed, of natural law is free from the hesitations and ambiguities which are characteristic of the teachings, not only of Plato and Cicero, but of Aristotle as well. In definiteness and noble simplicity it even surpasses the mitigated Stoic natural law teaching. No doubt is left, not only regarding the basic harmony between natural right and civil society, but likewise regarding the immutable character of the fundamental propositions of natural law; the principles of the moral law, especially as formulated in the Second Table of the Decalogue, suffer no exception, unless possibly by divine intervention. The doctrine of *synderesis* or of the conscience explains why the natural law can always be duly promulgated to all men and hence be universally obligatory. It is reasonable to assume that these profound changes were due to the influence of the belief in biblical revelation. If this assumption should prove to be correct, one would be forced to wonder, however, whether the natural law as Thomas Aquinas understands it is natural law strictly speaking, i.e., a law knowable to the unassisted human mind, to the human mind which is not illumined by divine revelation. This doubt is strengthened by the following consideration: The natural law which is knowable to the unassisted human mind and which prescribes chiefly actions in the strict sense is related to, or founded upon, the natural end of man; that end is twofold: moral perfection and intellectual perfection; intellectual perfection is higher in dignity than moral perfection; but intellectual perfection or wisdom, as unassisted human reason knows it, does not require moral virtue. Thomas solves this difficulty by virtually contending that, according to natural reason, the natural end of man is insufficient, or points beyond itself or, more precisely, that the end of man cannot consist in philosophic investigation, to say nothing of political activity. Thus natural reason itself creates a presumption in favor of the divine law, which completes or perfects the natural law. At any rate, the ultimate consequence of the Thomistic view of natural law is that natural law is practically inseparable not only from natural theology—i.e., from a natural theology which is, in fact, based on belief in biblical revelation—but even from revealed theology. Modern natural law was partly a reaction to this absorption of natural law by theology. The modern efforts were partly based on the premise, which would have been acceptable to the classics, that the moral principles have a greater evidence than the teachings even of natural theology and, therefore, that natural law or natural right should be kept independent of theology and its controversies. The second important respect in which modern political thought returned to the classics by opposing the Thomistic view is illustrated by such issues as the indissolubility of marriage and birth control. A work like Montesquieu's *Spirit of Laws* is misunderstood if one disregards the fact that it is directed against the Thomistic view of natural right. Montesquieu tried to recover for statesmanship a latitude which had been considerably restricted by the Thomistic teaching. What Montesquieu's private thoughts were will always remain controversial. But it is safe to say that what he explicitly teaches, as a student of politics and as politically sound and right, is nearer in spirit to the classics than to Thomas.

V

MODERN NATURAL RIGHT

✻

THE most famous and the most influential of all modern natural right teachers was John Locke. But Locke makes it particularly difficult for us to recognize how modern he is or how much he deviates from the natural right tradition. He was an eminently prudent man, and he reaped the reward of superior prudence: he was listened to by many people, and he wielded an extraordinarily great influence on men of affairs and on a large body of opinion. But it is of the essence of prudence that one know when to speak and when to be silent. Knowing this very well, Locke had the good sense to quote only the right kind of writers and to be silent about the wrong kind, although he had more in common, in the last analysis, with the wrong kind than with the right. His authority seems to be Richard Hooker, the great Anglican divine, distinguished by elevation of sentiment and sobriety; "the judicious Hooker," as Locke, following others, likes to call him. Now Hooker's conception of natural right is the Thomistic conception, and the Thomistic conception, in its turn, goes back to the Church Fathers, who, in their turn, were pupils of the Stoics, of the pupils of pupils of Socrates. We are then apparently confronted with an unbroken tradition of perfect respectability that stretches from Socrates to Locke. But the moment we take the trouble to confront Locke's teaching as a whole with Hooker's teaching as a whole, we become aware that, in spite of a certain agreement between Locke and Hooker, Locke's conception of natural right is fundamentally different from Hooker's. The notion of natural right had undergone a fundamental change between Hooker and Locke. A break in the natural right tradition had occurred on the way. This is not surprising. The period between Hooker and Locke had witnessed the emergence of modern natural science, of nonteleological natural science, and therewith the destruction of the basis of traditional natural right. The man who was the first to draw the consequences for natural right from this momentous change was Thomas Hobbes—that imprudent, impish, and iconoclastic extremist, that first plebeian philosopher, who is so enjoyable a writer because of his almost boyish straightforwardness, his never failing humanity, and his marvelous clarity and force. He was deservedly punished for his recklessness, especially by his countrymen. Still, he exercised a very great influence on all subsequent political thought, Continental and even English, and especially on Locke—on the judicious Locke, who judiciously refrained as much as he could from mentioning Hobbes's "justly decried name." To Hobbes we must turn if we desire to understand the specific character of modern natural right.

A. HOBBES

Thomas Hobbes regarded himself as the founder of political philosophy or political science. He knew, of course, that the great honor which he claimed for himself was awarded, by almost universal consent, to Socrates. Nor was he allowed to forget the notorious fact that the tradition which Socrates had originated was still powerful in his own age. But he was certain that traditional political philosophy "was rather a dream than science."[1]

Present-day scholars are not impressed by Hobbes's claim. They note that he was deeply indebted to the tradition which

---

1. *Elements of Law*, Ep. ded.; I, 1, sec. 1; 13, sec. 3, and 17, sec. 1. *De corpore*, Ep. ded.; *De cive*, Ep. ded. and praef.; *Opera Latina*, I, p. xc. *Leviathan*, chaps. xxxi (241) and xlvi (438). In the quotations from the *Leviathan*, figures in parentheses indicate the pages of the "Blackwell's Political Texts" edition.

he scorned. Some of them come close to suggesting that he was one of the last Schoolmen. Lest we overlook the wood for the trees, we shall reduce for a while the significant results of present-day polymathy into the compass of one sentence. Hobbes was indebted to tradition for a single, but momentous, idea: he accepted on trust the view that political philosophy or political science is possible or necessary.

To understand Hobbes's astonishing claim means to pay proportionate attention to his emphatic rejection of the tradition, on the one hand, and to his almost silent agreement with it, on the other. For this purpose one must first identify the tradition. More precisely, one must first see the tradition as Hobbes saw it and forget for a moment how it presents itself to the present-day historian. Hobbes mentions the following representatives of the tradition by name: Socrates, Plato, Aristotle, Cicero, Seneca, Tacitus, and Plutarch.[2] He then tacitly identifies the tradition of political philosophy with a particular tradition. He identifies it with that tradition whose basic premises may be stated as follows: the noble and the just are fundamentally distinguished from the pleasant and are by nature preferable to it; or, there is a natural right that is wholly independent of any human compact or convention; or, there is a best political order which is best because it is according to nature. He identifies traditional political philosophy with the quest for the best regime or for the simply just social order, and therefore with a pursuit that is political not merely because it deals with political matters but, above all, because it is animated by a political spirit. He identifies traditional political philosophy with that particular tradition that was public spirited or—to employ a term which is loose indeed but at present still easily intelligible—that was "idealistic."

When speaking of earlier political philosophers, Hobbes does not mention that tradition whose most famous represent-

2. *De cive*, praef., and XII, 3; *Opera Latina*, V, 358–59.

atives might be thought to be "the sophists," Epicurus and Carneades. The anti-idealistic tradition simply did not exist for him—as a tradition of political philosophy. For it was ignorant of the very idea of political philosophy as Hobbes understood it. It was indeed concerned with the nature of political things and especially of justice. It was also concerned with the question of the right life of the individual and therefore with the question of whether or how the individual could use civil society for his private, nonpolitical purposes: for his ease or for his glory. But it was not political. It was not public spirited. It did not preserve the orientation of statesmen while enlarging their views. It was not dedicated to the concern with the right order of society as with something that is choiceworthy for its own sake.

By tacitly identifying traditional political philosophy with the idealistic tradition, Hobbes expresses, then, his tacit agreement with the idealistic view of the function or the scope of political philosophy. Like Cicero before him, he sides with Cato against Carneades. He presents his novel doctrine as the first truly scientific or philosophic treatment of natural law; he agrees with the Socratic tradition in holding the view that political philosophy is concerned with natural right. He intends to show "what is law, as Plato, Aristotle, Cicero, and divers others have done"; he does not refer to Protagoras, Epicurus, or Carneades. He fears that his *Leviathan* might remind his readers of Plato's *Republic;* no one could dream of comparing the *Leviathan* to Lucretius' *De rerum natura*.[3]

Hobbes rejects the idealistic tradition on the basis of a fundamental agreement with it. He means to do adequately what the Socratic tradition did in a wholly inadequate manner. He means to succeed where the Socratic tradition had failed. He traces the failure of the idealistic tradition to one fundamental

3. *Elements*, Ep. ded.; *Leviathan*, chaps. xv (94–95), xxvi (172), xxxi (241), and xlvi (437–38).

mistake: traditional political philosophy assumed that man is by nature a political or social animal. By rejecting this assumption, Hobbes joins the Epicurean tradition. He accepts its view that man is by nature or originally an a-political and even an a-social animal, as well as its premise that the good is fundamentally identical with the pleasant.[4] But he uses that a-political view for a political purpose. He gives that a-political view a political meaning. He tries to instil the spirit of political idealism into the hedonistic tradition. He thus became the creator of political hedonism, a doctrine which has revolutionized human life everywhere on a scale never yet approached by any other teaching.

The epoch-making change which we are forced to trace to Hobbes was well understood by Edmund Burke: "Boldness formerly was not the character of atheists as such. They were even of a character nearly the reverse; they were formerly like the old Epicureans, rather an unenterprising race. But of late they are grown active, designing, turbulent, and seditious."[5] Political atheism is a distinctly modern phenomenon. No premodern atheist doubted that social life required belief in, and worship of, God or gods. If we do not permit ourselves to be deceived by ephemeral phenomena, we realize that political atheism and political hedonism belong together. They arose together in the same moment and in the same mind.

For in trying to understand Hobbes's political philosophy we must not lose sight of his natural philosophy. His natural

4. *De cive*, I, 2; *Leviathan*, chap. vi (33). Hobbes speaks more emphatically of self-preservation than of pleasure and thus seems to be closer to the Stoics than to the Epicureans. Hobbes's reason for putting the emphasis on self-preservation is that pleasure is an "appearance" whose underlying reality is "only motion," whereas self-preservation belongs to the sphere not only of "appearance" but of "motion" as well (cf. Spinoza, *Ethics*, III, 9 schol. and 11 schol.). Hobbes's emphasizing self-preservation rather than pleasure is then due to his notion of nature or of natural science and has therefore an entirely different motivation than the seemingly identical Stoic view.

5. *Thoughts on French Affairs*, in *Works of Edmund Burke* ("Bohn's Standard Library," Vol. III), p. 377.

philosophy is of the type classically represented by Democritean-Epicurean physics. Yet he regarded, not Epicurus or Democritus, but Plato, as "the best of the ancient philosophers." What he learned from Plato's natural philosophy was not that the universe cannot be understood if it is not ruled by divine intelligence. Whatever may have been Hobbes's private thoughts, his natural philosophy is as atheistic as Epicurean physics. What he learned from Plato's natural philosophy was that mathematics is "the mother of all natural science."[6] By being both mathematical and materialistic-mechanistic, Hobbes's natural philosophy is a combination of Platonic physics and Epicurean physics. From his point of view, premodern philosophy or science as a whole was "rather a dream than science" precisely because it did not think of that combination. His philosophy as a whole may be said to be the classic example of the typically modern combination of political idealism with a materialistic and atheistic view of the whole.

Positions that are originally incompatible with one another can be combined in two ways. The first way is the eclectic compromise which remains on the same plane as the original positions. The other way is the synthesis which becomes possible through the transition of thought from the plane of the original positions to an entirely different plane. The combination effected by Hobbes is a synthesis. He may or may not have been aware that he was, in fact, combining two opposed traditions. He was fully aware that his thought presupposed a radical break with all traditional thought, or the abandonment of the plane on which "Platonism" and "Epicureanism" had carried on their secular struggle.

Hobbes, as well as his most illustrious contemporaries, was overwhelmed or elated by a sense of the complete failure of traditional philosophy. A glance at present and past contro-

6. *Leviathan*, chap. xlvi (438); *English Works*, VII, 346.

versies sufficed to convince them that philosophy, or the quest for wisdom, had not succeeded in transforming itself into wisdom. This overdue transformation was now to be effected. To succeed where tradition had failed, one has to start with reflections on the conditions which have to be fulfilled if wisdom is to become actual: one has to start with reflections on the right method. The purpose of these reflections was to guarantee the actualization of wisdom.

The failure of traditional philosophy showed itself most clearly in the fact that dogmatic philosophy had always been accompanied, as by its shadow, by skeptical philosophy. Dogmatism had never yet succeeded in overcoming skepticism once and for all. To guarantee the actualization of wisdom means to eradicate skepticism by doing justice to the truth embodied in skepticism. For this purpose, one must first give free rein to extreme skepticism: what survives the onslaught of extreme skepticism is the absolutely safe basis of wisdom. The actualization of wisdom is identical with the erection of an absolutely dependable dogmatic edifice on the foundation of extreme skepticism.[7]

The experiment with extreme skepticism was then guided by the anticipation of a new type of dogmatism. Of all known scientific pursuits, mathematics alone had been successful. The new dogmatic philosophy must therefore be constructed on the pattern of mathematics. The mere fact that the only certain knowledge which was available is not concerned with ends but "consists in comparing figures and motions only" created a prejudice against any teleological view or a prejudice in favor of a mechanistic view.[8] It is perhaps more accurate to say that it strengthened a prejudice already in existence. For it is probable that what was foremost in Hobbes's mind was

7. Compare Hobbes's agreement with the thesis of Descartes's first *Meditation*.

8. *Elements*, Ep. ded., and I, 13, sec. 4; *De cive*, Ep. ded.; *Leviathan*, chap. xi (68); cf. Spinoza, *Ethics*, I, Appendix.

the vision, not of a new type of philosophy or science, but of a universe that is nothing but bodies and their aimless motions. The failure of the predominant philosophic tradition could be traced directly to the difficulty with which every teleological physics is beset, and the suspicion arose quite naturally that, owing to social pressures of various kinds, the mechanistic view had never been given a fair chance to show its virtues. But precisely if Hobbes was primarily interested in a mechanistic view, he was inevitably led, as matters stood, to the notion of a dogmatic philosophy based on extreme skepticism. For he had learned from Plato or Aristotle that if the universe has the character ascribed to it by Democritean-Epicurean physics, it excludes the possibility of any physics, of any science, or, in other words, that consistent materialism necessarily culminates in skepticism. "Scientific materialism" could not become possible if one did not first succeed in guaranteeing the possibility of science against the skepticism engendered by materialism. Only the anticipatory revolt against a materialistically understood universe could make possible a science of such a universe. One had to discover or to invent an island that would be exempt from the flux of mechanical causation. Hobbes had to consider the possibility of a natural island. An incorporeal mind was out of the question. On the other hand, what he had learned from Plato and Aristotle made him realize somehow that the corporeal mind, composed of very smooth and round particles with which Epicurus remained satisfied, was an inadequate solution. He was forced to wonder whether the universe did not leave room for an artificial island, for an island to be created by science.

The solution was suggested by the fact that mathematics, the model of the new philosophy, was itself exposed to skeptical attack and proved capable of resisting it by undergoing a specific transformation or interpretation. To "avoid the cavils of the skeptics" at "that so much renowned evidence of geometry . . . I thought it necessary in my definitions to express those motions by which lines, superficies, solids, and figures, were drawn and described." Generally stated, we have absolutely certain or scientific knowledge only of those subjects of which we are the causes, or whose construction is in our own power or depends on our arbitrary will. The construction would not be fully in our power if there were a single step of the construction that is not fully exposed to our supervision. The construction must be conscious construction; it is impossible to know a scientific truth without knowing at the same time that we have made it. The construction would not be fully in our power if it made use of any matter, i.e., of anything that is not itself our construct. The world of our constructs is wholly unenigmatic because we are its sole cause and hence we have perfect knowledge of its cause. The cause of the world of our constructs does not have a further cause, a cause that is not, or not fully, within our power; the world of our constructs has an absolute beginning or is a creation in the strict sense. The world of our constructs is therefore the desired island that is exempt from the flux of blind and aimless causation.[9] The discovery or invention of that island seemed to

9. *English Works*, VII, 179 ff.; *De homine*, X, 4–5; *De cive*, XVIII, 4, and XVII, 28; *De corpore*, XXV, 1; *Elements*, ed. Toennies, p. 168; fourth objection to Descartes's *Meditations*. The difficulty to which Hobbes's view of science is exposed is indicated by the fact that, as he says, all philosophy or science "weaves consequences" (cf. *Leviathan*, chap. ix) while taking its beginning from "experiences" (*De cive*, XVII, 12), i.e., that philosophy or science is ultimately dependent on what is given and not constructed. Hobbes tried to solve this difficulty by distinguishing between the sciences proper, which are purely constructive or demonstrative (mathematics, cinematics, and political science), and physics, which has a lower status than the former (*De corpore*, XXV, 1; *De homine*, X, 5). This solution creates a new difficulty, since political science presupposes the scientific study of the nature of man, which is a part of physics (*Leviathan*, chap. ix in both versions; *De homine*, Ep. ded.; *De corpore*, VI, 6). Hobbes apparently tried to solve this new difficulty in the following manner: it is possible to know the causes of the political phenomena both by descending from the more general phenomena (the nature of motion, the nature of living beings, the nature of man) to those causes and by ascending from the political phenomena themselves, as they are known

guarantee the possibility of a materialistic and mechanistic philosophy or science, without forcing one to assume a soul or mind that is irreducible to moved matter. That discovery or invention eventually permitted an attitude of neutrality or indifference toward the secular conflict between materialism and spiritualism. Hobbes had the earnest desire to be a "metaphysical" materialist. But he was forced to rest satisfied with a "methodical" materialism.

We understand only what we make. Since we do not make the natural beings, they are, strictly speaking, unintelligible. According to Hobbes, this fact is perfectly compatible with the possibility of natural science. But it leads to the consequence that natural science is and will always remain fundamentally hypothetical. Yet this is all we need in order to make ourselves masters and owners of nature. Still, however much man may succeed in his conquest of nature, he will never be able to understand nature. The universe will always remain wholly enigmatic. It is this fact that ultimately accounts for the persistence of skepticism and justifies skepticism to a certain extent. Skepticism is the inevitable outcome of the unintelligible character of the universe or of the unfounded belief in its intelligibility. In other words, since natural things are, as such, mysterious, the knowledge or certainty engendered by nature necessarily lacks evidence. Knowledge based on the natural working of the human mind is necessarily exposed to doubt. For this reason Hobbes parts company with premodern nominalism in particular. Premodern nominalism had faith in the natural working of the human mind. It showed this faith especially by teaching that *natura occulte operatur in universalibus*, or that the "anticipations" by virtue of which

---

to everyone from experience, to the same causes (*De corpore*, VI, 7). At any rate, Hobbes emphatically stated that political science may be based on, or consist of, "experience" as distinguished from "demonstrations" (*De homine*, Ep. ded.; *De cive*, praef.; *Leviathan*, Introd. and chap. xxxii, beginning).

we take our bearings in ordinary life and in science are products of nature. For Hobbes, the natural origin of the universals or of the anticipations was a compelling reason for abandoning them in favor of artificial "intellectual tools." There is no natural harmony between the human mind and the universe.

Man can guarantee the actualization of wisdom, since wisdom is identical with free construction. But wisdom cannot be free construction if the universe is intelligible. Man can guarantee the actualization of wisdom, not in spite of, but because of, the fact that the universe is unintelligible. Man can be sovereign only because there is no cosmic support for his humanity. He can be sovereign only because he is absolutely a stranger in the universe. He can be sovereign only because he is forced to be sovereign. Since the universe is unintelligible and since control of nature does not require understanding of nature, there are no knowable limits to his conquest of nature. He has nothing to lose but his chains, and, for all he knows, he may have everything to gain. Still, what is certain is that man's natural state is misery; the vision of the City of Man to be erected on the ruins of the City of God is an unsupported hope.

It is hard for us to understand how Hobbes could be so hopeful where there was so much cause for despair. Somehow the experience, as well as the legitimate anticipation, of unheard-of progress within the sphere which is subject to human control must have made him insensitive to "the eternal silence of those infinite spaces" or to the crackings of the *moenia mundi*. In fairness to him, one must add that the long series of disappointments which subsequent generations experienced have not yet succeeded in extinguishing the hope which he, together with his most illustrious contemporaries, kindled. Still less have they succeeded in breaking down the walls which he erected as if in order to limit his vision. The conscious constructs have indeed been replaced by the unplanned workings of "History." But "History" limits our vision in exactly the same way in which the conscious constructs limited the vision of Hobbes: "History," too, fulfils the function of enhancing the status of man and of his "world" by making him oblivious of the whole or of eternity.[10] In its final stage the typically modern limitation expresses itself in the suggestion that the highest principle, which, as such, has no relation to any possible cause or causes of the whole, is the mysterious ground of "History" and, being wedded to man and to man alone, is so far from being eternal that it is coeval with human history.

To return to Hobbes, his notion of philosophy or science has its root in the conviction that a teleological cosmology is impossible and in the feeling that a mechanistic cosmology fails to satisfy the requirement of intelligibility. His solution is that the end or the ends without which no phenomenon can be understood need not be inherent in the phenomena; the end inherent in the concern with knowledge suffices. Knowledge as the end supplies the indispensable teleological principle. Not

10. Two quotations taken from authors who belong to opposed camps but to the same spiritual family may serve as illustrations. We read in Friedrich Engels' *Ludwig Feuerbach und der Ausgang der deutschen klassischen Philosophie:* "nichts besteht vor [der dialektischen Philosophie] als der ununterbrochene Prozess des Werdens und Vergehens, des Aufsteigens *ohne Ende* vom Niedern zum Höhern. . . . Wir brauchen hier nicht auf die Frage einzugehn, ob diese Anschauungsweise durchaus mit dem jetzigen Stand der Naturwissenschaft stimmt, die der Existenz der Erde selbst ein mögliches, ihrer Bewohnbarkeit aber *ein ziemlich sicheres Ende* vorhersagt, die also auch der Menschengeschichte nicht nur einen aufsteigenden, sondern auch einen absteigenden Ast zuerkennt. Wir befinden uns *jedenfalls noch ziemlich weit von dem Wendepunkt.*" We read in J. J. Bachofen's *Die Sage von Tanaquil:* "Der Orient huldigt dem Naturstandpunkt, der Occident ersetzt ihn durch den geschichtlichen. . . . Man könnte sich versucht fühlen, in dieser *Unterordnung der göttlichen unter die menschliche Idee* die letzte Stufe des Abfalls von einem früheren erhabeneren Standpunkte zu erkennen. . . . Und dennoch enthält dieser Rückgang den Keim zu einem sehr wichtigen Fortschritt. Denn als solchen haben wir jede Befreiung unseres Geistes aus den lähmenden Fesseln einer kosmisch-physischen Lebensbetrachtung anzusehen. . . . Wenn der Etrusker bekümmerten Sinnes an die Endlichkeit seines Stammes glaubt, so freut der Römer sich der *Ewigkeit seines Staates, an welcher zu zweifeln er gar nicht fähig ist.*" (The italics are not in the originals.)

the new mechanistic cosmology but what later on came to be called "epistemology" becomes the substitute for teleological cosmology. But knowledge cannot remain the end if the whole is simply unintelligible: *Scientia propter potentiam.*[11] All intelligibility or all meaning has its ultimate root in human needs. The end, or the most compelling end posited by human desire, is the highest principle, the organizing principle. But if the human good becomes the highest principle, political science or social science becomes the most important kind of knowledge, as Aristotle had predicted. In the words of Hobbes, *Dignissima certe scientiarum haec ipsa est, quae ad Principes pertinet, hominesque in regendo genere humano occupatos.*[12] One cannot leave it, then, at saying that Hobbes agrees with the idealistic tradition in regard to the function and scope of political philosophy. His expectation from political philosophy is incomparably greater than the expectation of the classics. No Scipionic dream illumined by a true vision of the whole reminds his readers of the ultimate futility of all that men can do. Of political philosophy thus understood, Hobbes is indeed the founder.

It was Machiavelli, that greater Columbus, who had discovered the continent on which Hobbes could erect his structure. When trying to understand the thought of Machiavelli, one does well to remember the saying that Marlowe was inspired to ascribe to him: "I . . . hold there is no sin but ignorance." This is almost a definition of the philosopher. Besides, no one of consequence ever doubted that Machiavelli's study of political matters was public spirited. Being a public

11. *De corpore*, I, 6. The abandonment of the primacy of contemplation or theory in favor of the primacy of practice is the necessary consequence of the abandonment of the plane on which Platonism and Epicureanism had carried on their struggle. For the synthesis of Platonism and Epicureanism stands or falls with the view that to understand is to make.

12. Aristotle *Nicomachean Ethics* 1141^{a}20–22; *De cive*, praef.; cf. *Opera Latina*, IV, 487–88: the only serious part of philosophy is political philosophy.

spirited philosopher, he continued the tradition of political idealism. But he combined the idealistic view of the intrinsic nobility of statesmanship with an anti-idealistic view, if not of the whole, at any rate of the origins of mankind or of civil society.

Machiavelli's admiration for the political practice of classical antiquity and especially of republican Rome is only the reverse side of his rejection of classical political philosophy. He rejected classical political philosophy, and therewith the whole tradition of political philosophy in the full sense of the term, as useless: Classical political philosophy had taken its bearings by how man ought to live; the correct way of answering the question of the right order of society consists in taking one's bearings by how men actually do live. Machiavelli's "realistic" revolt against tradition led to the substitution of patriotism or merely political virtue for human excellence or, more particularly, for moral virtue and the contemplative life. It entailed a deliberate lowering of the ultimate goal. The goal was lowered in order to increase the probability of its attainment. Just as Hobbes later on abandoned the original meaning of wisdom in order to guarantee the actualization of wisdom, Machiavelli abandoned the original meaning of the good society or of the good life. What would happen to those natural inclinations of man or of the human soul whose demands simply transcend the lowered goal was of no concern to Machiavelli. He disregarded those inclinations. He limited his horizon in order to get results. And as for the power of chance, Fortuna appeared to him in the shape of a woman who can be forced by the right kind of men: chance can be conquered.

Machiavelli justified his demand for a "realistic" political philosophy by reflections on the foundations of civil society, and this means ultimately by reflections on the whole within which man lives. There is no superhuman, no natural, support for justice. All human things fluctuate too much to permit their subjection to stable principles of justice. Necessity rather than moral purpose determines what is in each case the sensible course of action. Therefore, civil society cannot even aspire to be simply just. All legitimacy has its root in illegitimacy; all social or moral orders have been established with the help of morally questionable means; civil society has its root not in justice but in injustice. The founder of the most renowned of all commonwealths was a fratricide. Justice in any sense is possible only after a social order has been established; justice in any sense is possible only within a man-made order. Yet the founding of civil society, the supreme case in politics, is imitated, within civil society, in all extreme cases. Machiavelli takes his bearings not so much by how men live as by the extreme case. He believes that the extreme case is more revealing of the roots of civil society and therefore of its true character than is the normal case.[13] The root or the efficient cause takes the place of the end or of the purpose.

It was the difficulty implied in the substitution of merely political virtue for moral virtue or the difficulty implied in Machiavelli's admiration for the lupine policies of republican Rome[14] that induced Hobbes to attempt the restoration of the moral principles of politics, i.e., of natural law, on the plane of Machiavelli's "realism." In making this attempt he was mindful of the fact that man cannot guarantee the actualization of the right social order if he does not have certain or exact or scientific knowledge of both the right social order and the conditions of its actualization. He attempted, therefore, in the first place a rigorous deduction of the natural or moral law. To "avoid the cavils of the skeptics," natural law had to be made independent of any natural "anticipations" and therefore of the *consensus gentium*.[15] The predominant tradition had

13. Cf. Bacon, *Advancement of Learning* ("Everyman's Library" ed.), pp. 70–71.

14. *De cive*, Ep. ded.

15. *Ibid.*, II, 1.

defined natural law with a view to the end or the perfection of man as a rational and social animal. What Hobbes attempted to do on the basis of Machiavelli's fundamental objection to the utopian teaching of the tradition, although in opposition to Machiavelli's own solution, was to maintain the idea of natural law but to divorce it from the idea of man's perfection; only if natural law can be deduced from how men actually live, from the most powerful force that actually determines all men, or most men most of the time, can it be effectual or of practical value. The complete basis of natural law must be sought, not in the end of man, but in his beginnings,[16] in the *prima naturae* or, rather, in the *primum naturae*. What is most powerful in most men most of the time is not reason but passion. Natural law will not be effectual if its principles are distrusted by passion or are not agreeable to passion.[17] Natural law must be deduced from the most powerful of all passions.

But the most powerful of all passions will be a natural fact, and we are not to assume that there is a natural support for justice or for what is human in man. Or is there a passion, or an object of passion, which is in a sense antinatural, which marks the point of indifference between the natural and the nonnatural, which is, as it were, the *status evanescendi* of nature and therefore a possible origin for the conquest of nature or for freedom? The most powerful of all passions is the fear of death and, more particularly, the fear of violent death at the hands of others: not nature but "that terrible enemy of nature, death," yet death insofar as man can do something about it,

16. In the alternative title of the *Leviathan* (*The Matter, Form, and Power of a Commonwealth*) the end is not mentioned. See also what Hobbes says about his method in the Preface to *De cive*. He claims that he deduced the end from the beginning. In fact, however, he takes the end for granted; for he discovers the beginning by analyzing human nature and human affairs with that end (peace) in view (cf. *De cive*, I, 1, and *Leviathan*, chap. xi beginning). Similarly, in his analysis of right or justice, Hobbes takes for granted the generally accepted view of justice (*De cive*, Ep. ded.).

17. *Elements*, Ep. ded.

i.e., death insofar as it can be avoided or avenged, supplies the ultimate guidance.[18] Death takes the place of the *telos*. Or, to preserve the ambiguity of Hobbes's thought, let us say that the fear of violent death expresses most forcefully the most powerful and the most fundamental of all natural desires, the initial desire, the desire for self-preservation.

If, then, natural law must be deduced from the desire for self-preservation, if, in other words, the desire for self-preservation is the sole root of all justice and morality, the fundamental moral fact is not a duty but a right; all duties are derivative from the fundamental and inalienable right of self-preservation. There are, then, no absolute or unconditional duties; duties are binding only to the extent to which their performance does not endanger our self-preservation. Only the right of self-preservation is unconditional or absolute. By nature, there exists only a perfect right and no perfect duty. The law of nature, which formulates man's natural duties, is not a law, properly speaking. Since the fundamental and absolute moral fact is a right and not a duty, the function as well as the limits of civil society must be defined in terms of man's natural right and not in terms of his natural duty. The state has the function, not of producing or promoting a virtuous life, but of safeguarding the natural right of each. And the power of the state finds its absolute limit in that natural right and in no other moral fact.[19] If we may call liberalism that political doctrine which regards as the fundamental political fact the rights, as distinguished from the duties, of man and which identifies the function of the state with the protection or the

18. *Ibid.*, I, 14, sec. 6; *De cive*, Ep. ded., I, 7, and III, 31; *Leviathan*, chaps. xiv (92) and xxvii (197). One would have to start from here in order to understand the role of the detective story in present-day moral orientation.

19. *De cive*, II, 10 end, 18–19; III, 14, 21, 27 and annot., 33; VI, 13; XIV, 3; *Leviathan*, chaps. xiv (84, 86–87), xxi (142–43), xxviii (202), and xxxii (243).

safeguarding of those rights, we must say that the founder of liberalism was Hobbes.

By transplanting natural law on the plane of Machiavelli, Hobbes certainly originated an entirely new type of political doctrine. The premodern natural law doctrines taught the duties of man; if they paid any attention at all to his rights, they conceived of them as essentially derivative from his duties. As has frequently been observed, in the course of the seventeenth and eighteenth centuries a much greater emphasis was put on rights than ever had been done before. One may speak of a shift of emphasis from natural duties to natural rights.[20] But quantitative changes of this character become intelligible only when they are seen against the background of a qualitative and fundamental change, not to say that such quantitative changes always become possible only by virtue of a qualitative and fundamental change. The fundamental change from an orientation by natural duties to an orientation by natural rights finds its clearest and most telling expression in the teaching of Hobbes, who squarely made an unconditional natural right the basis of all natural duties, the duties being therefore only conditional. He is the classic and the founder of the specifically modern natural law doctrine. The profound change under consideration can be traced directly to Hobbes's concern with a human guaranty for the actualization of the right social order or to his "realistic" intention. The actualization of a social order that is defined in terms of man's duties is necessarily uncertain and even improbable; such an order may well appear to be utopian. Quite different is the case of a social order that is defined in terms of the rights of man. For the rights in question express, and are meant to express,

20. Cf. Otto von Gierke, *The Development of Political Theory* (New York, 1939), pp. 108, 322, 352; and J. N. Figgis, *The Divine Right of Kings* (2d ed.; Cambridge: At the University Press, 1934), pp. 221–23. For Kant it is already a question why moral philosophy is called the doctrine of duties and not the doctrine of rights (see *Metaphysik der Sitten*, ed. Vorlaender, p. 45).

something that everyone actually desires anyway; they hallow everyone's self-interest as everyone sees it or can easily be brought to see it. Men can more safely be depended upon to fight for their rights than to fulfil their duties. In the words of Burke: "The little catechism of the rights of men is soon learned; and the inferences are in the passions."[21] With regard to Hobbes's classic formulation, we add that the premises already are in the passions. What is required to make modern natural right effective is enlightenment or propaganda rather than moral appeal. From this we may understand the frequently observed fact that during the modern period natural law became much more of a revolutionary force than it had been in the past. This fact is a direct consequence of the fundamental change in the character of the natural law doctrine itself.

The tradition which Hobbes opposed had assumed that man cannot reach the perfection of his nature except in and through civil society and, therefore, that civil society is prior to the individual. It was this assumption which led to the view that the primary moral fact is duty and not rights. One could not assert the primacy of natural rights without asserting that the individual is in every respect prior to civil society: all rights of civil society or of the sovereign are derivative from rights which originally belonged to the individual.[22] The individual as such, the individual regardless of his qualities—and not merely, as Aristotle had contended, the man who surpasses humanity—had to be conceived of as essentially complete independently of civil society. This conception is implied in the contention that there is a state of nature which antedates civil society. According to Rousseau, "the philosophers who have examined the foundations of civil society have all of them felt the necessity to go back to the state of nature." It is true that

21. *Thoughts on French Affairs*, p. 367.
22. *De cive*, VI, 5–7; *Leviathan*, chaps. xviii (113) and xxviii (202–3).

the quest for the right social order is inseparable from reflection on the origins of civil society or on the prepolitical life of man. But the identification of the prepolitical life of man with "the state of nature" is a particular view, a view by no means held by "all" political philosophers. The state of nature became an essential topic of political philosophy only with Hobbes, who still almost apologized for employing that term. It is only since Hobbes that the philosophic doctrine of natural law has been essentially a doctrine of the state of nature. Prior to him, the term "state of nature" was at home in Christian theology rather than in political philosophy. The state of nature was distinguished especially from the state of grace, and it was subdivided into the state of pure nature and the state of fallen nature. Hobbes dropped the subdivision and replaced the state of grace by the state of civil society. He thus denied, if not the fact, at any rate the importance of the Fall and accordingly asserted that what is needed for remedying the deficiencies or the "inconveniences" of the state of nature is, not divine grace, but the right kind of human government. This antitheological implication of "the state of nature" can only with difficulty be separated from its intra-philosophic meaning, which is to make intelligible the primacy of rights as distinguished from duties: the state of nature is originally characterized by the fact that in it there are perfect rights but no perfect duties.[23]

23. *De cive*, praef.: "conditionem hominum extra societatem civilem (quam conditionem appellare liceat statum naturae)." Cf. Locke, *Treatises of Civil Government*, II, sect. 15. For the original meaning of the term, cf. Aristotle *Physics* 246ª10–17; Cicero *Offices* i. 67; *De finibus* iii. 16, 20; *Laws* iii. 3 (cf. also *De cive*, III, 25). According to the classics, the state of nature would be the life in a healthy civil society and not the life antedating civil society. The conventionalists assert, indeed, that civil society is conventional or artificial, but this implies a depreciation of civil society. Most conventionalists do not identify the life antedating civil society with the state of nature: they identify the life according to nature with the life of human fulfilment (be it the life of the philosopher or the life of the tyrant); the life according to nature is therefore impossible in the primeval condition that antedates civil society. On the other hand, those

If everyone has by nature the right to preserve himself, he necessarily has the right to the means required for his self-preservation. At this point the question arises as to who is to be the judge of what means are required for a man's self-preservation or as to which means are proper or right. The classics would have answered that the natural judge is the man of practical wisdom, and this answer would finally lead back to the view that the simply best regime is the absolute rule of the wise and the best practicable regime is the rule of gentlemen. According to Hobbes, however, everyone is by nature the judge of what are the right means to his self-preservation. For, even granting that the wise man is, in principle, a better

conventionalists who identify the life according to nature, or the state of nature, with the life antedating civil society, regard the state of nature as preferable to civil society (cf. Montaigne, *Essais*, II, 12, *Chronique des lettres françaises*, III, 311). Hobbes's notion of the state of nature presupposes the rejection of both the classic and the conventionalist view, for he denies the existence of a natural end, of a *summum bonum*. He identifies, therefore, the natural life with the "beginning," the life dominated by the most elementary wants; and at the same time he holds that this beginning is defective and that the deficiency is remedied by civil society. There is, then, according to Hobbes, no tension between civil society and what is natural, whereas, according to conventionalism, there is a tension between civil society and what is natural. Hence, according to conventionalism, the life according to nature is superior to civil society, whereas, according to Hobbes, it is inferior to it. We add that conventionalism is not necessarily egalitarian, whereas Hobbes's orientation necessitates egalitarianism. According to Thomas Aquinas, the *status legis naturae* is the condition in which man lived prior to the revelation of the Mosaic law (*Summa theologica* i. 2. qu. 102, *a.* 3 ad 12). It is the state in which the Gentiles live and therefore a condition of civil society (cf. Suarez, *Tr. de legibus*, I, 3, sec. 12; III, 11 ["in pura natura, vel in gentibus"]; III, 12 ["in statu purae naturae, si in illo esset respublica verum Deum naturaliter colens"]; also Grotius *De jure belli* ii. 5, sec. 15. 2 uses "status naturae" in contradistinction to the "status legis Christianae"; when Grotius [iii. 7, sec. 1] says: "citra factum humanum aut primaevo naturae statu," he shows, by the addition of "primaevo," that the state of nature as such is not "citra factum humanum" and hence does not essentially antedate civil society. However, if the human law is regarded as the outcome of human corruption, the *status legis naturae* becomes that condition in which man was subject to the law of nature alone, and not yet to any human laws (Wyclif, *De civili dominio*, II, 13, ed. Poole, p. 154). For the prehistory of Hobbes's notion of the state of nature cf. also Soto's doctrine as reported by Suarez, *op. cit.*, II, 17, sec. 9.

judge, he is much less concerned with the self-preservation of a given fool than is the fool himself. But if everyone, however foolish, is by nature the judge of what is required for his self-preservation, everything may legitimately be regarded as required for self-preservation: everything is by nature just.[24] We may speak of a natural right of folly. Furthermore, if everyone is by nature the judge of what is conducive to his self-preservation, consent takes precedence over wisdom. But consent is not effective if it does not transform itself into subjection to the sovereign. For the reason indicated, the sovereign is sovereign not because of his wisdom but because he has been made sovereign by the fundamental compact. This leads to the further conclusion that command or will, and not deliberation or reasoning, is the core of sovereignty or that laws are laws by virtue, not of truth or reasonableness, but of authority alone.[25] In Hobbes's teaching, the supremacy of authority as distinguished from reason follows from an extraordinary extension of the natural right of the individual.

The attempt to deduce the natural law or the moral law from the natural right of self-preservation or from the inescapable power of the fear of violent death led to far-reaching modifications of the content of the moral law. The modification amounted, in the first place, to a considerable simplification. Sixteenth- and seventeenth-century thought in general tended toward a simplification of moral doctrine. To say the least, that tendency easily lent itself to absorption in the broader concern with the guaranty for the actualization of the right social order. One tried to replace the "unsystematic" multiplicity of irreducible virtues by a single virtue, or by a single basic virtue from which all other virtues could be deduced. There existed two well-paved ways in which this re-

24. *De cive*, I, 9; III, 13; *Leviathan*, chaps. xv (100) and xlvi (448).

25. *De cive*, VI, 19; XIV, 1 and 17; *Leviathan*, chap. xxvi (180); cf. also Sir Robert Filmer, *Observations concerning the Original of Government*, Preface.

duction could be achieved. In the moral teaching of Aristotle, "whose opinions are at this day, and in these parts of greater authority than any other human writings" (Hobbes), there occur two virtues which comprise all other virtues or, as we may say, two "general" virtues: magnanimity, which comprises all other virtues in so far as they contribute to the excellence of the individual, and justice, which comprises all other virtues in so far as they contribute to man's serving others. Accordingly, one could simplify moral philosophy by reducing morality either to magnanimity or else to justice. The first was done by Descartes, the second by Hobbes. The latter's choice had the particular advantage that it was favorable to a further simplification of moral doctrine: the unqualified identification of the doctrine of virtues with the doctrine of the moral or natural law. The moral law, in its turn, was to be greatly simplified by being deduced from the natural right of self-preservation. Self-preservation requires peace. The moral law became, therefore, the sum of rules which have to be obeyed if there is to be peace. Just as Machiavelli reduced virtue to the political virtue of patriotism, Hobbes reduced virtue to the social virtue of peaceableness. Those forms of human excellence which have no direct or unambiguous relation to peaceableness—courage, temperance, magnanimity, liberality, to say nothing of wisdom—cease to be virtues in the strict sense. Justice (in conjunction with equity and charity) does remain a virtue, but its meaning undergoes a radical change. If the only unconditional moral fact is the natural right of each to his self-preservation, and therefore all obligations to others arise from contract, justice becomes identical with the habit of fulfilling one's contracts. Justice no longer consists in complying with standards that are independent of human will. All material principles of justice—the rules of commutative and distributive justice or of the Second Table of the Decalogue—cease to have intrinsic validity. All material obligations arise from the agreement of the contractors, and therefore in practice from the will of the sovereign.[26] For the contract that makes possible all other contracts is the social contract or the contract of subjection to the sovereign.

If virtue is identified with peaceableness, vice will become identical with that habit or that passion which is per se incompatible with peace because it essentially and, as it were, of set purpose issues in offending others; vice becomes identical for all practical purposes with pride or vanity or *amour-propre* rather than with dissoluteness or weakness of the soul. In other words, if virtue is reduced to social virtue or to benevolence or kindness or "the liberal virtues," "the severe virtues" of self-restraint will lose their standing.[27] Here again we must have recourse to Burke's analysis of the spirit of the French Revolution; for Burke's polemical overstatements were and are indispensable for tearing away the disguises, both intentional and unintentional, in which "the new morality" introduced itself: "The Parisian philosophers . . . explode or render odious or contemptible, that class of virtues which restrain the appetite. . . . In the place of all this, they substitute a virtue which they call humanity or benevolence."[28] This substitution is the core of what we have called "political hedonism."

To establish the meaning of political hedonism in somewhat more precise terms, we must contrast Hobbes's teaching with the nonpolitical hedonism of Epicurus. The points in which Hobbes could agree with Epicurus, were these: the good is fundamentally identical with the pleasant; virtue is therefore not choiceworthy for its own sake but only with a view to the

26. *Elements*, I, 17, sec. 1; *De cive*, Ep. ded.; III, 3–6, 29, 32; VI, 16; XII, 1; XIV, 9–10, 17; XVII, 10; XVIII, 3; *De homine*, XIII, 9; *Leviathan*, chaps. xiv (92), xv (96, 97, 98, 104), and xxvi (186).

27. "Temperantia privatio potius vitiorum quae oriuntur ab ingeniis cupidis (*quibus non laeditur civitas*, sed ipsi) quam virtus moralis (est)" (*De homine*, XIII, 9). The step from this view to "private vices, public benefits," is short.

28. Letter to Rivarol of June 1, 1791.

attainment of pleasure or the avoidance of pain; the desire for honor and glory is utterly vain, i.e., sensual pleasures are, as such, preferable to honor or glory. Hobbes had to oppose Epicurus in two crucial points in order to make possible political hedonism. In the first place, he had to reject Epicurus' implicit denial of a state of nature in the strict sense, i.e., of a prepolitical condition of life in which man enjoys natural rights; for Hobbes agreed with the idealistic tradition in thinking that the claim of civil society stands or falls with the existence of natural right. Besides, he could not accept the implication of Epicurus' distinction between natural desires which are necessary and natural desires which are not necessary; for that distinction implied that happiness requires an "ascetic" style of life and that happiness consists in a state of repose. Epicurus' high demands on self-restraint were bound to be utopian as far as most men are concerned; they had therefore to be discarded by a "realistic" political teaching. The "realistic" approach to politics forced Hobbes to lift all restrictions on the striving for unnecessary sensual pleasures or, more precisely, for the *commoda hujus vitae*, or for power, with the exception of those restrictions that are required for the sake of peace. Since, as Epicurus said, "Nature has made [only] the necessary things easy to supply," the emancipation of the desire for comfort required that science be put into the service of the satisfaction of that desire. It required, above all, that the function of civil society be radically redefined: "the good life," for the sake of which men enter civil society, is no longer the life of human excellence but "commodious living" as the reward of hard work. And the sacred duty of the rulers is no longer "to make the citizens good and doers of noble things" but to "study, as much as by laws can be effected, to furnish the citizens abundantly with all good things . . . which are conducive to delectation."[29]

29. *De cive*, I, 2, 5, 7; XIII, 4–6; *Leviathan*, chaps. xi (63–64) and xiii end; *De corpore*, I, 6.

It is not necessary for our purpose to follow Hobbes's thought on its way from the natural right of everyone, or from the state of nature, to the establishment of civil society. This part of his doctrine is not meant to be more than the strict consequence from his premises. It culminates in the doctrine of sovereignty, of which he is generally recognized to be the classic exponent. The doctrine of sovereignty is a legal doctrine. Its gist is not that it is expedient to assign plenitude of power to the ruling authority but that that plenitude belongs to the ruling authority as of right. The rights of sovereignty are assigned to the supreme power on the basis not of positive law or of general custom but of natural law. The doctrine of sovereignty formulates natural public law.[30] Natural public law—*jus publicum universale seu naturale*—is a new discipline that emerged in the seventeenth century. It emerged in consequence of that radical change of orientation which we are trying to understand. Natural public law represents one of the two characteristically modern forms of political philosophy, the other form being "politics" in the sense of Machiavellian "reason of state." Both are fundamentally distinguished from classical political philosophy. In spite of their opposition to each other, they are motivated by fundamen-

---

30. *Leviathan*, chap. xxx, the third and fourth paragraphs of the Latin version; *De cive*, IX, 3; X, 2 beginning, and 5; XI, 4 end; XII, 8 end; XIV, 4; cf. also Malebranche, *Traité de morale*, ed. Joly, p. 214. There is this difference between natural law in the ordinary sense and natural public law, that natural public law and its subject matter (the commonwealth) are based on a fundamental fiction, on the fiction that the will of the sovereign is the will of all and of each or that the sovereign represents all and each (*De cive*, V, 6, 9, 11; VII, 14). The will of the sovereign has to be *regarded* as the will of all and of each, whereas, in fact, there is an essential discrepancy between the will of the sovereign and the wills of the individuals, the only wills that are natural: to obey the sovereign means precisely to do what the sovereign wills, not what I will. Even if my reason should habitually tell me to will what the sovereign wills, this rational will is not necessarily identical with my complete will, my actual or explicit will (cf. the reference to the "implicit wills" in *Elements*, II, 9, sec. 1; cf. also *De cive*, XII, 2). On the basis of Hobbes's premises, "representation" is then not a convenience but an essential necessity.

tally the same spirit.[31] Their origin is the concern with a right or sound order of society whose actualization is probable, if not certain, or does not depend on chance. Accordingly, they deliberately lower the goal of politics; they are no longer concerned with having a clear view of the highest political possibility with regard to which all actual political orders can be judged in a responsible manner. The "reason of state" school replaced "the best regime" by "efficient government." The "natural public law" school replaced "the best regime" by "legitimate government."

Classical political philosophy had recognized the difference between the best regime and legitimate regimes. It asserted, therefore, a variety of types of legitimate regimes; that is, what type of regime is legitimate in given circumstances depends on the circumstances. Natural public law, on the other hand, is concerned with that right social order whose actualization is possible under all circumstances. It therefore tries to delineate that social order that can claim to be legitimate or just in all cases, regardless of the circumstances. Natural public law, we may say, replaces the idea of the best regime, which does not supply, and is not meant to supply, an answer to the question of what is the just order here and now, by the idea of the just social order which answers the basic practical question once and for all, i.e., regardless of place and time.[32]

31. Cf. Fr. J. Stahl, *Geschichte der Rechtsphilosophie* (2d ed.), p. 325: "Es ist eine Eigentümlichkeit der neuern Zeit, dass ihre Staatslehre (das Naturrecht) und ihre Staatskunst (die vorzugsweise sogenannte Politik) zwei völlig verschiedene Wissenschaften sind. Diese Trennung ist das Werk des Geistes, welcher in dieser Periode die Wissenschaft beherrscht. Das Ethos wird in der Vernunft gesucht, diese hat aber keine Macht über die Begebenheiten und den natürlichen Erfolg; was die äusserlichen Verhältnisse fordern und abnöthigen, stimmt gar nicht mit ihr überein, verhält sich feindlich gegen sie, die Rücksicht auf dasselbe kann daher nicht Sache der Ethik des Staates sein." Cf. Grotius *De jure belli*, Prolegomena, sec. 57.

32. Cf. *De cive*, praef. toward the end, on the entirely different status of the question of the best form of government, on the one hand, and the question of the rights of the sovereign, on the other.

Natural public law intends to give such a universally valid solution to the political problem as is meant to be universally applicable in practice. In other words, whereas, according to the classics, political theory proper is essentially in need of being supplemented by the practical wisdom of the statesman on the spot, the new type of political theory solves, as such, the crucial practical problem: the problem of what order is just here and now. In the decisive respect, then, there is no longer any need for statesmanship as distinguished from political theory. We may call this type of thinking "doctrinairism," and we shall say that doctrinairism made its first appearance within political philosophy—for lawyers are altogether in a class by themselves—in the seventeenth century. At that time the sensible flexibility of classical political philosophy gave way to fanatical rigidity. The political philosopher became more and more indistinguishable from the partisan. The historical thought of the nineteenth century tried to recover for statesmanship that latitude which natural public law had so severely restricted. But since that historical thought was absolutely under the spell of modern "realism," it succeeded in destroying natural public law only by destroying in the process all moral principles of politics.

As regards Hobbes's teaching on sovereignty in particular, its doctrinaire character is shown most clearly by the denials which it implies. It implies the denial of the possibility of distinguishing between good and bad regimes (kingship and tyranny, aristocracy and oligarchy, democracy and ochlocracy) as well as of the possibility of mixed regimes and of "rule of law."[33] Since these denials are at variance with observed facts, the doctrine of sovereignty amounts in practice

33. De cive, VII, 2–4; XII, 4–5; Leviathan, chap. xxix (216). See, however, the reference to legitimate kings and to illegitimate rulers in De cive, XII, 1 and 3. De cive, VI, 13 end, and VII, 14, show that natural law, as Hobbes understands it, supplies a basis for objectively distinguishing between kingship and tyranny. Cf. also ibid., XII, 7, with XIII, 10.

to a denial not of the existence, but of the legitimacy, of the possibilities mentioned: Hobbes's doctrine of sovereignty ascribes to the sovereign prince or to the sovereign people an unqualified right to disregard all legal and constitutional limitations according to their pleasure,[34] and it imposes even on sensible men a natural law prohibition against censuring the sovereign and his actions. But it would be wrong to overlook the fact that the basic deficiency of the doctrine of sovereignty is shared, if to different degrees, by all other forms of natural public law doctrines as well. We merely have to remind ourselves of the practical meaning of the doctrine that the only legitimate regime is democracy.

The classics had conceived of regimes (*politeiai*) not so much in terms of institutions as in terms of the aims actually pursued by the community or its authoritative part. Accordingly, they regarded the best regime as that regime whose aim is virtue, and they held that the right kind of institutions are indeed indispensable for establishing and securing the rule of the virtuous, but of only secondary importance in comparison with "education," i.e., the formation of character. From the point of view of natural public law, on the other hand, what is needed in order to establish the right social order is not so much the formation of character as the devising of the right kind of institutions. As Kant put it in rejecting the view that the establishment of the right social order requires a nation of angels: "Hard as it may sound, the problem of establishing the state [i.e., the just social order] is soluble even for a nation of devils, provided they have sense," i.e., provided that they are guided by enlightened selfishness; the fundamental political problem is simply one of "a good organization of the state, of

34. As for the discrepancy between Hobbes's doctrine and the practice of mankind, see *Leviathan*, chaps. xx end, and xxxi end. As for the revolutionary consequences of Hobbes's doctrine of sovereignty, see *De cive*, VII, 16 and 17, as well as *Leviathan*, chaps. xix (122) and xxix (210): there is no right of prescription; the sovereign is the present sovereign (see *Leviathan*, chap. xxvi [175]).

which man is indeed capable." In the words of Hobbes, "when [commonwealths] come to be dissolved, not by external violence, but intestine disorder, the fault is not in men, as they are the *matter*, but as they are the *makers*, and orderers of them."[35] Man as the maker of civil society can solve once and for all the problem inherent in man as the matter of civil society. Man can guarantee the actualization of the right social order because he is able to conquer human nature by understanding and manipulating the mechanism of the passions.

There is a term that expresses in the most condensed form the result of the change which Hobbes has effected. That term is "power." It is in Hobbes's political doctrine that power becomes for the first time *eo nomine* a central theme. Considering the fact that, according to Hobbes, science as such exists for the sake of power, one may call Hobbes's whole philosophy the first philosophy of power. "Power" is an ambiguous term. It stands for *potentia*, on the one hand, and for *potestas* (or *jus* or *dominium*), on the other.[36] It means both "physical" power and "legal" power. The ambiguity is essential: only if *potentia* and *potestas* essentially belong together, can there be a guaranty of the actualization of the right social order. The state, as such, is both the greatest human force and the highest human authority. Legal power is irresistible force.[37] The necessary coincidence of the greatest human force and the highest human authority corresponds strictly to the necessary coincidence of the most powerful passion (fear of violent death) and

35. *Leviathan*, chap. xxix (210); Kant, *Eternal Peace*, Definitive Articles, First Addition.

36. Cf., e.g., the headings of chap. x in the English and Latin versions of the *Leviathan*, and the headings of *Elements*, II, 3 and 4, with those of *De cive*, VIII and IX. For an example of the synonymous use of *potentia* and *potestas* see *De cive*, IX, 8. A comparison of the title of the *Leviathan* with the Preface of *De cive* (beginning of the section on method) suggests that "power" is identical with "generation." Cf. *De corpore*, X, 1: *potentia* is the same as *causa*. In opposition to Bishop Bramhall, Hobbes insists on the identity of "power" with "potentiality" (*English Works*, IV, 298).

37. *De cive*, XIV, 1, and XVI, 15; *Leviathan*, chap. x (56).

the most sacred right (the right of self-preservation). *Potentia* and *potestas* have this in common, that they are both intelligible only in contradistinction, and in relation, to the *actus:* the *potentia* of a man is what a man *can* do, and the *potestas* or, more generally expressed, the right of a man, is what a man *may* do. The predominance of the concern with "power" is therefore only the reverse of a relative indifference to the *actus*, and this means to the purposes for which man's "physical" as well as his "legal" power is or ought to be used. This indifference can be traced directly to Hobbes's concern with an exact or scientific political teaching. The sound use of "physical" power as well as the sound exercise of rights depends on *prudentia*, and whatever falls within the province of *prudentia* is not susceptible of exactness. There are two kinds of exactness: mathematical and legal. From the point of view of mathematical exactness, the study of the *actus* and therewith of the ends is replaced by the study of *potentia*. "Physical" power as distinguished from the purposes for which it is used is morally neutral and therefore more amenable to mathematical strictness than is its use: power can be measured. This explains why Nietzsche, who went much beyond Hobbes and declared the will to power to be the essence of reality, conceived of power in terms of "quanta of power." From the point of view of legal exactness, the study of the ends is replaced by the study of *potestas*. The rights of the sovereign, as distinguished from the exercise of these rights, permit of an exact definition without any regard to any unforeseeable circumstances, and this kind of exactness is again inseparable from moral neutrality: right declares what is permitted, as distinguished from what is honorable.[38] Power, as distinguished from the end for which

---

38. *De cive*, X, 16, and VI, 13 annot. end. Cf. *Leviathan*, chap. xxi (143), for the distinction between the permitted and the honorable (cf. Salmasius, *Defensio regia* [1649], pp. 40–45). Cf. *Leviathan*, chap. xi (64) with Thomas Aquinas *Summa contra Gentiles* iii. 31.

power is used or ought to be used, becomes the central theme of political reflections by virtue of that limitation of horizon which is needed if there is to be a guaranty of the actualization of the right social order.

Hobbes's political doctrine is meant to be universally applicable and hence to be applicable also and especially in extreme cases. This indeed may be said to be the boast of the classic doctrine of sovereignty: that it gives its due to the extreme case, to what holds good in emergency situations, whereas those who question that doctrine are accused of not looking beyond the pale of normality. Accordingly, Hobbes built his whole moral and political doctrine on observations regarding the extreme case; for the experience on which his doctrine of the state of nature is based is the experience of civil war. It is in the extreme situation, when the social fabric has completely broken down, that there comes to sight the solid foundation on which every social order must ultimately rest: the fear of violent death, which is the strongest force in human life. Yet Hobbes was forced to concede that the fear of violent death is only "commonly" or in most cases the most powerful force. The principle which was supposed to make possible a political doctrine of universal applicability, then, is not universally valid and therefore is useless in what, from Hobbes's point of view, is the most important case—the extreme case. For how can one exclude the possibility that precisely in the extreme situation the exception will prevail?[39]

---

39. *Leviathan*, chaps. xiii (83) and xv (92). One may state this difficulty also as follows: In the spirit of the dogmatism based on skepticism, Hobbes identified what the skeptic Carneades apparently regarded as the conclusive refutation of the claims raised on behalf of justice, with the only possible justification of these claims: the extreme situation—the situation of the two shipwrecked men on a plank on which only one man can save himself—reveals, not the impossibility of justice, but the basis of justice. Yet Carneades did not contend that in such a situation one is compelled to kill one's competitor (Cicero *Republic* iii. 29–30): the extreme situation does not reveal a real necessity.

To speak in more specific terms, there are two politically important phenomena which would seem to show with particular clarity the limited validity of Hobbes's contention regarding the overwhelming power of the fear of violent death. In the first place, if the only unconditional moral fact is the individual's right of self-preservation, civil society can hardly demand from the individual that he resign that right both by going to war and by submitting to capital punishment. As regards capital punishment, Hobbes was consistent enough to grant that, by being justly and legally condemned to death, a man does not lose the right to defend his life by resisting "those that assault him": a justly condemned murderer retains—nay, he acquires—the right to kill his guards and everyone else who stands in his way to escape, in order to save dear life.[40] But, by granting this, Hobbes in fact admitted that there exists an insoluble conflict between the rights of the government and the natural right of the individual to self-preservation. This conflict was solved in the spirit, if against the letter, of Hobbes by Beccaria, who inferred from the absolute primacy of the right of self-preservation the necessity of abolishing capital punishment. As regards war, Hobbes, who proudly declared that he was "the first of all that fled" at the outbreak of the Civil War, was consistent enough to grant that "there is allowance to be made for natural timorousness." And as if he desired to make it perfectly clear to what lengths he was prepared to go in opposing the lupine spirit of Rome, he continues as follows: "When armies fight, there is on one side, or both, a running away: yet when they do it not out of treachery, but fear, they are not esteemed to do it unjustly, but dishonourably."[41] But, by granting this, he destroyed the moral basis of national defense. The only solution to this difficulty which

40. *Leviathan*, chap. xxi (142–43); cf. also *De cive*, VIII, 9.

41. *Leviathan*, chap. xxi (143); *English Works*, IV, 414. Cf. *Leviathan*, chap. xxx (227) and *De cive*, XIII, 14, with Locke's chapter on conquest.

preserves the spirit of Hobbes's political philosophy is the outlawry of war or the establishment of a world state.

There was only one fundamental objection to Hobbes's basic assumption which he felt very keenly and which he made every effort to overcome. In many cases the fear of violent death proved to be a weaker force than the fear of hell fire or the fear of God. The difficulty is well illustrated by two widely separated passages of the *Leviathan*. In the first passage Hobbes says that the fear of the power of men (i.e., the fear of violent death) is "commonly" greater than the fear of the power of "spirits invisible," i.e., than religion. In the second passage he says that "the fear of darkness and ghosts is greater than other fears."[42] Hobbes saw his way to solve this contradiction: the fear of invisible powers is stronger than the fear of violent death as long as people believe in invisible powers, i.e., as long as they are under the spell of delusions about the true character of reality; the fear of violent death comes fully into its own as soon as people have become enlightened. This implies that the whole scheme suggested by Hobbes requires for its operation the weakening or, rather, the elimination of the fear of invisible powers. It requires such a radical change of orientation as can be brought about only by the disenchantment of the world, by the diffusion of scientific knowledge, or by popular enlightenment. Hobbes's is the first doctrine that necessarily and unmistakably points to a thoroughly "enlightened," i.e., a-religious or atheistic society as the solution of the social or political problem. This most important implication of Hobbes's doctrine was made explicit not many years after his death by Pierre Bayle, who attempted to prove that an atheistic society is possible.[43]

42. *Leviathan*, chaps. xiv (92) and xxix (215); cf. also *ibid.*, chap. xxxviii beginning; *De cive*, VI, 11; XII, 2, 5; XVII, 25 and 27.

43. A good reason for connecting Bayle's famous thesis with Hobbes's doctrine rather than with that of Faustus Socinus, e.g., is supplied by the following statement

It is, then, only through the prospect of popular enlightenment that Hobbes's doctrine acquired such consistency as it
possesses. The virtues which he ascribed to enlightenment are
indeed extraordinary. The power of ambition and avarice, he
says, rests on the false opinions of the vulgar regarding right
and wrong; therefore, once the principles of justice are known
with mathematical certainty, ambition and avarice will become powerless and the human race will enjoy lasting peace.
For, obviously, mathematical knowledge of the principles of
justice (i.e., the new doctrine of natural right and the new
natural public law that is built on it) cannot destroy the
wrong opinions of the vulgar, if the vulgar are not apprised of
the results of that mathematical knowledge. Plato had said
that evils will not cease from the cities if the philosophers do
not become kings or if philosophy and political power do not
coincide. He had expected such salvation for mortal nature as
can reasonably be expected, from a coincidence over which

---

of Bayle (*Dictionnaire*, art. "Hobbes," rem. D): "Hobbes se fit beaucoup d'ennemis par
cet ouvrage [*De cive*]; mais il fit avouer aux plus clairvoyants, qu'on n'avait jamais si
bien pénétré les fondements de la politique." I cannot prove here that Hobbes was an
atheist, even according to his own view of atheism. I must limit myself to asking the
reader to compare *De cive*, XV, 14, with *English Works*, IV, 349. Many present-day
scholars who write on subjects of this kind do not seem to have a sufficient notion of
the degree of circumspection or of accommodation to the accepted views that was required, in former ages, of "deviationists" who desired to survive or to die in peace.
Those scholars tacitly assume that the pages in Hobbes's writings devoted to religious
subjects can be understood if they are read in the way in which one ought to read the
corresponding utterances, say, of Lord Bertrand Russell. In other words, I am familiar
with the fact that there are innumerable passages in Hobbes's writings which were
used by Hobbes and which can be used by everyone else for proving that Hobbes was a
theist and even a good Anglican. The prevalent procedure would merely lead to historical errors, if to grave historical errors, but for the fact that its results are employed for
buttressing the dogma that the mind of the individual is incapable of liberating itself
from the opinions which rule his society. Hobbes's last word on the question of public
worship is that the commonwealth *may* establish public worship. If the commonwealth
fails to establish public worship, i.e., if it allows "many sorts of worship," as it may,
"it cannot be said . . . that the commonwealth is of any religion at all" (cf. *Leviathan*,
chap. xxxi [240] with the Latin version [p.m. 171]).

philosophy has no control but for which one can only wish or pray. Hobbes, on the other hand, was certain that philosophy itself can bring about the coincidence of philosophy and political power by becoming popularized philosophy and thus public opinion. Chance will be conquered by systematic philosophy issuing in systematic enlightenment: *Paulatim eruditur vulgus*.[44] By devising the right kind of institutions and by enlightening the citizen body, philosophy guarantees the solution of the social problem, whose solution cannot be guaranteed by man if it is thought to depend on moral discipline.

Opposing the "utopianism" of the classics, Hobbes was concerned with a social order whose actualization is probable and even certain. The guaranty of its actualization might seem to be supplied by the fact that the sound social order is based on the most powerful passion and therewith on the most powerful force in man. But if the fear of violent death is truly the strongest force in man, one should expect the desired social order always, or almost always, to be in existence, because it will be produced by natural necessity, by the natural order. Hobbes overcomes this difficulty by assuming that men in their stupidity interfere with the natural order. The right social order does not normally come about by natural necessity on account of man's ignorance of that order. The "invisible

44. *De cive*, Ep. ded.; cf. *De corpore*, I, 7: the cause of civil war is ignorance of the causes of wars and of peace; hence the remedy is moral philosophy. Accordingly Hobbes, characteristically deviating from Aristotle (*Politics* 1302ᵃ35 ff.), seeks the causes of rebellion chiefly in false doctrines (*De cive*, XII). The belief in the prospects of popular enlightenment—*De homine*, XIV, 13; *Leviathan*, chaps. xviii (119), xxx (221, 224–25), and xxxi end—is based on the view that the natural inequality of human beings in regard to intellectual gifts is inconsiderable (*Leviathan*, chaps. xiii [80] and xv [100]; *De cive*, III, 13). Hobbes's expectation from enlightenment seems to be contradicted by his belief in the power of passion, and especially of pride or ambition. The contradiction is solved by the consideration that the ambition which endangers civil society is characteristic of a minority: of "the rich and potent subjects of a kingdom, or those that are accounted the most learned"; if "the common people," whom necessity "keepeth attent on their trades, and labour," are properly taught, the ambition and avarice of the few will become powerless. Cf. also *English Works*, IV, 443–44.

hand" remains ineffectual if it is not supported by the *Leviathan* or, if you wish, by the *Wealth of Nations*.

There is a remarkable parallelism and an even more remarkable discrepancy between Hobbes's theoretical philosophy and his practical philosophy. In both parts of his philosophy, he teaches that reason is impotent and that it is omnipotent, or that reason is omnipotent because it is impotent. Reason is impotent because reason or humanity have no cosmic support: the universe is unintelligible, and nature "dissociates" men. But the very fact that the universe is unintelligible permits reason to rest satisfied with its free constructs, to establish through its constructs an Archimedean basis of operations, and to anticipate an unlimited progress in its conquest of nature. Reason is impotent against passion, but it can become omnipotent if it co-operates with the strongest passion or if it puts itself into the service of the strongest passion. Hobbes's rationalism, then, rests ultimately on the conviction that, thanks to nature's kindness, the strongest passion is the only passion which can be "the origin of large and lasting societies" or that the strongest passion is the most rational passion. In the case of human things, the foundation is not a free construct but the most powerful natural force in man. In the case of human things, we understand not merely what we make but also what makes our making and our makings. Whereas the philosophy or science of nature remains fundamentally hypothetical, political philosophy rests on a nonhypothetical knowledge of the nature of man.[45] As long as Hobbes's approach prevails, "the philosophy concerned with the human things" will remain the last refuge of nature. For at some point nature succeeds in getting a hearing. The modern contention that man can "change the world" or "push back nature" is not unreasonable. One can even safely go much beyond it and say that man can expel nature with a hayfork. One ceases

45. Cf. n. 9 above.

to be reasonable only if one forgets what the philosophic poet adds, *tamen usque recurret*.

B. LOCKE

At first glance Locke seems to reject altogether Hobbes's notion of natural law and to follow the traditional teaching. He certainly speaks of man's natural rights as if they were derivative from the law of nature, and he accordingly speaks of the law of nature as if it were a law in the strict sense of the term. The law of nature imposes perfect duties on man as man, regardless of whether he lives in the state of nature or in civil society. "The law of nature stands as an eternal rule to all men," for it is "plain and intelligible to all rational creatures." It is identical with "the law of reason." It is "knowable by the light of nature; that is, without the help of positive revelation." Locke considers it entirely possible for the law of nature or the moral law to be raised to the rank of a demonstrative science. That science would make out "from self-evident propositions, by necessary consequences . . . the measures of right and wrong." Man would thus become able to elaborate "a body of ethics, proved to be the law of nature, from principles of reason, and teaching all the duties of life," or "the entire body of the 'law of nature,' " or "complete morality," or a "code" which gives us the law of nature "entire." That code would contain, among other things, the natural penal law.[46] Yet Locke never made a serious effort to elaborate that code. His failure to embark on this great enterprise was due to the problem posed by theology.[47]

The law of nature is a declaration of the will of God. It is "the voice of God" in man. It can therefore be called the "law

46. *Treatises of Government*, I, secs. 86, 101; II, secs. 6, 12, 30, 96, 118, 124, 135. *An Essay concerning Human Understanding*, I, 3, sec. 13, and IV, 3, sec. 18. *The Reasonableness of Christianity* (*The Works of John Locke in Nine Volumes*, VI [London, 1824], 140–42).

47. Cf. Descartes's "Auctor non libenter scribit ethica" (*Œuvres*, ed. Adam-Tannery, V, 178).

of God" or "divine law" or even the "eternal law"; it is "the highest law." It is the law of God not only in fact. It must be known to be the law of God in order to be law. Without such knowledge man cannot act morally. For "the true ground of morality . . . can only be the will and law of a God." The law of nature can be demonstrated because the existence and the attributes of God can be demonstrated. This divine law is promulgated, not only in or by reason, but by revelation as well. In fact, it first became known to man in its entirety by revelation, but reason confirms this divine law thus revealed. This does not mean that God did not reveal to man some laws which are purely positive: the distinction between the law of reason, which obliges man as man, and the law revealed in the gospel, which obliges Christians, is preserved by Locke.[48]

One may wonder whether what Locke says about the relation between the law of nature and the revealed law is free from difficulties. However this may be, his teaching is exposed to a more fundamental and more obvious difficulty, to a difficulty which seems to endanger the very notion of a law of nature. He says, on the one hand, that, in order to be a law, the law of nature must not only have been given by God and be known to have been given by God, but it must in addition have as its sanctions divine "rewards and punishments, of infinite weight and duration, in another life." On the other hand, however, he says that reason cannot demonstrate that there is another life. Only through revelation do we know of the sanctions for the law of nature or of "the only true touchstone of moral rectitude." Natural reason is therefore unable

48. *Treatises*, I, secs. 39, 56, 59, 63, 86, 88, 89, 111, 124, 126, 128, 166; II, secs. 1, 4, 6, 25, 52, 135, 136 n., 142, 195; *Essay*, I, 3, secs. 6 and 13; II, 28, sec. 8; IV, 3, sec. 18, and 10, sec. 7; *Reasonableness*, pp. 13, 115, 140, 144 ("the highest law, the law of nature"), 145; *A Second Vindication of the Reasonableness of Christianity (Works*, VI, 229): "As men, we have God for our king, and are under the law of reason: as Christians, we have Jesus the Messiah for our king, and are under the law revealed by him in the gospel. And though every Christian, both as a deist and a Christian, be obliged to study both the law of nature and the revealed law. . . ." Cf. n. 51 below.

to know the law of nature as a law.[49] This would mean that there does not exist a law of nature in the strict sense.

This difficulty is apparently overcome by the fact that "the veracity of God is a demonstration of the truth of what he has revealed."[50] That is to say, natural reason is indeed unable to demonstrate that the souls of men shall live forever. But natural reason is able to demonstrate that the New Testament is the perfect document of revelation. And since the New Testament teaches that the souls of men shall live forever, natural reason is able to demonstrate the true ground of morality and therewith to establish the dignity of the law of nature as a true law.

By demonstrating that the New Testament is a document of revelation, one demonstrates that the law promulgated by Jesus is a law in the proper sense of the term. This divine law

49. *Essay*, I, 3, secs. 5, 6, 13; II, 28, sec. 8; IV, 3, sec. 29; *Reasonableness*, p. 144: "But where was it that their obligation [the obligation of the just measures of right and wrong] was thoroughly known and allowed, and they received as precepts of a *law;* of the highest law, the law of nature? That *could not be*, without a clear knowledge and acknowledgment of the law-maker, and the great rewards and punishments, for those that would, or would not obey him." *Ibid.*, pp. 150–51: "The view of heaven and hell will cast a slight upon the short pleasures of this present state, and give attractions and encouragements to virtue which reason and interest, and the care of ourselves, cannot but allow and prefer. Upon this foundation, and upon this *only*, morality stands firm, and may defy all competition." *Second Reply to the Bishop of Worcester* (*Works*, III, 489; see also 474 and 480): "So unmovable is that truth delivered by the Spirit of truth, that though the light of nature gave some obscure glimmering, some uncertain hopes of a future state, yet human reason could attain to no clearness, no certainty about it, but that it was Jesus Christ alone who had 'brought life and immortality to light through the gospel' . . . this article of revelation, which . . . the Scripture assures us is established and made certain *only* by revelation." (The italics are not in the original.)

50. *Second Reply to the Bishop of Worcester*, p. 476. Cf. *ibid.*, p. 281: "I think it is possible to be certain upon the testimony of God . . . where I know that it is the testimony of God; because in such a case, that testimony is capable not only to make me believe, but, if I consider it right, to make me know the thing to be so; and so I may be certain. For the veracity of God is as capable of making me know a proposition to be true, as any other way of proof can be, and therefore I do not in such a case barely believe, but know such a proposition to be true, and attain certainty." See also *Essay*, IV, 16, sec. 14.

proves to be in full conformity with reason; it proves to be the absolutely comprehensive and perfect formulation of the law of nature. One is thus led to see that unassisted reason would have been unable to discover the law of nature in its entirety, but that the reason which has learned from revelation can recognize the thoroughly reasonable character of the law revealed in the New Testament. A comparison of the New Testament teaching with all other moral teachings shows that the entire law of nature is available in the New Testament, and only in the New Testament. The entire law of nature is available only in the New Testament, and it is there available in perfect clarity and plainness.[51]

If "the surest, the safest and most effectual way of teaching" the entire law of nature, and hence any part of it, is supplied by "the inspired books"; the complete and perfectly clear natural law teaching concerning government in particular would consist of properly arranged quotations from Scripture and especially from the New Testament. Accordingly, one would expect that Locke would have written a "Politique tirée des propres paroles de l'Écriture Sainte." But, in fact, he wrote his *Two Treatises of Government*. What he did stands in striking

---

51. *Reasonableness*, p. 139: "It should seem, by the little that has hitherto been done in it, that it is too hard a task for unassisted reason to establish morality in all its parts, upon its true foundation, with a clear and convincing light." *Ibid.*, pp. 142–43: "It is true, there is a law of nature: but who is there who ever did, or undertook to give it us all entire, as a law; *no more, nor no less*, than what was contained in, and had the obligation of that law? Who ever made out all the parts of it, put them together, and showed the world their obligation? Where was there any such code, that mankind might have recourse to, as their unerring rule, before our Saviour's time? . . . Such a law of morality Jesus Christ hath given us in the New Testament . . . by revelation. We have from him a full and sufficient rule for our direction, and conformable to that of reason." *Ibid.*, p. 147: "And then there needs no more, but to read the inspired books, to be instructed: all the duties of morality lie there clear, and plain, and easy to be understood. And here I appeal, whether this be not the surest, the safest, and most effectual way of teaching: especially, if we add this further consideration, that as it suits the lowest capacities of reasonable creatures, so it reaches and satisfies, nay, enlightens the highest." (The italics are not in the original.)

contrast to what he said. He himself "always thought the actions of men the best interpreters of their thoughts."[52] If we apply this rule to what was perhaps his greatest action, we are forced to suspect that he encountered some hidden obstacles on his way toward a strictly scriptural natural law teaching regarding government. He might have become aware of difficulties obstructing either the demonstration of the revealed character of Scripture or the equation of the New Testament law with the law of nature or both.

Locke would not have dwelt on these difficulties. He was a cautious writer. The fact that he is generally known as a cautious writer shows, however, that his caution is obtrusive, and therefore perhaps not what is ordinarily understood by caution. At any rate, the scholars who note that Locke was cautious do not always consider that the term "caution" designates a variety of phenomena and that the only authentic interpreter of Locke's caution is Locke himself. In particular, present-day scholars do not consider the possibility that procedures which they, from their point of view, justly regard as verging on the unseemly might have been regarded in other ages, and by men of another type, as entirely unobjectionable.

Caution is a kind of noble fear. "Caution" means something different when applied to theory than when applied to practice or politics. A theoretician will not be called cautious if he does not make clear in each case the value of the various arguments which he employs or if he suppresses any relevant fact. A man of affairs who is cautious in this sense would be blamed as lacking in caution. There may be extremely relevant facts which, if stressed, would inflame popular passion and thus prevent the wise handling of those very facts. A cautious political writer would state the case for the good cause in a manner which could be expected to create general good will toward the good cause. He would avoid the mention of every-

52. *Essay*, I, 3, sec. 3.

thing which would "displace the veil beneath which" the respectable part of society "dissembles its divisions." Whereas the cautious theoretician would scorn the appeal to prejudices, the cautious man of affairs would try to enlist all respectable prejudices in the service of the good cause. "Logic admits of no compromise. The essence of politics is compromise." Acting in this spirit, the statesmen who were responsible for the settlement of 1689 which Locke defended in the *Two Treatises*, "cared little whether their major agreed with their conclusion, if their major secured two hundred votes, and the conclusion two hundred more."[53] Acting in the same spirit, Locke, in his defense of the revolutionary settlement, appealed as frequently as he could to the authority of Hooker— of one of the least revolutionary men who ever lived. He took every advantage of his partial agreement with Hooker. And he avoided the inconveniences which might have been caused by his partial disagreement with Hooker by being practically silent about it. Since to write means to act, he did not proceed in an altogether different manner when composing his most theoretical work, the *Essay:* "since not all, nor the most of those that believe a God, are at the pains, or have the skill, to examine and clearly comprehend the demonstrations of his being, I was unwilling to show the weakness of the argument there spoken of [in *Essay*, IV, 10, sec. 7]; since possibly by it some men might be confirmed in the belief of a God, which is enough to preserve in them true sentiments of religion and morality."[54] Locke was always, as Voltaire liked to call him, "le sage Locke."

Locke has explained his view of caution most fully in some passages of his *Reasonableness of Christianity*. Speaking of the ancient philosophers, he says: "The rational and thinking part of mankind . . . when they sought after him, they found the

53. Macaulay, *The History of England* (New York: Allison, n.d.), II, 491.
54. *Letter to the Bishop of Worcester* (*Works*, III, 53–54).

one supreme, invisible God; but if they acknowledged and worshipped him, it was only in their own minds. They kept this truth locked up in their own breasts as a secret, nor ever durst venture it amongst the people; much less amongst the priests, those wary guardians of their own creeds and profitable inventions." Socrates indeed "opposed and laughed at their polytheism, and wrong opinions of the deity; and we see how they rewarded him for it. Whatsoever Plato, and the soberest of the philosophers, thought of the nature and being of the one God, they were fain, in their outward professions and worship, to go with the herd, and keep to their religion established by law. . . ." It does not appear that Locke regarded the conduct of the ancient philosophers as reprehensible. Still that conduct might be thought to be incompatible with biblical morality. Locke did not think so. When speaking of Jesus' "caution" or "reservedness" or his "concealing himself," he says that Jesus used "words too doubtful to be laid hold on against him" or words "obscure and doubtful, and less liable to be made use of against him," and that he tried "to keep himself out of the reach of any accusation, that might appear just or weighty to the Roman deputy." Jesus "perplexed his meaning," "his circumstances being such, that without such a prudent carriage and reservedness, he could not have gone through with the work which he came to do. . . . He so involved his sense, that it was not easy to understand him." If he had acted differently, both the Jewish and the Roman authorities would "have taken away his life; at least they would have . . . hindered the work he was about." In addition, if he had not been cautious, he would have created "manifest danger of tumult and sedition"; there would have been "room to fear that [his preaching the truth] should cause . . . disturbance in civil societies, and the governments of the world."[55] We see, then, that, according to Locke, cautious

55. *Reasonableness*, pp. 35, 42, 54, 57, 58, 59, 64, 135-36.

speech is legitimate if unqualified frankness would hinder a noble work one is trying to achieve or expose one to persecution or endanger the public peace; and legitimate caution is perfectly compatible with going with the herd in one's outward professions or with using ambiguous language or with so involving one's sense that one cannot easily be understood.

Let us assume for a moment that Locke was a thoroughgoing rationalist, i.e., that he regarded unassisted reason not only as man's "only star and compass"[56] but as sufficient for leading man to happiness, and hence rejected revelation as superfluous and therefore as impossible. Even in that case his principles would hardly have permitted him, given the circumstances in which he wrote, to go beyond contending that he accepted the New Testament teaching as true because its being revealed has been demonstrated and because the rules of conduct which it conveys express in the most perfect manner the entire law of reason. However, to understand why he wrote his *Two Treatises of Government*, and not a "Politique tirée des propres paroles de l'Écriture Sainte," it is not necessary to assume that he himself had any doubts regarding the truth of the two contentions mentioned. It suffices to assume that he had some misgivings as to whether what he was inclined to regard as solid demonstrations was likely to appear in the same light to all his readers. For if he had any misgivings of this kind, he was forced to make his political teaching, i.e., his natural law teaching concerning the rights and duties of rulers and of subjects, as independent of Scripture as it could possibly be.

To see why Locke could not be sure whether all his readers would regard the revealed character of the New Testament as demonstratively certain, one merely has to look at what he considered the proof of Jesus' divine mission. That proof is supplied by "the multitude of miracles he did before all sorts

56. *Treatises*, I, sec. 58.

of people." Now, according to Locke, who in this point is tacitly following Spinoza, one cannot prove that a given phenomenon is a miracle by proving that the phenomenon in question is supernatural; for, in order to prove that a phenomenon cannot be due to natural causes, one must know the limits of the power of nature, and such knowledge is hardly available. It is sufficient that the phenomenon which is said to attest a man's divine mission shows greater power than the phenomena which are said to disprove his claim. It may be doubted whether one can thus establish a clear distinction between miracles and nonmiracles, or whether a demonstrative argument can be based on Locke's notion of miracles. At any rate, in order to carry weight with people who were not eyewitnesses, the miracles must be sufficiently attested. The Old Testament miracles were not sufficiently attested to convince the pagans, but the miracles of Jesus and the Apostles were sufficiently attested to convince all men, so much so, that "the miracles [Jesus] did . . . never were, nor could be denied by any of the enemies, or opposers of Christianity."[57] This extraordinarily bold statement is particularly surprising in the mouth of a most competent contemporary of Hobbes and Spinoza. One could perhaps find Locke's remark less strange if one could be certain that he was not well read in "those justly

57. "A discourse of miracles," *Works*, VIII, 260–64; *Reasonableness*, pp. 135 and 146. *Ibid.*, pp. 137–38: the Old Testament "revelation was shut up in a little corner of the world. . . . The gentile world, in our Saviour's time, and several ages before, could have no attestation of the miracles on which the Hebrews built their faith, but from the Jews themselves, a people not known to the greatest part of mankind; contemned and thought vilely of, by those nations that did know them. . . . But our Saviour . . . did not confine his miracles or message to the land of Canaan, or the worshippers at Jerusalem. But he himself preached at Samaria, and did miracles in the borders of Tyre and Sidon, and before multitudes of people gathered from all quarters. And after his resurrection, sent apostles amongst the nations, accompanied with miracles; which were done in all parts so frequently, and before so many witnesses of all sorts, in broad day-light, that . . . the enemies of Christianity have never dared to deny them; no, not Julian himself: who neither wanted skill nor power to inquire into the truth." Cf. n. 59 below.

decried" authors.[58] But must one be well read in Hobbes and Spinoza in order to know that they deny the reality, or at least the certainty, of any miracles? And would not Locke's lack of familiarity with Hobbes's and Spinoza's writings considerably detract from his competence as a late-seventeenth-century writer on subjects of this kind? Quite apart from this, if no one denies the miracles reported in the New Testament, it would seem to follow that all men are Christians, for "where the miracle is admitted, the doctrine cannot be rejected."[59] Yet Locke knew that there were men who were familiar with the New Testament without being believing Christians; his *Reasonableness of Christianity*, in which his most emphatic statements regarding the New Testament miracles occur, was "chiefly designed for deists," of whom there was apparently "a great number" in his time.[60] Since Locke knew, as he admitted, of the existence of deists in his age and country, he must have been aware of the fact that a political teaching based on Scripture would not be universally accepted as unquestionably true, at least not without a previous and very

58. *Second Reply to the Bishop of Worcester*, p. 477: "I am not so well read in Hobbes or Spinoza, as to be able to say what were their opinions in this matter [the life after death]. But possibly there be those who will think your Lordship's authority of more use to them in the case, than those justly decried names." *A Second Vindication of the Reasonableness of Christianity* (*Works*, VI, 420): "I . . . did not know these words, he quoted out of the Leviathan, were there or any thing like them. Nor do I know yet, any farther than as I believe them to be there, from his quotation."

59. "A Discourse of Miracles," p. 259. Perhaps it will be suggested that Locke made a subtle distinction between "not denying the miracles" and "admitting the miracles." In that case the fact that the miracles reported in the New Testament were never denied and cannot be denied would not prove the divine mission of Jesus, and there would not exist any demonstrative proof of it. At any rate, the suggestion mentioned is contradicted by what Locke says elsewhere. Cf. *Second Vindication*, p. 340: "The principal of these [marks peculiarly appropriated to the Messiah] is his resurrection from the dead; which being the great and demonstrative proof of his being a Messiah . . ." with *ibid.*, p. 342: "His being or not being the Messiah, stands or falls with [his resurrection] . . . believe one, and you believe both; deny one of them, and you can believe neither."

60. *Second Vindication*, pp. 164, 264–65, 375.

complex argument for which we seek in vain in his writings.

One can state the issue in simpler terms as follows: The veracity of God is indeed a demonstration of any proposition which he has revealed. Yet "the whole strength of the certainty depends upon our knowledge that God revealed" the proposition in question, or "our assurance can be no greater than our knowledge is, that it is a revelation from God." And at least as regards all men who know of revelation only through tradition, "the knowledge we have that this revelation came at first from God, can never be so sure as the knowledge we have from the clear and distinct perception of the agreement or disagreement of our own ideas." Accordingly, our assurance that the souls of men shall live forever belongs to the province of faith and not to that of reason.[61] Yet since without that assurance "the just measures of right and wrong" do not have the character of a law, those just measures are not a law for reason. This would mean that there does not exist a law of nature. Therefore, if there is to be "a law knowable by the light of nature, that is, without the help of positive revelation," that law must consist of a set of rules whose validity does not presuppose life after death or belief in a life after death.

Such rules were established by the classical philosophers. The pagan philosophers, "who spoke from reason, made not much mention of the Deity in their ethics." They showed that virtue "is the perfection and the excellency of our nature; that she is herself a reward, and will recommend our names to future ages," but they left "her unendowed."[62] For they were

61. *Essay*, IV, 18, secs. 4–8; cf. n. 50 above.

62. From this it follows that, "however strange it may seem, the law-maker hath nothing to do with moral virtues and vices" but is limited in his function to the preservation of property (cf. *Treatises*, II, sec. 124; and J. W. Gough, *John Locke's Political Philosophy* [Oxford: Clarendon Press, 1950], p. 190). If virtue by itself is ineffectual, civil society must have a foundation other than human perfection or the inclination toward it; it must be based on the strongest desire in man, the desire for self-preservation, and therefore on his concern with property.

unable to show a necessary connection between virtue and prosperity or happiness, a connection which is not visible in this life and which can be guaranteed only if there is a life after death.[63] Still, while unassisted reason cannot establish a necessary connection between virtue and prosperity or happiness, the classical philosophers realized, and practically all men realize, a necessary connection between a kind of prosperity or happiness and a kind or part of virtue. There exists, indeed, a visible connection between "public happiness" or "the prosperity and temporal happiness of any people" and the general compliance with "*several* moral rules." These rules, which apparently are a part of the complete law of nature, "may receive from mankind a very general approbation, *without* either knowing or admitting *the true ground* of morality; which can only be the will and law of a God, who sees men in the dark, has in his hands rewards and punishments, and power enough to call to account the proudest offender." But even if, and precisely if, those rules are divorced from "the true ground of morality," they stand "on their true foundations": "[Prior to Jesus], those just measures of right and wrong, which necessity had anywhere introduced, the civil laws prescribed, or philosophers recommended, stood on *their true foundations*. They were looked on as bonds of society, and conveniencies of common life, and laudable practices."[64] However doubtful the status of the complete law of nature may have become in Locke's thought, the partial law of nature

63. *Reasonableness*, pp. 148–49: "Virtue and prosperity do not often accompany one another; and therefore virtue seldom had any followers. And it is no wonder she prevailed not much in a state, where the inconveniencies that attended her were visible, and at hand; and the rewards doubtful, and at a distance. Mankind, who are and must be allowed to pursue their happiness, nay, cannot be hindered; could not but think themselves excused from a strict observation of rules, which appeared so little to consist of their chief end, happiness; whilst they kept them from the enjoyments of this life; and they had little evidence and security of another." Cf. *ibid.*, pp. 139, 142–44, 150–51; *Essay*, I, 3, sec. 5, and II, 28, sec. 10–12.

64. *Reasonableness*, pp. 144 and 139; *Essay*, I, 3, secs. 4, 6, and 10 (the italics are not in the original); *Treatises*, II, secs. 7, 42, and 107.

which is limited to what "political happiness"—a "good of mankind in this world"—evidently requires would seem to have stood firm. Only this partial law of nature can have been recognized by him, in the last analysis, as a law of reason and therewith as truly a law of nature.

We must now consider the relation between what we call for the time being the partial law of nature and the New Testament law. If "no more nor no less" than the entire law of nature is supplied by the New Testament, if "all the parts" of the law of nature are made out in the New Testament in a manner which is "clear, plain, and easy to be understood," the New Testament must contain in particular clear and plain expressions of those prescriptions of the law of nature with which men must comply for the sake of political happiness.[65] According to Locke, one of the rules of "the law of God and nature" is to the effect that the government "must not raise taxes on the property of the people without the consent of the people, given by themselves or their deputies." Locke does not even attempt to confirm this rule by clear and plain statements of Scripture. Another very important and characteristic rule of the law of nature as Locke understands it, denies to the conqueror a right and title to the possessions of the vanquished: even in a just war the conqueror may not "dispossess the posterity of the vanquished." Locke himself admits that this "will seem a strange doctrine," i.e., a novel doctrine. In fact, it would seem that the opposite doctrine is at least as much warranted by Scripture as is Locke's. He quotes more than once Jephtha's saying "the Lord the Judge be judge"; but he fails even to allude to the fact that Jephtha's statement is made in the context of a controversy about the right of conquest, as well as to Jephtha's entirely un-Lockean view of the rights of the conqueror.[66] One is tempted to say that Jephtha's state-

65. Cf. also *Essay*, II, 28, sec. 11.

66. *Treatises*, II, secs. 142 (cf. sec. 136 n.), 180, 184; cf. also n. 51 above. *Ibid.*, secs. 21, 176, 241; cf. Judges 11:12–24; cf. also Hobbes's *Leviathan*, chap. xxiv (162).

ment, which refers to a controversy between two nations, is used by Locke as the *locus classicus* concerning controversies between the government and the people. The statement of Jephtha takes the place in Locke's doctrine of Paul's statement "Let every soul be subject to the higher powers," which he hardly, if ever, quotes.[67]

In addition, Locke's political teaching stands or falls by his natural law teaching concerning the beginnings of political societies. The latter teaching cannot well be based on Scripture because that beginning of a political society with which the Bible is chiefly concerned—that of the Jewish state—was the only beginning of a political society which was not natural.[68] Furthermore, Locke's entire political teaching is based on the assumption of a state of nature. This assumption is wholly alien to the Bible. The following fact is sufficiently revealing: in the *Second Treatise of Government*, in which Locke sets forth his own doctrine, explicit references to the state of nature abound; in the *First Treatise*, in which he criticizes Filmer's allegedly scriptural doctrine of the divine right of kings and therefore uses much more biblical material than in the *Second Treatise*, there occurs, if I am not mistaken, only one mention of the state of nature.[69] From the biblical point of view, the important distinction is the distinction, not between the state of nature and the state of civil society, but between the state of innocence and the state after the Fall. The state of nature, as Locke conceives of it, is not identical with either the state of innocence or the state after the Fall. If there is any place at all in biblical history for Locke's state of na-

67. Cf. especially the quotation from Hooker in *Treatises*, II, sec. 90 n., with the context in Hooker: in Hooker the passage quoted by Locke is immediately preceded by the quotation of Romans 13:1. Paul's statement occurs in a quotation (*Treatises*, sec. 237). Cf. also *ibid.*, sec. 13, where Locke refers to an objection in which the statement occurs that "God hath certainly appointed government," a statement which does not occur in Locke's rejoinder.

68. *Treatises*, II, secs. 101, 109, and 115.

69. *Ibid.*, I, sec. 90.

ture, the state of nature would begin after the flood, i.e., a long time after the Fall; for prior to God's grant to Noah and his sons, men did not have the natural right to meat which is a consequence of the natural right to self-preservation, and the state of nature is the state in which every man has "all the rights and privileges of the law of nature."[70] Now, if the state of nature begins a long time after the Fall, the state of nature would seem to partake of all characteristics of "the corrupt state of degenerate men." In fact, however, it is a "poor but virtuous age," an age characterized by "innocence and sincerity," not to say the golden age.[71] Just like the Fall itself, the punishment for the Fall ceased to be of any significance for Locke's political doctrine. He holds that even God's curse on Eve does not impose a duty on the female sex "not to endeavor to avoid" that curse: women may avoid the pangs of childbirth "if there could be found a remedy for it."[72]

The tension between Locke's natural law teaching and the New Testament is perhaps best illustrated by his teaching about marriage and related topics.[73] In the *First Treatise* he characterizes adultery, incest, and sodomy as sins. He indicates there that they are sins independently of the fact that

70. *Ibid.*, I, secs. 27 and 39; II, sec. 25; cf. also II, secs. 6 and 87; and II, secs. 36 and 38. In II, secs. 56–57, Locke seemingly says that Adam was in the state of nature prior to the Fall. According to *ibid.*, sec. 36 (cf. 107, 108, 116), the state of nature is situated in "the first ages of the world" or in "the beginning of things" (cf. Hobbes, *De cive*, V, 2); cf. also *Treatises*, II, sec. 11, end, with Gen. 4:14–15 and 9:5–6.

71. Cf. *Reasonableness*, p. 112, and *Treatises*, I, secs. 16 and 44–45 with *ibid.*, II, secs. 110–11 and 128. Note the plural "all those [ages]" *ibid.*, sec. 110; there have been many examples of the state of nature, whereas there was only once a state of innocence.

72. *Treatises*, I, sec. 47.

73. As regards the relation between Locke's teaching concerning property and the New Testament teaching, it suffices here to mention his interpretation of Luke 18:22: "This I look on to be the meaning of the place; this, of selling all he had, and giving it to the poor, not being a standing law of [Jesus'] kingdom; but a probationary command to this young man; to try whether he truly believed him to be the Messiah, and was ready to obey his commands, and relinquish all to follow him, when he, his prince, required it" (*Reasonableness*, p. 120).

"they cross the main intention of nature." One is therefore forced to wonder whether their being sins is not chiefly due to "positive revelation." Later on he raises the question "what in nature is the difference betwixt a wife and a concubine?" He does not answer that question, but the context suggests that natural law is silent about that difference. Furthermore, he indicates that the distinction between those whom men may and may not marry is based exclusively on the revealed law. In his thematic discussion of conjugal society in the *Second Treatise*,[74] he makes it quite clear that, according to natural law, conjugal society is not necessarily for life; the end of conjugal society (procreation and education) merely requires that "the male and female in mankind are tied to a longer conjunction than other creatures." He does not leave it at saying that "the conjugal bonds" must be more "lasting in man than the other species of animals"; he also demands that those bonds be "more firm . . . in man than the other species of animals"; he fails to tell us, however, how firm they should be.

74. The thematic discussion of conjugal society occurs in chap. vii of the *Second Treatise*, in a chapter entitled, not "Of Conjugal Society," but "Of Political or Civil Society." That chapter happens to be the only chapter of the entire *Treatises* which opens with the word "God." It happens to be followed by the only chapter of the entire *Treatises* which opens with the word "Men." Chapter vii begins with a clear reference to the divine institution of marriage as recorded in Genesis 2:18; all the more striking is the contrast between the biblical doctrine (especially in its Christian interpretation) and Locke's own doctrine. It so happens that there is also only one chapter in the *Essay* which opens with the word "God" and which is followed by the only chapter of the *Essay* whose first word is "Man" (III, 1 and 2). In the only chapter of the *Essay* which opens with the word "God," Locke tries to show that words are "ultimately derived from such as signify sensible ideas," and he remarks that, by the observations to which he refers, "we may give some kind of guess *what kind of notions they were*, and whence they derived, *which filled their minds who were the first beginners of languages*." (The italics are not in the original.) Locke thus cautiously contradicts the biblical doctrine which he adopts in the *Treatises* (II, sec. 56) and according to which the first beginner of language, Adam, "was created a perfect man, his body and mind in full possession of their strength and reason, and so was capable from the first instant of his being to . . . govern his actions according to the dictates of the law of reason which God had implanted in him."

Certainly, polygamy is perfectly compatible with natural law. It should also be noted that what Locke says about the difference between conjugal society among human beings and conjugal society among brutes—viz., that the former is, or ought to be, "more firm and lasting" than the latter—does not require any prohibition against incest and that he therefore remains silent about such prohibitions. In accordance with all this, he declares later on, in full agreement with Hobbes and in full disagreement with Hooker, that civil society is the sole judge of which "transgressions" are, and which are not, deserving of punishment.[75]

Locke's doctrine concerning conjugal society naturally affects his teaching regarding the rights and duties of parents and children. He does not tire of quoting "Honour your parents." But he gives the biblical commands an unbiblical meaning by disregarding entirely the biblical distinctions between lawful and unlawful unions of men and women. Furthermore, as regards the obedience which children owe to their parents, he teaches that that duty "terminates with the minority of the child." If parents retain "a strong tie" on the obedience of their children after the latter have come of age, this is due merely to the fact that "it is commonly in the father's power to bestow [his estate] with a more sparing or liberal hand, according as the behaviour of this or that child hath comported with his will and humour." "This is," to quote Locke's understatement, "no small tie on the obedience of children." But it is certainly, as he states explicitly, "no natural tie": children who are of age are under no natural law obligation to obey their parents. Locke insists all the more strongly on the children's "perpetual obligation of honouring their parents."

75. *Treatises*, I, secs. 59, 123, 128; II, secs. 65 and 79–81. Cf. *Treatises*, II, secs. 88 and 136 (and note) with Hooker, *Laws of Ecclesiastical Polity*, I, 10, sec. 10, and III, 9, sec. 2, on the one hand, and Hobbes, *De cive*, XIV, 9, on the other. Cf. Gough, *op. cit.*, p. 189. As for the higher right of the mother, as compared with the father, see especially *Treatises*, I, sec. 55, where Locke tacitly follows Hobbes (*De cive*, IX, 3). Cf. n. 84 below.

"Nothing can cancel" this duty. It "is always due from children to their parents." Locke finds the natural law basis of that perpetual duty in the fact that the parents have begotten their children. He admits, however, that if the parents have been "unnaturally careless" of their children, they "might" "perhaps" forfeit their right "to much of that duty comprehended in the command, 'Honour your parents.' " He goes beyond this. In the *Second Treatise*, he indicates that "the bare act of begetting" does not give the parents any claim to being honored by their children: "the honour due from a child places in the parents a perpetual right to respect, reverence, support, and compliance, too, more or less, as the father's care, cost, and kindness in his education have been more or less."[76] It follows from this that if the father's care, cost, and kindness have been zero, his right to honor will become zero too. The categoric imperative "Honour thy father and thy mother" becomes the hypothetical imperative "Honour thy father and thy mother if they have deserved it of you."

It can safely be said, we think, that Locke's "partial law of nature" is not identical with clear and plain teachings of the New Testament or of Scripture in general. If "all the parts" of the law of nature are made out in the New Testament in a clear and plain manner, it follows that the "partial law of nature" does not belong at all to the law of nature. This conclusion is supported also by the following consideration: In order to be a law in the proper sense of the term, the law of nature must be known to have been given by God. But the "partial law of nature" does not require belief in God. The "partial law of nature" circumscribes the conditions which a nation must fulfil in order to be civil or civilized. Now the Chinese are "a very

76. *Treatises*, I, secs. 63, 90, 100; II, secs. 52, 65–67, 69, 71–73. Locke seems to imply that, other things being equal, the children of the rich are under a stricter obligation to honor their parents than the children of the poor. This would be in perfect agreement with the fact that wealthy parents have a stronger tie on their children's obedience than poor parents.

great and civil people" and the Siamites are a "civilized nation," and both the Chinese and the Siamites "want the idea and knowledge of God."[77] The "partial law of nature" is, then, not a law in the proper sense of the term.[78]

We thus arrive at the conclusion that Locke cannot have recognized any law of nature in the proper sense of the term. This conclusion stands in shocking contrast to what is generally thought to be his doctrine, and especially the doctrine of the *Second Treatise*. Before turning to an examination of the *Second Treatise*, we beg the reader to consider the following facts: The accepted interpretation of Locke's teaching leads to the consequence that "Locke is full of illogical flaws and inconsistencies,"[79] of inconsistencies, we add, which are so obvious that they cannot have escaped the notice of a man of his rank and his sobriety. Furthermore, the accepted interpretation is based on what amounts to a complete disregard of Locke's caution, of a kind of caution which is, to say the least, compatible with so involving one's sense that one cannot easily be understood and with going with the herd in one's outward professions. Above all, the accepted interpretation does not pay sufficient attention to the character of the *Treatise;* it somehow assumes that the *Treatise* contains the philosophic presentation of Locke's political doctrine, whereas it contains, in fact, only its "civil" presentation. In the *Treatise*, it is less Locke the philosopher than Locke the Englishman who ad-

77. *Treatises*, I, sec. 141; *Essay*, I, 4, sec. 8; *Second Reply to the Bishop of Worcester*, p. 486. *Reasonableness*, p. 144: "Those just measures of right and wrong . . . stood on their true foundations. They were looked on as bonds of society, and conveniences of common life, and laudable practices. But where was it that their obligation was thoroughly known and allowed [prior to Jesus], and they received as precepts of a law; of the highest law, the law of nature? That could not be, without a clear knowledge and acknowledgment of the law-maker" (compare p. 213 above and n. 49 above).

78. Accordingly, Locke sometimes identifies the law of nature not with the law of reason but with reason simply (cf. *Treatises*, I, sec. 101, with II, secs. 6, 11, 181; cf. also *ibid.*, I, sec. 111, toward the end).

79. Gough, *op. cit.*, p. 123.

dresses not philosophers, but Englishmen.[80] It is for this reason that the argument of that work is based partly on generally accepted opinions, and even to a certain extent on scriptural principles: "The greatest part cannot know, and therefore they must believe," so much so, that even if philosophy had "given us ethics in a science like mathematics, in every part demonstrable, . . . the instruction of the people were best still to be left to the precepts and principles of the gospel."[81]

Yet, however much Locke may have followed tradition in the *Treatise*, already a summary comparison of its teaching with the teachings of Hooker and of Hobbes would show that Locke deviated considerably from the traditional natural law teaching and followed the lead given by Hobbes.[82] There is, indeed, only one passage in the *Treatise* in which Locke explicitly notes that he deviates from Hooker. But the passage draws our attention to a radical deviation. After having quoted Hooker, Locke says: "But I, moreover, affirm that all men are naturally in [the state of nature]." He thus suggests

80. Cf. *Treatises*, II, sec. 52 beginning, and I, sec. 109 beginning, with *Essay*, III, 9, secs. 3, 8, 15, and chap. xi, sec. 11; *Treatises*, Preface, I, secs. 1 and 47; II, secs. 165, 177, 223, and 239.

81. *Reasonableness*, p. 146. Cf. the reference to the other life in *Treatises*, II, secs. 21 end, with sec. 13 end. Cf. the references to religion in *Treatises*, II, secs. 92, 112, 209–10.

82. In *Treatises*, II, secs. 5–6, Locke quotes Hooker, I, 8, sec. 7. The passage is used by Hooker for establishing the duty of loving one's neighbor as one's self; it is used by Locke for establishing the natural equality of all men. In the same context Locke replaces the duty of mutual love, of which Hooker had spoken, by the duty of refraining from harming others, i.e., he drops the duty of charity (cf. Hobbes, *De cive*, IV, 12, and 23). According to Hooker (I, 10, sec. 4), fathers have by nature "a supreme power in their families"; according to Locke (*Treatises*, II, secs. 52 ff.), any natural right of the father is, to say the least, fully shared by the mother (cf. n. 75 above). According to Hooker (I, 10, sec. 5), natural law enjoins civil society; according to Locke (*Treatises*, II, secs. 95 and 13), "any number of men *may*" form a civil society (the italics are not in the original). Cf. Hobbes, *De cive*, VI, 2, and n. 67 above. Cf. the interpretation of self-preservation in Hooker, I, 5, sec. 2, with the entirely different interpretation in *Treatises*, I, secs. 86 and 88. Consider, above all, the radical disagreement between Hooker (I, 8, secs. 2–3) and Locke (*Essay*, I, 3) in regard to the *consensus gentium* evidence for the law of nature.

that, according to Hooker, some men were in fact or accidentally in the state of nature. Actually, Hooker had not said anything about the state of nature: the whole doctrine of the state of nature is based on a break with Hooker's principles, i.e., with the principles of the traditional nature law doctrine. Locke's notion of the state of nature is inseparable from the doctrine "that in the state of nature everyone has the executive power of the law of nature." He states twice in the context referred to that this doctrine is "strange," i.e., novel.[83]

For what is the reason why, according to Locke, the admission of a law of nature requires the admission of a state of nature, and more particularly the admission that in the state of nature "every man hath the right to . . . be executioner of the law of nature"? ". . . Since it would be utterly in vain to suppose a rule set to the free actions of man, without annexing to it some enforcement of good or evil to determine his will, we must wherever we suppose a law, suppose also some reward or punishment annexed to that law." In order to be a law, the law of nature must have sanctions. According to the traditional view those sanctions are supplied by the judgment of the conscience, which is the judgment of God. Locke rejects this view. According to him, the judgment of the conscience is so far from being the judgment of God that the conscience "is nothing else but our own opinion or judgment of the moral rectitude or pravity of our own actions." Or to quote Hobbes, whom Locke tacitly follows: "private consciences . . . are but private opinions." Conscience cannot therefore be a guide; still less can it supply sanctions. Or if the verdict of the con-

83. *Treatises*, II, secs. 9, 13, and 15; cf. sec. 91 n., where Locke, quoting Hooker, refers in an explanatory remark to the state of nature which is not mentioned by Hooker; cf. also sec. 14 with Hobbes, *Leviathan*, chap. xiii (83). As regards the "strange" character of the doctrine that in the state of nature everyone has the executive power of the law of nature, cf. Thomas Aquinas *Summa theologica* ii. 2. qu. 64, *a*. 3, and Suarez, *Tr. de legibus*, III, 3, secs. 1 and 3, on the one hand, and Grotius *De jure belli* ii. 20. secs. 3 and 7 and ii. 25. sec. 1, as well as Richard Cumberland, *De legibus naturae*, chap. 1, sec. 26, on the other.

science is identified with right opinion about the moral quality of our actions, it is utterly powerless by itself: "View but an army at the sacking of a town, and see what observation or sense of moral principles, or what touch of conscience, for all the outrages they do." If there are to be sanctions for the law of nature in this world, those sanctions must be supplied by human beings. But any "enforcement" of the law of nature which takes place in and through civil society appears to be the outcome of human convention. Therefore, the law of nature will not be effective in this world and hence not be a true law, if it is not effective in the state antedating civil society or government—in the state of nature; even in the state of nature everyone must be effectively responsible to other human beings. This, however, requires that everyone in the state of nature have the right to be the executioner of the law of nature: "the law of nature would, as all other laws that concern men in this world, be in vain, if there were nobody that in the state of nature had a power to execute that law." The law of nature is indeed given by God, but its being a law does not require that it be known to be given by God, because it is immediately enforced, not by God or by the conscience, but by human beings.[84]

<hr />

84. *Reasonableness*, p. 114: ". . . if there were no punishment for the transgressors of [Jesus' laws], his laws would not be the laws of a king, . . . but empty talk, without force, and without influence." *Treatises*, II, secs. 7, 8, 13 end, 21 end; cf. *ibid.*, sec. 11, with I, sec. 56. *Essay*, I, 3, secs. 6–9, and II, 28, sec. 6; Hobbes, *Leviathan*, chap. xxix (212). When speaking of everyone's natural right to be the executioner of the law of nature, Locke refers to "that great law of nature, 'Whoso sheddeth man's blood, by man shall his blood be shed' " (Gen. 9:6). But he omits the biblical reason, "for in the image of God made he man." The Lockean reason for the right to inflict capital punishment on murderers is that man may "destroy *things* noxious" to men (the italics are not in the original). Locke disregards the fact that both the murdered and the murderer are made in the image of God: the murderer "may be destroyed as a lion or a tiger, one of those wild savage beasts with whom men can have no society nor security" (*Treatises*, II, secs. 8, 10, 11, 16, 172, 181; cf. I, sec. 30). Cf. Thomas Aquinas *Summa theologica* i. qu. 79, *a.* 13 and ii. 1. qu. 96, *a.* 5 ad 3 (cf. *a.* 4, obj. 1); Hooker, I, 9, sec.2—10, sec. 1; Grotius *De jure belli*, Prolegomena, secs. 20 and 27; Cumberland, *loc. cit.*

The law of nature cannot be truly a law if it is not effective in the state of nature. It cannot be effective in the state of nature if the state of nature is not a state of peace. The law of nature imposes on everyone the perfect duty of preserving the rest of mankind "as much as he can," but only "when his own preservation comes not in competition." If the state of nature were characterized by habitual conflict between self-preservation and the preservation of others, the law of nature which "willeth the peace and preservation of all mankind" would be ineffectual: the higher claim of self-preservation would leave no room for concern with others. The state of nature must therefore be "a state of peace, good-will, mutual assistance, and preservation." This means that the state of nature must be a social state; in the state of nature all men "make up one society" by virtue of the law of nature, although they have no "common superior on earth." Inasmuch as self-preservation requires food and other necessities, and scarcity of such things leads to conflict, the state of nature must be a state of plenty: "God has given us all things richly." The law of nature cannot be a law if it is not known; it must be known and therefore it must be knowable in the state of nature.[85]

After having drawn or suggested this picture of the state of nature especially in the first pages of the *Treatise*, Locke demolishes it as his argument proceeds. The state of nature, which at first glance seems to be the golden age ruled by God or good demons, is literally a state without government, "pure anarchy." It could last forever, "were it not for the corruption and viciousness of degenerate men"; but unfortunately "the greater part" are "no strict observers of equity and justice." For this reason, to say nothing of others, the state of nature has great "inconveniences." Many "mutual grievances, injuries and wrongs . . . attend men in the state of nature"; "strife and troubles would be endless" in it. It "is full of fears

85. *Treatises*, I, sec. 43; II, secs. 6, 7, 11, 19, 28, 31, 51, 56–57, 110, 128, 171, 172.

and continual dangers." It is "an ill condition." Far from being a state of peace, it is a state in which peace and quiet are uncertain. The state of peace is civil society; the state antedating civil society is the state of war.[86] This is either the cause or the effect of the fact that the state of nature is a state not of plenty but of penury. Those living in it are "needy and wretched." Plenty requires civil society.[87] Being "pure anarchy," the state of nature is not likely to be a social state. In fact, it is characterized by "want of society." "Society" and "civil society" are synonymous terms. The state of nature is "loose." For "the first and strongest desire God planted in man" is not the concern with others, not even concern with one's offspring, but the desire for self-preservation.[88]

The state of nature would be a state of peace and good will if men in the state of nature were under the law of nature. But "nobody can be under a law which is not promulgated to him." Man would know the law of nature in the state of nature if "the dictates of the law of nature" were "implanted in him" or "writ in the hearts of mankind." But no moral rules are "imprinted in our minds" or "written on [our] hearts" or "stamped upon [our] minds" or "implanted." Since there is no *habitus* of moral principles, no *synderesis* or conscience, all knowledge of the law of nature is acquired by study: to know the law of nature, one must be "a studier of that law." The law of nature becomes known only through demonstration. The question, therefore, is whether men in the state of nature are capable of becoming studiers of the law of nature. "The greatest part of mankind want leisure or capacity for demonstration. . . . And you may as soon hope to have all the day-

86. *Ibid.*, II, secs. 13, 74, 90, 91 and note, 94, 105, 123, 127, 128, 131, 135 n., 136, 212, 225–27.

87. *Ibid.*, secs. 32, 37, 38, 41–43, 49.

88. *Ibid.*, secs. 21, 74, 101, 105, 116, 127, 131 beginning, 132 beginning, 134 beginning (cf. 124 beginning), 211, 220, 243; cf. I, sec. 56, with sec. 88. Cf. both passages, as well as I, sec. 97, and II, secs. 60, 63, 67, 170, with *Essay*, I, 3, secs. 3, 9, 19.

labourers and tradesmen, and spinsters and dairy-maids, perfect mathematicians, as to have them perfect in ethics this way." Yet a day laborer in England is better off than a king of the Americans, and "in the beginning all the world was America, and more so than it is now." "The first ages" are characterized by "negligent and unforeseeing innocence" rather than by habits of study.[89] The condition in which man lives in the state of nature—"continual dangers" and "penury"—make impossible knowledge of the law of nature: the law of nature is not promulgated in the state of nature. Since the law of nature must be promulgated in the state of nature if it is to be a law in the proper sense of the term, we are again forced to conclude that the law of nature is not a law in the proper sense of the term.[90]

What, then, is the status of the law of nature in Locke's doctrine? What is its foundation? There is no rule of the law of nature which is innate, "that is, . . . imprinted on the mind as a duty." This is shown by the fact that there are no rules of the law of nature, "which, as practical principles ought, do continue constantly to operate and influence all our actions without ceasing [and which] may be observed in all persons and all ages, steady and universal." However, "Nature . . . has put into man a desire of happiness, and an aversion to misery; these, indeed, are innate practical principles": they are universally and unceasingly effective. The desire for happiness and the pursuit of happiness to which it gives rise are not duties. But "men . . . must be allowed to pursue their happiness, nay, cannot be hindered." The desire for happiness and the pursuit of happiness have the character of an absolute right, of a natural right. There is, then, an innate natural right, while

89. Cf., above all, *Treatises*, II, secs. 11 end, and 56, with *Essay*, I, 3, sec. 8, and I, 4, sec. 12; *Treatises*, II, secs. 6, 12, 41, 49, 57, 94, 107, 124, 136; *Essay*, I, 3, secs. 1, 6, 9, 11–13, 26, 27; *Reasonableness*, pp. 146, 139, 140. Cf. n. 74 above.

90. Cf. the use of the term "crime" (as distinguished from "sin ') in *Treatises*, II, secs. 10, 11, 87, 128, 218, 230, with *Essay*, II, 28, secs. 7–9.

there is no innate natural duty. To understand how this is possible, one merely has to reformulate our last quotation: pursuit of happiness is a right, it "must be allowed," because "it cannot be hindered." It is a right antedating all duties for the same reason that, according to Hobbes, establishes as the fundamental moral fact the right of self-preservation: man must be allowed to defend his life against violent death because he is driven to do so by some natural necessity which is not less than that by which a stone is carried downward. Being universally effective, natural right, as distinguished from natural duty, is effective in the state of nature: man in the state of nature is "absolute lord of his own person and possessions."[91] Since the right of nature is innate, whereas the law of nature is not, the right of nature is more fundamental than the law of nature and is the foundation of the law of nature.

Since happiness presupposes life, the desire for life takes precedence over the desire for happiness in case of conflict. This dictate of reason is at the same time a natural necessity: "the first and strongest desire God planted in men, and wrought into the very principles of their nature, is that of self-preservation." The most fundamental of all rights is therefore the right of self-preservation. While nature has put into man "a strong desire of preserving his life and being," it is only man's reason which teaches him what is "necessary and useful to his being." And reason—or, rather, reason applied to a subject to be specified presently—is the law of nature. Reason teaches that "he that is master of himself and his own life has a right, too, to the means of preserving it." Reason further teaches that, since all men are equal in regard to the desire, and hence to the right, of self-preservation, they are equal in the decisive respect, notwithstanding any natural inequalities

91. *Essay*, I, 3, secs. 3 and 12; *Reasonableness*, p. 148; *Treatises*, II, sec. 123 (cf. sec. 6). Cf. Hobbes, *De cive*, I, 7, and III, 27 n.

in other respects.[92] From this Locke concludes, just as Hobbes did, that in the state of nature everyone is the judge of what means are conducive to his self-preservation, and this leads him, as it did Hobbes, to the further conclusion that in the state of nature "any man may do what he thinks fit."[93] No wonder, therefore, that the state of nature is "full of fears and continual dangers." But reason teaches that life cannot be preserved, let alone enjoyed, except in a state of peace: reason wills peace. Reason therefore wills such courses of action as are conducive to peace. Reason dictates, accordingly, that "no one ought to harm another," that he who harms another—who therefore has renounced reason—may be punished by everyone and that he who is harmed may take reparations. These are the fundamental rules of the law of nature on which the argument of the *Treatise* is based: the law of nature is nothing other than the sum of the dictates of reason in regard to men's "mutual security" or to "the peace and safety" of mankind. Since in the state of nature all men are judges in their own cases and since, therefore, the state of nature is characterized by constant conflict that arises from the very law of nature, the state of nature is "not to be endured": the only remedy is government or civil society. Reason accordingly dictates how civil society must be constructed and what its rights or bounds are: there is a rational public law or a natural constitutional law. The principle of that public law is that all social or governmental power is derivative from powers which by nature belong to the individuals. The contract of the individuals actually con-

92. *Treatises*, I, secs. 86–88, 90 beginning, 111 toward the end; II, secs. 6, 54, 149, 168, 172. One may describe the relation of the right of self-preservation to the right to the pursuit of happiness as follows: the former is the right to "subsist" and implies the right to what is necessary to man's being; the second is the right to "enjoy the conveniences of life" or to "comfortable preservation" and implies, therefore, also the right to what is useful to man's being without being necessary for it (cf. *Treatises*, I, secs. 86, 87, 97; II, secs. 26, 34, 41).

93. *Ibid.*, II, secs. 10, 13, 87, 94, 105, 129, 168, 171.

cerned with their self-preservation—not the contract of the fathers qua fathers or divine appointment or an end of man that is independent of the actual wills of all individuals—creates the whole power of society: "the supreme power in every commonwealth [is] but the joint power of every member of the society."[94]

Locke's natural law teaching can then be understood perfectly if one assumes that the laws of nature which he admits are, as Hobbes put it, "but conclusions, or theorems concerning what conduces to the conservation and defense" of man over against other men. And it must be thus understood, since the alternative view is exposed to the difficulties which have been set forth. The law of nature, as Locke conceives of it, formulates the conditions of peace or, more generally stated, of "public happiness" or "the prosperity of any people." There is therefore a kind of sanction for the law of nature in this world: the disregard of the law of nature leads to public misery and penury. But this sanction is insufficient. Universal compliance with the law of nature would indeed guarantee perpetual peace and prosperity everywhere on earth. Failing such universal compliance, however, it may well happen that a society which complies with the law of nature enjoys less of temporal happiness than a society which transgresses the law of nature. For in both foreign and domestic affairs victory does not always favor "the right side": the "great robbers . . . are too big for the weak hands of justice in this world." There remains, however, at least this difference between those who strictly comply with the law of nature and those who do not, that only the former can act and speak consistently; only the former can consistently maintain that there is a fundamental difference between civil societies and gangs of robbers, a distinction to which every society and every government is forced to appeal time and again. In a word, the law of nature

94. *Ibid.*, secs. 4, 6–11, 13, 96, 99, 127–30, 134, 135, 142, 159.

is "a creature of the understanding rather than a work of nature"; it is "barely in the mind," a "notion," and not "in the things themselves." This is the ultimate reason why ethics can be raised to the rank of a demonstrative science.[95]

One cannot clarify the status of the law of nature without considering the status of the state of nature. Locke is more definite than Hobbes in asserting that men actually lived in the state of nature or that the state of nature is not merely a hypothetical assumption.[96] By this he means, in the first place, that men actually lived, and may live, without being subject to a common superior on earth. He means, furthermore, that men living in that condition, who are studiers of the law of nature, would know how to set about remedying the inconveniences of their condition and to lay the foundations for public happiness. But only such men could know the law of nature while living in a state of nature who have already lived in civil society, or rather in a civil society in which reason has been properly cultivated. An example of men who are in the state of nature under the law of nature would therefore be an elite among the English colonists in America rather than the wild Indians. A better example would be that of any highly civilized men after the breakdown of their society. It is only one step from this to the view that the most obvious example

95. *Ibid.*, secs. 1, 12, 176–77, 202; *Essay*, III, 5, sec. 12, and IV, 12, secs. 7–9 (cf. Spinoza, *Ethics*, IV, praef. and 18 schol.). As for the element of legal fiction involved in "the law of nature and reason," cf. *Treatises*, II, sec. 98 beginning, with sec. 96. Cf. *Reasonableness*, p. 11: "the law of reason, or, as it is called, the law of nature." Cf. also Section A, n. 8 above, and nn. 113 and 119 below. Hobbes, *De cive*, Ep. ded., and *Leviathan*, chap. xv (96 and 104–5).

96. Cf. *Leviathan*, chap. xiii (83)—see also the Latin version—with *Treatises*, II, secs. 14, 100–103, 110. The reason for Locke's deviation from Hobbes is that, according to Hobbes, the state of nature is worse than any kind of government, whereas, according to Locke, the state of nature is preferable to arbitrary and lawless government. Hence Locke teaches that the state of nature is more viable from the point of view of sensible men than "absolute monarchy": the state of nature must be, or have been, actual.

of men in the state of nature under the law of nature is that of men living in civil society, in so far as they reflect on what they could justly demand from civil society or on the conditions under which civil obedience would be reasonable. Thus it becomes ultimately irrelevant whether the state of nature understood as a state in which men are subject only to the law of nature, and not to any common superior on earth, was ever actual or not.[97]

It is on the basis of Hobbes's view of the law of nature that Locke opposes Hobbes's conclusions. He tries to show that Hobbes's principle—the right of self-preservation—far from favoring absolute government, requires limited government. Freedom, "freedom from arbitrary, absolute power," is "the fence" to self-preservation. Slavery is therefore against natural law except as a substitute for capital punishment. Nothing which is incompatible with the basic right of self-preservation, and hence nothing to which a rational creature cannot be supposed to have given free consent, can be just; hence civil society or government cannot be established lawfully by force or conquest: consent alone "did or could give beginning to any lawful government in the world." For the same reason Locke condemns absolute monarchy or, more precisely, "absolute arbitrary power . . . of any one or more" as well as "governing without settled standing laws."[98] In spite of the limitations which Locke demands, the commonwealth remains for him, as it was for Hobbes, "the mighty leviathan": in entering civil society, "men give up all their natural power to the society which they enter into." Just as Hobbes did, so Locke admits only one contract: the contract of union which every

97. Cf. *Treatises*, II, secs. 111, 121, 163; cf. Hobbes, *De cive*, praef.: "in jure civitatis, civiumque officiis investigandis opus est, non quidem ut dissolvatur civitas, sed tamen ut tamquam dissoluta consideretur."

98. *Treatises*, I, secs. 33 and 41; II, secs. 13, 17, 23, 24, 85, 90–95, 99, 131, 132, 137, 153, 175–76, 201–2; cf. Hobbes, *De cive*, V, 12, and VIII, 1–5.

individual makes with every other individual of the same multitude is identical with the contract of subjection. Just as Hobbes did, so Locke teaches that, by virtue of the fundamental contract, every man "puts himself under an obligation to everyone of that society to submit to the determination of the majority, and to be concluded by it"; that, therefore, the fundamental contract establishes immediately an unqualified democracy; that this primary democracy may by majority vote either continue itself or transform itself into another form of government; and that the social contract is therefore in fact identical with a contract of subjection to the "sovereign" (Hobbes) or to the "supreme power" (Locke) rather than to society.[99] Locke opposes Hobbes by teaching that wherever "the people" or "the community," i.e., the majority, have placed the supreme power, they still retain "a supreme power to remove or alter" the established government, i.e., they still retain a right of revolution.[100] But this power (which is normally dormant) does not qualify the subjection of the individual to the community or society. On the contrary, it is only fair to say that Hobbes stresses more strongly than does Locke the individual's right to resist society or the government whenever his self-preservation is endangered.[101]

99. *Treatises*, II, secs. 89, 95–99, 132, 134, 136; Hobbes, *De cive*, V, 7; VI, 2, 3, 17; VIII, 5, 8, 11; cf. also *Leviathan*, chaps. xviii (115) and xix (126).

100. *Treatises*, II, secs. 149, 168, 205, 208, 209, 230. Locke teaches, on the one hand, that society can exist without government (*ibid.*, secs. 121 end and 211) and, on the other hand, that society cannot exist without government (*ibid.*, secs. 205 and 219). The contradiction disappears if one considers the fact that society exists, and acts, without government only in the moment of revolution. If society, or "the people," could not exist and hence not act while there is no government, i.e., no lawful government, there could be no action of "the people" against the *de facto* government. The revolutionary action thus understood is a kind of majority decision which establishes a new legislative or supreme power in the very moment in which it abolishes the old one.

101. In accordance with this, Locke asserts more emphatically than did Hobbes the individual's duty of military service (cf. *Treatises*, II, secs. 88, 130, 168, 205, and 208, with *Leviathan*, chaps. xxi [142–43], xiv [86–87], and xxviii [202]).

Locke would nevertheless have been justified in contending that the mighty leviathan, as he had constructed it, offered a greater guarantee for the individual's self-preservation than Hobbes's Leviathan. The individual's right of resistance to organized society, which Hobbes had stressed and which Locke did not deny, is an ineffectual guaranty for the individual's self-preservation.[102] Since the only alternative to pure anarchy—to a condition in which everyone's self-preservation is in continual danger—is that "men give up all their natural power to the society which they enter into"; the only effective guaranty for the rights of the individual is that society be so constructed as to be incapable of oppressing its members: only a society or a government thus constructed is legitimate or in accordance with natural law; only such a society can justly demand that the individual surrender to it all his natural power. According to Locke, the best institutional safeguards for the rights of the individuals are supplied by a constitution that, in practically all domestic matters, strictly subordinates the executive power (which must be strong) to law, and ultimately to a well-defined legislative assembly. The legislative assembly must be limited to the making of laws as distinguished from "extemporary, arbitrary decrees"; its members must be elected by the people for fairly short periods of tenure and therefore be "themselves subject to the laws they have made"; the electoral system must take account of both numbers and wealth.[103] For, although Locke seems to have thought that the individual's self-preservation is less seriously threatened by the majority than by monarchic or oligarchic rulers, he cannot be said to have had an implicit faith in the majority as a guarantor of the rights of the individual.[104] In the pas-

102. *Treatises*, II, secs. 168 and 208.

103. *Ibid.*, secs. 94, 134, 136, 142, 143, 149, 150, 153, 157–59.

104. See the examples of tyranny mentioned in *Treatises*, II, sec. 201: no example of tyranny by the majority is given. Cf. also Locke's remarks on the character of the people, *ibid.*, sec. 223: the people are "slow" rather than "unsteady."

sages in which he seems to describe the majority as such a guarantor, he is speaking of cases in which the individuals' self-preservation is threatened by tyrannical monarchic or oligarchic rulers and wherein, therefore, the last and only hope for the suffering individual obviously rests on the dispositions of the majority. Locke regarded the power of the majority as a check on bad government and a last resort against tyrannical government; he did not regard it as a substitute for government or as identical with government. Equality, he thought, is incompatible with civil society. The equality of all men in regard to the right of self-preservation does not obliterate completely the special right of the more reasonable men. On the contrary, the exercise of that special right is conducive to the self-preservation and happiness of all. Above all, since self-preservation and happiness require property, so much so that the end of civil society can be said to be the preservation of property, the protection of the propertied members of society against the demands of the indigent —or the protection of the industrious and rational against the lazy and quarrelsome—is essential to public happiness or the common good.[105]

Locke's doctrine of property, which is almost literally the central part of his political teaching, is certainly its most characteristic part.[106] It distinguishes his political teaching most clearly not only from that of Hobbes but from the traditional teachings as well. Being a part of his natural law teaching, it partakes of all the complexities of the latter. Its peculiar difficulty can be provisionally stated as follows: Property is an institution of natural law; natural law defines the manner and

105. *Ibid.*, secs. 34, 54, 82, 94, 102, 131, 157–58.

106. After I had finished this chapter, my attention was drawn to C. B. Macpherson's article, "Locke on Capitalist Appropriation," *Western Political Quarterly*, 1951, pp. 550–66. There is considerable agreement between Mr. Macpherson's interpretation of the chapter on property and the interpretation set forth in the text. Cf. *American Political Science Review*, 1950, pp. 767–70.

the limitations of just appropriation. Men own property prior to civil society; they enter civil society in order to preserve or protect the property which they acquired in the state of nature. But, once civil society is formed, if not before, the natural law regarding property ceases to be valid; what we may call "conventional" or "civil" property—the property which is owned within civil society—is based on positive law alone. Yet, while civil society is the creator of civil property, it is not its master: civil society must respect civil property; civil society has, as it were, no other function but to serve its own creation. Locke claims for civil property a much greater sanctity than for natural property, i.e., the property which is acquired and owned exclusively on the basis of natural law, of "the highest law." Why, then, is he so anxious to prove that property antedates civil society?[107]

The natural right to property is a corollary of the fundamental right of self-preservation; it is not derivative from compact, from any action of society. If everyone has the natural right to preserve himself, he necessarily has the right to everything that is necessary for his self-preservation. What is necessary for self-preservation is not so much, as Hobbes may seem to have believed, knives and guns as victuals. Food is conducive to self-preservation only if it is eaten, i.e., appropriated in such a manner that it becomes the exclusive property of the individual; there is then a natural right to some "private dominion exclusive of the rest of mankind." What is true of food applies *mutatis mutandis* to all other things required for

107. "There seems some inconsistency between this acceptance of 'consent' as the basis of actual property rights and the theory that government exists for the purpose of defending the natural right of property. Locke would doubtless have solved the contradiction by passing, as he constantly does, from the phraseology of the 'law of nature' to utilitarian considerations" (R. H. I. Palgrave, *Dictionary of Political Economy, s.v.* "Locke"). Locke does not have to "pass" from the law of nature to utilitarian considerations because the law of nature, as he understands it, namely, as the formulation of the conditions of peace and public happiness, is in itself "utilitarian."

self-preservation and even for comfortable self-preservation, for man has a natural right not only to self-preservation but to the pursuit of happiness as well.

The natural right of everyone to appropriate everything that is useful to him must be limited if it is not to be incompatible with the peace and preservation of mankind. That natural right must exclude any right to appropriate things which have already been appropriated by others; taking things which others have appropriated, i.e., harming others, is against the natural law. Nor does natural law encourage begging; need as such is not a title to property. Persuasion gives as little a title to property as does force. The only honest way of appropriating things is by taking them, not from other men, but directly from nature, "the common mother of all"; by making one's own what previously belonged to no one and therefore might be taken by anyone; the only honest way of appropriating things is by one's own labor. Everyone is by nature the exclusive owner of his body and hence of the work of his body, i.e., of his labor. Therefore, if a man mixes his labor—be it only the labor involved in picking berries—with things of which no one is the owner, those things become an indissoluble mixture of his exclusive property with no one's property, and therefore they become his exclusive property. Labor is the only title to property which is in accordance with natural right. "Man, by being master of himself and proprietor of his own person and the actions or labour of it, [has] in himself the great foundation of property."[108] Not society, but the individual—the individual prompted by his self-interest alone—is the originator of property.

Nature has set "a measure of property": there are natural law limitations to what a man may appropriate. Everyone may appropriate by his labor as much as is necessary and useful for his self-preservation. He may therefore appropriate in par-

108. *Treatises*, II, secs. 26–30, 34, 44.

ticular as much land as he can use for tilling or grazing. If he has more than he can use of one kind of things (*a*) and less than he can use of another kind (*b*), he could make *a* useful to himself by bartering it away from *b*. Hence every man may appropriate by his labor not only what is in itself useful to him but also what could become useful to him if bartered away for other useful things. Man may appropriate by his labor all those things, but only those things, which are, or may become, useful to him; he may not appropriate things which through his appropriating them would cease to be useful; he may appropriate as much as he "can make use of to any advantage of life before it spoils." He may therefore accumulate many more nuts which "last good for his eating a whole year" than plums which would "rot in a week." As for things which never spoil and, in addition, are of no "real use," such as gold, silver, and diamonds, he may "heap" as much of them as he pleases. For it is not "the largeness" of what a man appropriates by his labor (or by bartering the products of his labor) but "the perishing anything uselessly in [his] possession" which makes him guilty of a crime against the natural law. He may therefore accumulate very little of perishable and useful things. He may accumulate very much of durable and useful things. He may accumulate infinitely much of gold and silver.[109] The terrors of the natural law no longer strike the covetous, but the waster. The natural law regarding property is concerned with the prevention of waste; in appropriating things by his labor, man must think exclusively of the prevention of waste; he does not have to think of other human beings.[110] *Chacun pour soi; Dieu pour nous tous.*

The law of nature regarding property, as hitherto summa-

109. *Ibid.*, secs. 31, 37, 38, 46.

110. Cf. *Ibid.*, secs. 40–44, with Cicero *Offices* ii. 12–14: the same type of example which Cicero uses for proving the virtue of man's helping man is used by Locke for proving the virtue of labor.

rized, applies only to the state of nature or to a certain stage of the state of nature. It is the "original law of nature" which obtained "in the first ages of the world" or "in the beginning."[111] And it obtained in that remote past only because the conditions in which men then lived required it. The law of nature could remain silent about the interests or needs of other men because these needs were taken care of by "the common mother of all"; however much a man might appropriate by his labor, there was "enough and as good left in common for others." The original law of nature was the dictate of reason in the beginning, because in the beginning the world was sparsely populated and there was "plenty of natural provisions."[112] This cannot mean that early men lived in a state of abundance showered upon them by their common mother; for if this had been the case, man would not have been compelled from the very beginning to work for his living, and the law of nature would not have prohibited so sternly every kind of waste. The natural plenty is only a potential plenty: "nature and the earth furnished only the almost worthless materials as in themselves"; they furnished "acorn, water, and leaves, or skins," the food and drink and clothing of the golden age or of the Garden of Eden, as distinguished from "bread, wine, and cloth." The natural plenty, the plenty of the first ages, never became actual plenty during the first ages; it was actual penury. This being the case, it was plainly impossible for man to appropriate by his labor more than the bare necessities of life or what was absolutely necessary for mere self-preservation (as distinguished from comfortable self-preservation); the natural right to comfortable self-preservation was illusory. But precisely for this reason, every man was forced to appropriate by his labor what he needed for his self-preservation without any

111. *Treatises*, II, secs. 30, 36, 37, 45. Consider the transition from the present tense to the past tense in secs. 32–51; consider especially sec. 51.

112. *Ibid.*, secs. 27, 31, 33, 34, 36.

concern for other men. For man is obliged to be concerned with the preservation of others only if and when "his own preservation comes not in competition."[113] Locke explicitly justifies man's natural right to appropriate and to own without concern for the needs of others by referring to the plenty of natural provisions which was available in the beginning; but such unconcern can be justified equally well on his principles if one assumes that men lived in a state of penury; and it must be justified in the latter manner, since Locke says that the only men to whom the original law of nature applied lived in a state of penury. It is the poverty of the first ages of the world which explains why the original law of nature (1) commanded appropriation by labor alone, (2) commanded the prevention of waste, and (3) permitted unconcern for the need of other human beings. Appropriation without concern for the need of others is simply justified because it is justified regardless of whether men lived in a state of plenty or in a state of penury.

Let us now consider that form of the law of nature regarding property which has taken the place of the original law of nature, or which regulates property within civil society. According to the original law of nature, man may appropriate by his labor as much as he can use before it spoils; no other limita-

113. *Ibid.*, secs. 6, 32, 37, 41, 42, 43, 49, 107, 110. Locke says that early men did not desire to have "more than man needed." But one must wonder whether "the needy and wretched" individuals who peopled the earth in the beginning always had what man needs. For the reason given in the text, man must have the natural right to appropriate by his labor what he needs for his self-preservation, regardless of whether or not there is enough left for others. The same reasoning seems to lead to the further conclusion that lawful appropriation cannot be limited to appropriation by labor; for in a state of extreme scarcity everyone may take away from others what he needs for mere self-preservation, regardless of whether or not the others starve. But this merely means that in a condition of extreme scarcity peace is altogether impossible, and natural law formulates how men have to act for the sake of peace, if peace is not altogether impossible: the natural law regarding property necessarily remains within the limits set to the law of nature as such. But in the misty wilds that stretch out beyond those limits, there exists merely the right of self-preservation, which is as precarious there as it is everywhere indefeasible.

tions are required because there is enough and as good left for others which has not yet been appropriated by anyone. According to the original law of nature, man may appropriate by his labor as much gold and silver as he pleases because these things are of no value in themselves.[114] In civil society almost everything has been appropriated; land in particular has become scarce. Gold and silver are not only scarce but, through the invention of money, they have become "so valuable to be hoarded up."[115] One should therefore expect that the original law of nature has been replaced by rules imposing much severer restrictions on appropriation than those which existed in the state of nature.[116] Since there is no longer enough and as good left in common for everyone, equity would seem to demand that man's natural right to appropriate as much as he can use should be restricted to the right to appropriate as much as he needs, lest the poor be "straitened." And, since gold and silver are now immensely valuable, equity would seem to demand that man should lose the natural right to accumulate as much money as he pleases. Yet Locke teaches exactly the opposite: the right to appropriate is much more restricted in the state of nature than in civil society. One privilege enjoyed by man in the state of nature is indeed denied to man living in civil society: labor no longer creates a sufficient title to property.[117] But this loss is only a part of the enormous gain which the right of appropriation makes after "the first ages" have come to their end. In civil society the right of appropriation is completely freed from the shackles by which it

114. *Ibid.*, secs. 33, 34, 37, 46.

115. *Ibid.*, secs. 45 and 48.

116. "The obligations of the law of nature cease not in society but only *in many cases* are drawn closer" (*ibid.*, sec. 135) (the italics are not in the original). The case of property does not belong to the "many cases" of which Locke speaks.

117. "Labour, *in the beginning*, gave a right to property" (*ibid.*, sec. 45); "labour could *at first begin* a title of property" (sec. 51); cf. also secs. 30 and 35 (the italics are not in the original).

was still fettered under Locke's original law of nature: the introduction of money has introduced "larger possessions and a right to them"; man may now "rightfully and without injury, possess more than he himself can make use of."[118] Although Locke stresses the fact that the invention of money has revolutionized property, he does not say a word to the effect that the natural right to heap as much gold and silver as one pleases has been affected by that revolution. According to the natural law—and this means according to the moral law—man in civil society may acquire as much property of every kind, and in particular as much money, as he pleases; and he may acquire it in every manner permitted by the positive law, which keeps the peace among the competitors and in the interest of the competitors. Even the natural law prohibition against waste is no longer valid in civil society.[119]

118. *Ibid.*, secs. 36, 48, 50.

119. Luigi Cossa, *An Introduction to the Study of Political Economy* (London, 1893), p. 242: Locke "escapes, by roundly asserting the productive power of labour, the old error of Hobbes, who counted the soil and thrift as components of production." According to Locke, the original law of nature regarding property remains valid in relations between civil societies, for "all commonwealths are in the state of nature one with another" (*Treatises*, II, secs. 183 and 184; cf. Hobbes, *De cive*, XIII, 11, and XIV, 4, as well as *Leviathan*, chaps. xiii [83] and xxx [226]). Hence the original law of nature determines the rights over the vanquished which the conqueror in a just war acquires; e.g., the conqueror in a just war does not acquire title to the landed property of the conquered, but he may take away their money as reparation for damages received, for "such riches and treasure . . . have but a fantastical imaginary value; nature has put no such upon them" (*Treatises*, II, secs. 180-84). In making this statement, Locke is not oblivious of the fact that money is immensely valuable in civil societies and that conquest presupposes the existence of civil societies. The difficulty is resolved by the following consideration: The primary function of Locke's disquisition on conquest is to show that conquest cannot give title to lawful government. He had, therefore, to show in particular that the conqueror does not become the lawful governor of the conquered by becoming the proprietor of their land; hence he had to stress the essential difference between land and money and the greater value for self-preservation of the former. Furthermore, he speaks in this context of a situation where trade and industry have come to a standstill, and not comfortable self-preservation but bare self-preservation (of the innocent part of the conquered people) is at stake. This situation is radically different from the situation which exists in the state of nature proper: in the former situa-

Locke does not commit the absurdity of justifying the emancipation of acquisitiveness by appealing to a nonexistent absolute right of property. He justifies the emancipation of acquisitiveness in the only way in which it can be defended: he shows that it is conducive to the common good, to public happiness or the temporal prosperity of society. Restrictions on acquisitiveness were required in the state of nature because the state of nature is a state of penury. They can safely be abandoned in civil society because civil society is a state of plenty: ". . . a king of a large and fruitful territory [in America] feeds, lodges, and is clad worse than a day-labourer in England."[120] The day laborer in England has no natural right even to complain about the loss of his natural right to appropriate land and other things by his labor: the exercise of all the rights and privileges of the state of nature would give him less wealth than he gets by receiving "subsistence" wages for his work. Far from being straitened by the emancipation of acquisitiveness, the poor are enriched by it. For the emancipation of acquisitiveness is not merely compatible with general

---

tion, the conqueror "hath, and to spare" and there is nothing left in common for use by the conquered; the conqueror is therefore under an obligation to be charitable (*Treatises*, II, sec. 183); but in the state of nature proper, either no one "hath, and to spare" or else there is enough left in common for other men. Locke refrains from discussing what conquerors may do if they do not "have, and to spare," or, in other words, "when all the world is overcharged with inhabitants." Since, according to his principles, the conquerors are under no obligation to consider the claims of the conquered if their own preservation comes into competition, he must have answered that question as Hobbes did: "then the last remedy of all is war; which provideth for every man, by victory, or death" (*Leviathan*, chap. xxx [227]; cf. *De cive*, Ep. ded.).

120. *Treatises*, II, sec. 41. "I look on a right of property—on the right of the individuals, to have and to own, for their own separate and selfish use and enjoyment, the produce of their own industry, with power freely to dispose of the whole of that in the manner most agreeable to themselves, as essential to the welfare and even to the continued existence of society . . . believing . . . with Mr. Locke that nature establishes such a right" (Thomas Hodgskin, *The Natural and Artificial Right of Property Contrasted* [1832], p. 24; quoted from W. Stark, *The Ideal Foundations of Economic Thought* [London, 1943], p. 59).

plenty but is the cause of it. Unlimited appropriation without concern for the need of others is true charity.

Labor no doubt supplies the original title to property. But labor is also the origin of almost all value: "labour makes the far greatest part of the value of things we enjoy in this world." Labor ceases to supply a title to property in civil society; but it remains, what it always has been, the origin of value or of wealth. Labor is eventually important, not as creating a title to property, but as the origin of wealth. What, then, is the cause of labor? What is it that induces men to work? Man is induced to work by his wants, his selfish wants. Yet what he needs for his bare self-preservation is very little and therefore does not require much work; the picking-up of acorns and the gathering of apples from trees suffice. Real work—the improvement of the spontaneous gifts of nature—presupposes that man is not satisfied with what he needs. His appetites will not be enlarged if his views are not enlarged first. The men of larger views are "the rational," who are a minority. Real work presupposes, furthermore, that man is willing and able to undergo the present hardship of work for the sake of future convenience; and "the industrious" are a minority. "The lazy and inconsiderate part of men" makes "the far greater number." The production of wealth requires, therefore, that the industrious and rational, who work hard spontaneously, take the lead and force the lazy and inconsiderate to work against their will, if for their own good. The man who works hard at improving the gifts of nature in order to have not merely what he needs but what he can use, and for no other reason, "does not lessen but increase the common stock of mankind." He is a greater benefactor of mankind than those who give alms to the poor; the latter lessen rather than increase the common stock of mankind. More than that. By appropriating as much as they can use, the industrious and rational reduce the extent of "the great commons of the world" which lies waste; through "such enclosure," they create a kind of scarcity which forces the lazy and inconsiderate to work much harder than they otherwise would and thus to improve their own condition by improving the condition of all. But real plenty will not be produced if the individual does not have an incentive to appropriate more than he can use. Even the industrious and rational will relapse into the drowsy laziness so characteristic of early man, as long as their *amor habendi* can have no other objects than things which are useful in themselves, like fertile land, useful animals, and commodious houses. The labor required for creating plenty will not be forthcoming if there exists no money: "Find out something that hath the use and value of money among his neighbours, you shall see the same man will begin presently to enlarge his possessions" "beyond the use of his family and a plentiful supply to its consumption." While labor is then the necessary cause of plenty, it is not its sufficient cause; the incentive to that labor which is productive of real plenty is the acquisitiveness—the desire for having more than man can use—which comes into being through the invention of money. We must add the remark that that which money began comes to its fruition only through the discoveries and inventions fostered by natural science: "the study of nature . . . may be of greater benefit to mankind than the monuments of exemplary charity that have, at so great charge, been raised by the founders of hospitals and alms-houses. He that first . . . made public the virtue and right use of *kin-kina* . . . saved more from the grave, than those who built . . . hospitals."[121]

If the end of government is nothing but "the peace, the safety, and public good of the people"; if peace and safety are the indispensable conditions of plenty, and the public good of

121. *Treatises*, II, secs. 34, 37, 38, 40–44, 48–49; *Essay*, I, 4, sec. 15, and IV, 12, sec. 12; cf. Hobbes, *Leviathan*, chap. xxiv: "Money the blood of a commonwealth."

the people is identical with plenty; if the end of government is therefore plenty; if plenty requires the emancipation of acquisitiveness; and if acquisitiveness necessarily withers away whenever its rewards do not securely belong to those who deserve them—if all this is true, it follows that the end of civil society is "the preservation of property." "The great and chief end . . . of men's uniting into commonwealths and putting themselves under government is the preservation of their property." By this central statement Locke does not mean that men enter civil society in order to preserve those "narrow bounds of each man's small property" within which their desires were confined by "the simple, poor way of living" "in the beginning of things" or in the state of nature. Men enter society in order not so much to preserve as to enlarge their possessions. The property which is to be "preserved" by civil society is not "static" property—the small farm which one has inherited from one's fathers and which one will hand down to one's children—but "dynamic" property. Locke's thought is perfectly expressed by Madison's statement: "The protection of [different and unequal faculties of *acquiring* property] is the first object of government."[122]

It is one thing to say that the end of government or of society is the preservation of property or the protection of the unequal acquisitive faculties; it is an entirely different thing and, as it would seem, an entirely superfluous thing to say, as Locke does, that property antedates society. Yet, by saying that property antedates civil society, Locke says that even civil property—the property owned on the basis of positive law—is in the decisive respect independent of society: it is not the creation of society. "Man," i.e., the individual, has "still in himself the great foundation of property." Property is cre-

122. *Treatises*, II, secs. 42, 107, 124, 131; *The Federalist*, No. 10 (the italics are not in the original). Cf. n. 104 above.

ated by the individual and in different degrees by different individuals. Civil society merely creates the conditions under which the individuals can pursue their productive-acquisitive activity without obstruction.

Locke's doctrine of property is directly intelligible today if it is taken as the classic doctrine of "the spirit of capitalism" or as a doctrine regarding the chief objective of public policy. Since the nineteenth century, readers of Locke have found it hard to understand why he used "the phraseology of the law of nature" or why he stated his doctrine in terms of natural law. But to say that public happiness requires the emancipation and the protection of the acquisitive faculties amounts to saying that to accumulate as much money and other wealth as one pleases is right or just, i.e., intrinsically just or by nature just. And the rules which enable us to distinguish between what is by nature just and by nature unjust, either absolutely or under specific conditions, were called the "propositions of the law of nature." Locke's followers in later generations no longer believed that they needed "the phraseology of the law of nature" because they took for granted what Locke did not take for granted: Locke still thought that he had to prove that the unlimited acquisition of wealth is not unjust or morally wrong.

It was indeed easy for Locke to see a problem where later men saw only an occasion for applauding progress or themselves, since in his age most people still adhered to the older view according to which the unlimited acquisition of wealth is unjust or morally wrong. This also explains why, in stating his doctrine of property, Locke "so involved his sense, that it is not easy to understand him" or went as much as possible "with the herd." While therefore concealing the revolutionary character of his doctrine of property from the mass of his readers, he yet indicated it clearly enough. He did this by occasionally mentioning and apparently approving the older view. He traced the introduction of "larger possessions and a right to them" to "the desire of having more than man" needs, or to an increase in "covetousness," or to "*amor scelera-tus habendi*, evil concupiscence." In the same vein he speaks disparagingly of "little pieces of yellow metal" and of "sparkling pebbles."[123] But he soon drops these *niaiseries:* the burden of his chapter on property is that covetousness and concupiscence, far from being essentially evil or foolish, are, if properly channeled, eminently beneficial and reasonable, much more so than "exemplary charity." By building civil society on "the low but solid ground" of selfishness or of certain "private vices," one will achieve much greater "public benefits" than by futilely appealing to virtue, which is by nature "unendowed." One must take one's bearings not by how men should live but by how they do live. Locke almost quotes the words of the apostle, "God who giveth us richly all things to enjoy," and he speaks of "God's blessings poured on [man] with a liberal hand," and yet "nature and the earth furnish only the almost worthless materials as in themselves."[124] He says that God is "sole lord and proprietor of the whole world," that men are God's property, and that "man's propriety in the creatures is nothing but that liberty to use them which God has permitted"; but he also says that "man in the state of nature [is] absolute lord of his own person and possessions."[125] He

123. *Treatises*, II, secs. 37, 46, 51 end, 75, 111.

124. *Ibid.*, I, secs. 40, 43; II, secs. 31, 43. Cf. Locke's statements about the relative importance of the gifts of nature and human labor with a statement from Ambrose's *Hexaemeron*, translated by George Boas, in *Essays on Primitivism and Related Ideas in the Middle Ages* (Baltimore: Johns Hopkins Press, 1948), p. 42.

125. *Treatises*, I, sec. 39; II, secs. 6, 27, 123. Incidentally, it may be remarked that if "man in the state of nature [is] absolute lord of his own . . . possessions" or if property is "for the benefit and sole advantage of the proprietor," the natural right of children "to inherit the goods of their parents" (*ibid.*, I, secs. 88, 93, 97; II, sec. 190) is subject to the crucial qualification that the children have this right if the parents do not dispose of their property otherwise, as they may, according to Locke (I, sec. 87; II, secs. 57, 65, 72, 116 end). The natural right of the children to inherit their parents' property amounts, then, merely to this, that if the parents die intestate, it is assumed that they would have preferred their children to strangers as heirs of their estate. Cf. I, sec. 89, with Hobbes, *De cive*, IX, 15.

says that "it will always be a sin in any man of estate to let his brother perish for want of affording him relief out of his plenty." But in his thematic discussion of property, he is silent about any duties of charity.[126]

Locke's teaching on property, and therewith his whole political philosophy, are revolutionary not only with regard to the biblical tradition but with regard to the philosophic tradition as well. Through the shift of emphasis from natural duties or obligations to natural rights, the individual, the ego, had become the center and origin of the moral world, since man—as distinguished from man's end—had become that center or origin. Locke's doctrine of property is a still more "advanced" expression of this radical change than was the political philosophy of Hobbes. According to Locke, man and not nature, the work of man and not the gift of nature, is the origin of almost everything valuable: man owes almost everything valuable to his own efforts. Not resigned gratitude and consciously obeying or imitating nature but hopeful self-reliance and creativity become henceforth the marks of human nobility. Man is effectively emancipated from the bonds of nature, and therewith the individual is emancipated from those social bonds which antedate all consent or compact, by the emancipation of his productive acquisitiveness, which is necessarily, if accidentally, beneficent and hence susceptible of becoming the strongest social bond: restraint of the appetites is replaced by a mechanism whose effect is humane. And that emancipation is achieved through the intercession of the prototype of conventional things, i.e., money. The world in which human creativity seems to reign supreme is, in fact, the world which has replaced the rule of nature by the rule of con-

126. *Treatises*, I, sec. 42 (as for the use of the term "sin," cf. n. 90 above). Cf. *ibid.*, sec. 92: "Property . . . is for the benefit and *sole* advantage of the proprietor" (the italics are not in the original). As regards the mention of the duty of charity in the chapter on conquest (ii, sec. 183), see n. 119 above. Cf. n. 73 above.

vention. From now on, nature furnishes only the worthless materials as in themselves; the forms are supplied by man, by man's free creation. For there are no natural forms, no intelligible "essences": "the abstract ideas" are "the inventions and creatures of the understanding, made by it for its own use." Understanding and science stand in the same relation to "the given" in which human labor, called forth to its supreme effort by money, stands to the raw materials. There are, therefore, no natural principles of understanding: all knowledge is acquired; all knowledge depends on labor and is labor.[127]

Locke is a hedonist: "That which is properly good or bad, is nothing but barely pleasure or pain." But his is a peculiar hedonism: "The greatest happiness consists" not in enjoying the greatest pleasures but "in the having those things which produce the greatest pleasures." It is not altogether an accident that the chapter in which these statements occur, and which happens to be the most extensive chapter of the whole *Essay*, is entitled "Power." For if, as Hobbes says, "the power of a man . . . is his present means, to obtain some future apparent good," Locke says in effect that the greatest happiness consists in the greatest power. Since there are no knowable natures, there is no nature of man with reference to which we could distinguish between pleasures which are according to nature and pleasures which are against nature, or between pleasures which are by nature higher and pleasures which are by nature lower: pleasure and pain are "for different men . . . very different things." Therefore, "the philosophers of old did in vain inquire, whether *summum bonum* consisted in riches, or bodily delights, or virtue, or contemplation?" In the absence of a *summum bonum*, man would lack completely a star and

127. Speaking of a concession which his opponents ought not to make, Locke says: "For this would be to destroy that *bounty of nature they seem so fond of*, whilst they make the knowledge of those principles to depend on the *labour* of our thoughts" (*Essay*, I, 2, sec. 10) (the italics are not in the original).

compass for his life if there were no *summum malum*. "Desire is always moved by evil, to fly it."[128] The strongest desire is the desire for self-preservation. The evil from which the strongest desire recoils is death. Death must then be the greatest evil: Not the natural sweetness of living but the terrors of death make us cling to life. What nature firmly establishes is that from which desire moves away, the point of departure of desire; the goal toward which desire moves is secondary. The primary fact is want. But this want, this lack, is no longer understood as pointing to something complete, perfect, whole. The necessities of life are no longer understood as necessary *for* the complete life or the good life, but as mere inescapabilities. The satisfaction of wants is therefore no longer limited by the demands of the good life but becomes aimless. The goal of desire is defined by nature only negatively—the denial of pain. It is not pleasure more or less dimly anticipated which elicits human efforts: "the chief, if not only, spur to human industry and action is uneasiness." So powerful is the natural primacy of pain that the active denial of pain is itself painful. The pain which removes pain is labor.[129] It is this pain, and hence a defect, which gives man originally the most important of all rights: sufferings and defects, rather than merits or virtues, originate rights. Hobbes identified the rational life with the life dominated by the fear of fear, by the fear which relieves us from fear. Moved by the same spirit, Locke identifies the rational life with the life dominated by the pain which relieves pain. Labor takes the place of the art which imitates nature; for labor is, in the words of Hegel, a negative attitude toward nature. The starting point of human efforts is misery: the state of nature is a state of wretchedness. The way toward happiness is a movement away from the state of nature, a movement away from nature: the negation of nature is the way

128. *Essay*, II, 21, secs. 55, 61, 71; chap. 20, sec. 6.
129. *Treatises*, II, secs. 30, 34, 37, 42.

toward happiness. And if the movement toward happiness is the actuality of freedom, freedom is negativity. Just like the primary pain itself, the pain which relieves pain "ceaseth only in death." Since there are therefore no pure pleasures, there is no necessary tension between civil society as the mighty leviathan or coercive society, on the one hand, and the good life, on the other: hedonism becomes utilitarianism or political hedonism. The painful relief of pain culminates not so much in the greatest pleasures as "in the having those things which produce the greatest pleasures." Life is the joyless quest for joy.

VI

THE CRISIS OF MODERN NATURAL RIGHT

�֎

A. ROUSSEAU

THE first crisis of modernity occurred in the thought of Jean-Jacques Rousseau. Rousseau was not the first to feel that the modern venture was a radical error and to seek the remedy in a return to classical thought. It suffices to mention the name of Swift. But Rousseau was not a "reactionary." He abandoned himself to modernity. One is tempted to say that only through thus accepting the fate of modern man was he led back to antiquity. At any rate, his return to antiquity was, at the same time, an advance of modernity. While appealing from Hobbes, Locke, or the Encyclopedists to Plato, Aristotle, or Plutarch, he jettisoned important elements of classical thought which his modern predecessors had still preserved. In Hobbes, reason, using her authority, had emancipated passion; passion acquired the status of a freed woman; reason continued to rule, if only by remote control. In Rousseau, passion itself took the initiative and rebelled; usurping the place of reason and indignantly denying her libertine past, passion began to pass judgment, in the severe accents of Catonic virtue, on reason's turpitudes. The fiery rocks with which the Rousseauan eruption had covered the Western world were used, after they had cooled and after they had been hewn, for the imposing structures which the great thinkers of the late eighteenth and early nineteenth centuries erected. His disciples clarified his views indeed, but one may wonder whether they preserved the breadth of his vision. His passionate and forceful attack on modernity in the name of what was at the same time

classical antiquity and a more advanced modernity was repeated, with no less passion and force, by Nietzsche, who thus
ushered in the second crisis of modernity—the crisis of our
time.

Rousseau attacked modernity in the name of two classical
ideas: the city and virtue, on the one hand, and nature, on the
other.[1] "The ancient politicians spoke unceasingly of manners and virtue; ours speak of nothing but trade and money."
Trade, money, enlightenment, the emancipation of acquisitiveness, luxury, and the belief in the omnipotence of legislation are characteristic of the modern state, be it the absolute
monarchy or the representative republic. Manners and virtue
are at home in the city. Geneva is a city, indeed, but it is less a
city than the cities of classical antiquity, especially Rome: in
his very eulogy of Geneva, Rousseau calls, not the Genevans,
but the Romans, the model of all free peoples and the most
respectable of all free peoples. The Romans are the most respectable of all peoples because they were the most virtuous,
the most powerful, and the freest people that ever were. The
Genevans are not Romans or Spartans or even Athenians, because they lack the public spirit or the patriotism of the ancients. They are more concerned with their private or domestic
affairs than with the fatherland. They lack the greatness of
soul of the ancients. They are bourgeois rather than citizens.
The sacred unity of the city has been destroyed in postclassical
times by the dualism of power temporal and power spiritual,

1. In the notes to this section, the following abbreviated forms of the titles are used:
"*D'Alembert*" = *Lettre à d'Alembert sur les spectacles*, ed. Léon Fontaine; "*Beaumont*" =
Lettre à M. de Beaumont (Garnier ed.); "*Confessions*" = *Les Confessions*, ed. Ad. Van
Bever; "*C.S.*" = *Contrat social;* "*First Discourse*" = *Discours sur les sciences et sur les arts*,
ed. G. R. Havens; "*Second Discourse*" = *Discours sur l'origine de l'inégalité* (Flammarion
ed.); "*Émile*" = *Émile* (Garnier ed.); "*Hachette*" = *Œuvres complètes*, Hachette ed.;
"*Julie*" = *Julie ou la Nouvelle Héloïse* (Garnier ed.); "*Montagne*" = *Lettres écrites de la
Montagne* (Garnier ed.); "*Narcisse*" = *Préface de Narcisse* (Flammarion ed.); "*Rêveries*" = *Les Rêveries du promeneur solitaire*, ed. Marcel Raymond.

and ultimately by the dualism of the earthly and the heavenly fatherland.[2]

The modern state presented itself as an artificial body which comes into being through convention and which remedies the deficiencies of the state of nature. For the critic of the modern state, therefore, a question arose as to whether the state of nature is not preferable to civil society. Rousseau suggested the return to the state of nature, the return to nature, from a world of artificiality and conventionality. Throughout his entire career, he never was content merely to appeal from the modern state to the classical city. He appealed almost in the same breath from the classical city itself to "the man of nature," the prepolitical savage.[3]

There is an obvious tension between the return to the city and the return to the state of nature. This tension is the substance of Rousseau's thought. He presents to his readers the confusing spectacle of a man who perpetually shifts back and forth between two diametrically opposed positions. At one moment he ardently defends the rights of the individual or the rights of the heart against all restraint and authority; at the next moment he demands with equal ardor the complete submission of the individual to society or the state and favors the most rigorous moral or social discipline. Today most serious students of Rousseau incline to the view that he eventually succeeded in overcoming what they regard as a temporary vacillation. The mature Rousseau, they hold, found a solution which he thought satisfied equally the legitimate claims of the

2. *First Discourse*, p. 134; *Narcisse*, pp. 53–54, 57 n.; *Second Discourse*, pp. 66, 67, 71–72; *D'Alembert*, pp. 192, 237, 278; *Julie*, pp. 112–13; *C.S.*, IV, 4, 8; *Montagne*, pp. 292–93. No modern thinker has understood better than Rousseau the philosophic conception of the *polis:* the *polis* is that complete association which corresponds to the natural range of man's power of knowing and of loving. See especially *Second Discourse*, pp. 65–66, and *C.S.*, II, 10.

3. *First Discourse*, pp. 102 n., 115 n., 140. "On me reproche d'avoir affecté de prendre chez les anciens mes examples de vertu. Il y a bien de l'apparence que j'en aurais trouvé encore davantage, si j'avais pu remonter plus haut" (Hachette, I, 35–36).

individual and those of society, the solution consisting in a certain type of society.[4] This interpretation is exposed to a decisive objection. Rousseau believed to the end that even the right kind of society is a form of bondage. Hence he cannot have regarded his solution to the problem of the conflict between the individual and society as more than a tolerable approximation to a solution—an approximation which remains open to legitimate doubts. The farewell to society, authority, restraint, and responsibility or the return to the state of nature remains therefore for him a legitimate possibility.[5] The question is, then, not how he solved the conflict between the individual and society but rather how he conceived of that insoluble conflict.

Rousseau's *First Discourse* provides a key to a more precise formulation of this question. In that earliest of his important writings he attacked the sciences and the arts in the name of virtue: the sciences and the arts are incompatible with virtue, and virtue is the only thing which matters.[6] Virtue apparently requires support by faith or theism, although not necessarily by monotheism.[7] Yet the emphasis rests on virtue itself. Rousseau indicates the meaning of virtue clearly enough for his purpose by referring to the examples of the citizen-philosopher Socrates, of Fabricius, and, above all, of Cato: Cato was "the greatest of men."[8] Virtue is primarily political virtue, the

4. The classic formulation of this interpretation of Rousseau is to be found in Kant's "Idee zu einer allgemeinen Geschichte in weltbürgerlicher Absicht," Siebenter Satz (*The Philosophy of Kant*, ed. Carl J. Friedrich ["Modern Library" ed.], pp. 123–27).

5. *C.S.*, I, 1; II, 7, 11; III, 15; *Émile*, I, 13–16, 79–80, 85; *Second Discourse*, pp. 65, 147, 150, 165.

6. *First Discourse*, pp. 97–98, 109–10, 116. Hachette, I, 55: Morality is infinitely more sublime than the marvels of the understanding.

7. *First Discourse*, pp. 122, 140–41; *Émile*, II, 51; *Julie*, pp. 502 ff., 603; *Montagne*, p. 180.

8. *First Discourse*, pp. 120–22; *Second Discourse*, p. 150; *Julie*, p. 325. Hachette, I, 45–46: Original equality is "the source of all virtue." *Ibid.*, p. 59: Cato has given the human race the spectacle and the model of the purest virtue which has ever existed.

virtue of the patriot or the virtue of a whole people. Virtue presupposes free society, and free society presupposes virtue: virtue and free society belong together.[9] Rousseau deviates from his classical models at two points. Following Montesquieu, he regards virtue as the principle of democracy: virtue is inseparable from equality or from the recognition of equality.[10] Secondly, he believes that the knowledge which is required for virtue is supplied, not by reason, but by what he calls the "conscience" (or "the sublime science of the simple souls") or by sentiment or by instinct. The sentiment which he has in mind will prove to be originally the sentiment of compassion, the natural root of all genuine beneficence. Rousseau saw a connection between his inclination toward democracy and his preference for sentiment above reason.[11]

Since Rousseau assumed that virtue and free society belong together, he could prove that science and virtue are incompatible by proving that science and free society are incompatible. The reasoning underlying the *First Discourse* can be reduced to five chief considerations, which are indeed only insufficiently developed in that work but which become sufficiently clear if, in reading the *First Discourse*, one takes into account Rousseau's later writings.[12]

9. *Narcisse*, pp. 54, 56, 57 n.; *Émile*, I, 308; *C.S.*, I, 8; *Confessions*, I, 244.

10. Hachette, I, 41, 45–46; *Second Discourse*, pp. 66, 143–44; *Montagne*, p. 252. Compare the quotation from Plato's *Apology of Socrates* (21ᵇ ff.) in the *First Discourse* (pp. 118–20) with the Platonic original: Rousseau fails to quote Socrates' censure of the (democratic or republican) statesmen; and he substitutes for Socrates' censure of the artisans a censure of the artists.

11. *First Discourse*, p. 162; *Second Discourse*, pp. 107–10; *Émile*, I, 286–87, 307; *Confessions*, I, 199; Hachette, I, 31, 35, 62–63.

12. This procedure is unobjectionable, since Rousseau himself said that he did not yet reveal his principles fully in the *First Discourse* and that that work is inadequate also for other reasons (*First Discourse*, pp. 51, 56, 92, 169–70); and, on the other hand, the *First Discourse* reveals more clearly than do the later writings the unity of Rousseau's fundamental conception.

According to Rousseau, civil society is essentially a particular or, more precisely, a closed society. Civil society, he holds, can be healthy only if it has a character of its own, and this requires that its individuality be produced or fostered by national and exclusive institutions. These institutions must be animated by a national "philosophy," by a way of thinking that is not transferable to other societies: "the philosophy of each people is little apt for another people." On the other hand, science or philosophy is essentially universal. Science or philosophy necessarily weakens the power of the national "philosophies" and therewith the attachment of the citizens to the particular way of life, or the manners, of their community. In other words, whereas science is essentially cosmopolitan, society must be animated by a spirit of patriotism, by a spirit which is by no means irreconcilable with national hatreds. Political society being a society that has to defend itself against other states, it must foster the military virtues, and it normally develops a warlike spirit. Philosophy or science, on the contrary, is destructive of the warlike spirit.[13] Furthermore, society requires that its members be fully devoted to the common good or that they be busy or active on behalf of their fellows: "Every idle citizen is a scoundrel." On the other hand, the element of science is admittedly leisure, which is falsely distinguished from idleness. In other words, the true citizen is devoted to duty, whereas the philosopher or scientist selfishly pursues his pleasure.[14] In addition, society requires that its members adhere without question to certain religious beliefs. These salutary certainties, "our dogmas" or "the sacred dogmas authorized by the laws," are endangered by

13. *First Discourse*, pp. 107, 121–23, 141–46; *Narcisse*, pp. 49 n., 51–52, 57 n.; *Second Discourse*, pp. 65–66, 134–35, 169–70; *C.S.*, II, 8 (toward the end); *Émile*, I, 13; *Gouvernement de Pologne*, chaps. ii and iii; *Montagne*, pp. 130–33.

14. *First Discourse*, pp. 101, 115, 129–32, 150; Hachette, I, 62; *Narcisse*, pp. 50–53; *Second Discourse*, p. 150; *D'Alembert*, pp. 120, 123, 137; *Julie*, p. 517; *Émile*, I, 248.

science. Science is concerned with truth as such, regardless of its utility, and thus by reason of its intention is exposed to the danger of leading to useless or even harmful truths. In fact, however, the truth is inaccessible, and therefore the quest for truth leads to dangerous error or to dangerous skepticism. The element of society is faith or opinion. Therefore, science, or the attempt to replace opinion by knowledge, necessarily endangers society.[15] Moreover, free society presupposes that its members have abandoned their original or natural freedom in favor of conventional freedom, that is, in favor of obedience to the laws of the community or to uniform rules of conduct, to the making of which everyone can have contributed. Civil society requires conformity or the transformation of man as natural being into the citizen. But the philosopher or scientist must follow his "own genius" with absolute sincerity or without any regard to the general will or the communal way of thinking.[16] Finally, free society comes into being through

15. *First Discourse*, pp. 107, 125–26, 129–33, 151, 155–57; *Narcisse*, pp. 56, 57 n.; *Second Discourse*, pp. 71, 152; *C.S.*, II, 7; *Confessions*, II, 226. Hachette, I, 38 n.: "Ce serait en effet un détail bien flétrissant pour la philosophie, que l'exposition des maximes pernicieuses et des dogmes impies de ses diverses sectes ... y-a-t-il une seule de toutes ces sectes qui ne soit tombée dans quelque erreur dangereuse? Et que devons-nous dire de la distinction des deux doctrines, si avidement reçu de *tous* les philosophes, et par laquelle ils professaient en secret des sentiments contraires à ceux qu'ils enseignaient publiquement? Pythagore fit le premier qui fut usage de la doctrine intérieure; il ne la découvrait à ses disciples qu'après de longues épreuves et avec le plus grand mystère. Il leur donnait en secret des leçons d'athéisme, et offrit solennellement des hécatombes à Jupiter. Les philosophes se trouvaient si bien de cette méthode, qu'elle se répandit rapidement dans la Grèce, et de là dans Rome, comme on le voit par les ouvrages de Cicéron, qui se moquait avec ses amis des dieux immortels, qu'il attestait avec tant d'emphase sur le tribunal aux harangues. La doctrine intérieure n'a point été portée d'Europe à la Chine; mais elle y est née aussi avec la philosophie; et c'est à elle que les Chinois sont redevables de cette foule d'athées ou de philosophes qu'ils ont parmi eux. L'histoire de cette fatale doctrine, faite par un homme instruit et sincère, serait un terrible coup porté à *la philosophie ancienne et moderne*." (The italics are not in the original.) Cf. *Confessions*, II, 329.

16. *First Discourse*, pp. 101–2, 105–6, 158–59; *Second Discourse*, p. 116; *C.S.*, I, 6, 8; II, 7; *Émile*, I, 13–15.

the substitution of conventional equality for natural inequality. The pursuit of science, however, requires the cultivation of talents, that is, of natural inequality; its fostering of inequality is so characteristic of it that one is justified in saying that concern with superiority, or pride, is the root of science or philosophy.[17]

It was by means of science or philosophy that Rousseau established the thesis that science or philosophy is incompatible with free society and hence with virtue. In so doing, he tacitly admitted that science or philosophy can be salutary, i.e., compatible with virtue. He did not leave it at this tacit admission. In the very *First Discourse*, he bestowed high praise upon the learned societies whose members must combine learning and morality; he called Bacon, Descartes, and Newton the teachers of the human race; he demanded that scholars of the first rank should find honorable asylum at the courts of princes, in order from there to enlighten the peoples concerning their duties and thus contribute to the peoples' happiness.[18]

Rousseau has suggested three different solutions to this contradiction. According to the first suggestion, science is bad for a good society and good for a bad society. In a corrupt society, in a society ruled despotically, the attack on all sacred opinions or prejudices is legitimate because social morality cannot become worse than it already is. In such a society, only science can provide man with a measure of relief: the discussion of the foundations of society may lead to the discovery of palliatives for the prevailing abuses. This solution would suffice if Rousseau had addressed his works only to his contemporaries, i.e., to members of a corrupt society. But he wished to live as a writer beyond his time, and he foresaw a revolution. He wrote, therefore, also with a view to the requirements of a

17. *First Discourse*, pp. 115, 125–26, 128, 137, 161–62; *Narcisse*, p. 50; *Second Discourse*, p. 147; *C.S.*, I, 9 (end); Hachette, I, 38 n.

18. *First Discourse*, pp. 98–100, 127–28, 138–39, 151–52, 158–61; *Narcisse*, pp. 45, 54.

good society and, in fact, of a more perfect society than had ever existed before, which might be established after the revolution. This best solution to the political problem is discovered by philosophy and only by philosophy. Hence philosophy cannot merely be good for a bad society; it is indispensable for the emergence of the best society.[19]

According to Rousseau's second suggestion, science is good for "the individuals," i.e., for "some great geniuses" or "some privileged souls" or "the small number of true philosophers," among whom he counts himself, but bad for "the peoples" or "the public" or "the common men" (*les hommes vulgaires*). Hence he attacked in the *First Discourse*, not science as such, but popularized science or the diffusion of scientific knowledge. The diffusion of scientific knowledge is disastrous not only for society but for science or philosophy itself; through popularization, science degenerates into opinion, or the fight against prejudice becomes itself a prejudice. Science must remain the preserve of a small minority; it must be kept secret from the common man. Since every book is accessible not only to the small minority but to all who can read, Rousseau was forced by his principle to present his philosophic or scientific teaching with a great deal of reserve. He believed, indeed, that in a corrupt society, like the one in which he lived, the diffusion of philosophic knowledge can no longer be harmful; but, as was said before, he wrote not merely for his contemporaries. The *First Discourse* must be understood in the light of these facts. The function of that work is to warn away from science, not all men, but only the common men. When Rousseau rejects science as simply bad, he speaks in the character of a common man addressing common men. But he intimates that, far from being a common man, he is a philosopher

19. *First Discourse*, p. 94 (cf. 38, 46, 50); *Narcisse*, pp. 54, 57–58, 60 n.; *Second Discourse*, pp. 66, 68, 133, 136, 141, 142, 145, 149; *Julie*, Preface (beginning); *C.S.*, I, 1; *Beaumont*, pp. 471–72.

who merely appears in the guise of a common man and that, far from ultimately addressing "the people," he addresses only those who are not subjugated by the opinions of their century, of their country, or of their society.[20]

It might then seem that it was Rousseau's belief in the fundamental disproportion between science and society (or "the people") which was the primary reason for his belief that the conflict between the individual and society is insoluble or for his making an ultimate reservation on behalf of "the individual," i.e., of the few "privileged souls" against the claims of even the best society. This impression is confirmed by the fact that Rousseau finds the foundations of society in the needs of the body and that he says of himself that nothing related to the interest of his body could ever truly occupy his soul; he himself finds in the joys and raptures of pure and disinterested contemplation—for example, the study of plants in the spirit of Theophrastus—perfect happiness and a godlike self-sufficiency.[21] Thus the impression grows that Rousseau sought to restore the classical idea of philosophy as opposed to the En-

20. *First Discourse*, pp. 93–94, 108 n., 120, 125, 132–33, 152, 157–62, 227; Hachette, I, 23, 26, 31, 33, 35, 47 n. 1, 48, 52, 70; *Second Discourse*, pp. 83, 170, 175; *D'Alembert*, pp. 107–8; *Beaumont*, p. 471; *Montagne*, pp. 152–53, 202, 283. A critic of the *First Discourse* had said: "On ne saurait mettre dans un trop grand jour des vérités qui heurtent autant de front le goût général...." Rousseau replied to him as follows: "Je ne suis pas tout-à-fait de cet avis, et je crois qu'il faut laisser des osselets aux enfants" (Hachette, I, 21; cf. also *Confessions*, II, 247). Rousseau's principle was to say the truth "en toute chose *utile*" (*Beaumont*, pp. 472, 495; *Rêveries*, IV); hence one may not only suppress or disguise truths devoid of all possible utility but may even be positively deceitful about them by asserting their contraries, without thus committing the sin of lying. The consequence regarding harmful or dangerous truths is obvious (cf. also *Second Discourse*, end of the First Part, and *Beaumont*, p. 461). Compare Dilthey, *Gesammelte Schriften*, XI, 92: "[Johannes von Mueller spricht] von der sonderbaren Aufgabe: 'sich so auszudrücken, dass die Obrigkeiten die Wahrheit lernen, ohne dass ihn die Untertanen verstünden, und die Untertanen so zu unterrichten, dass sie vom Glück ihres Zustandes recht überzeugt sein möchten.' "

21. *First Discourse*, p. 101; *Montagne*, p. 206; *Confessions*, III, 205, 220–21; *Rêveries*, V–VII.

lightenment. It is certainly in opposition to the Enlightenment that he reasserts the crucial importance of the natural inequality of men in regard to intellectual gifts. But one must add at once that the instant Rousseau takes hold of the classical view he succumbs again to the powers from which he sought to liberate himself. The same reason which forces him to appeal from civil society to nature forces him to appeal from philosophy or science to nature.[22]

The contradiction of the *First Discourse* regarding the value of science is solved as completely as Rousseau ever solved it by his third suggestion, of which the first and second suggestions are parts. The first and second suggestions solve the contradiction by distinguishing between two kinds of addressees of science. The third suggestion solves the contradiction by distinguishing between two kinds of science: a kind of science which is incompatible with virtue and which one may call "metaphysics" (or purely theoretical science) and a kind of science which is compatible with virtue and which one may call "Socratic wisdom." Socratic wisdom is self-knowledge; it is knowledge of one's ignorance. It is therefore a kind of skepticism, an "involuntary skepticism" but not a dangerous one. Socratic wisdom is not identical with virtue, for virtue is "the science of the simple souls," and Socrates was not a simple soul. Whereas all men can be virtuous, Socratic wisdom is the preserve of a small minority. Socratic wisdom is essentially ancillary; the humble and silent practice of virtue is the only thing that matters. Socratic wisdom has the function of defending "the science of the simple souls," or the conscience, against all kinds of sophistry. The need for such defense is not accidental and not limited to times of corruption. As one of Rousseau's greatest disciples put it, simplicity or innocence is a wonderful thing indeed, but it can easily be misled; "therefore

---

22. *First Discourse*, p. 115 n.; *Narcisse*, pp. 52–53; *Second Discourse*, pp. 89, 94, 109, 165; *Julie*, pp. 415–17; *Émile*, I, 35–36, 118, 293–94, 320–21. Hachette, I, 62–63: "osera-t-on prendre le parti de l'instinct contre la raison? C'est précisément ce que je demande."

wisdom which otherwise consists in doing or in forbearing to do rather than in knowing, is in need of science." Socratic wisdom is needed, not for the sake of Socrates, but for the sake of the simple souls or of the people. The true philosophers fulfil the absolutely necessary function of being the guardians of virtue or of free society. Being the teachers of the human race, they, and they alone, can enlighten the peoples as to their duties and as to the precise character of the good society. In order to fulfil this function, Socratic wisdom requires as its basis the whole of theoretical science; Socratic wisdom is the end and crown of theoretical science. Theoretical science, which is not intrinsically in the service of virtue and is therefore bad, must be put into the service of virtue in order to become good.[23] It can become good, however, only if its study remains the preserve of the few who are by nature destined to guide the peoples; only an esoteric theoretical science can become good. This is not to deny that, in times of corruption, the restriction on the popularization of science can and must be relaxed.

This solution might be regarded as final if the virtuous citizen and not "natural man" were Rousseau's ultimate standard. But according to him, the very philosopher comes closer to natural man in certain respects than does the virtuous citizen. It suffices here to refer to the "idleness" which the philosopher shares with natural man.[24] In the name of nature, Rousseau questioned not only philosophy but the city and virtue as well. He was forced to do so because his Socratic wisdom is ultimately based on theoretical science or, rather on a particular kind of theoretical science, namely, modern natural science.

23. *First Discourse*, pp. 93, 97, 99–100, 107, 118–22, 125, 128, 129, 130 n., 131–32, 152–54, 161–62; Hachette, I, 35; *Narcisse*, pp. 47, 50–51, 56; *Second Discourse*, pp. 74, 76; *Émile*, II, 13, 72, 73; *Beaumont*, p. 452. Cf. Kant, *Grundlegung zur Metaphysik der Sitten*, Erster Abschnitt (toward the end).

24. *First Discourse*, pp. 105–6; *Second Discourse*, pp. 91, 97, 122, 150–51, 168; *Confessions*, II, 73; III, 205, 207–9, 220–21; *Rêveries*, VI (end) and VII.

To understand Rousseau's theoretical principles, one must turn to his *Discourse on the Origin of Inequality*. Contrary to the inclinations of most present-day students, he always regarded this work (the *Second Discourse*) as "a work of the greatest importance." He claimed that in it he had developed his principles "completely," or that the *Second Discourse* is the writing in which he had revealed his principles "with the greatest boldness, not to say audacity."[25] The *Second Discourse* is indeed Rousseau's most philosophic work; it contains his fundamental reflections. In particular, the *Social Contract* rests on the foundations laid in the *Second Discourse*.[26] The *Second Discourse* is decidedly the work of a "philosopher." Morality is regarded there, not as an unquestioned or unquestionable presupposition, but as an object or as a problem.

The *Second Discourse* is meant to be a "history" of man. That history is modeled on the account of the fate of the human race which Lucretius gave in the fifth book of his poem.[27] But Rousseau takes that account out of its Epicurean context and puts it into a context supplied by modern natural and social science. Lucretius had described the fate of the human race in order to show that that fate can be perfectly understood without recourse to divine activity. The remedies for the ills which he was forced to mention, he sought in philosophic withdrawal from political life. Rousseau, on the other hand, tells the story of man in order to discover that political order which is in accordance with natural right. Furthermore, at least at the outset, he follows Descartes rather than Epicurus: he assumes that animals are machines and that man transcends

25. *Confessions*, II, 221, 246.

26. Cf. especially *C.S.*, I, 6 (beginning), which shows that the *raison d'être* of the social contract is set forth, not in the *C.S.*, but in the *Second Discourse*. Cf. also *C.S.*, I, 9.

27. *Second Discourse*, p. 84; cf. also *Confessions*, II, 244. See Jean Morel, "Recherches sur les sources du discours de l'inégalité," *Annales de la Société J.-J. Rousseau*, V (1909), 163–64.

the general mechanism, or the dimension of (mechanical) necessity, only by virtue of the spirituality of his soul. Descartes had integrated the "Epicurean" cosmology into a theistic framework: God having created matter and established the laws of its motions, the universe with the exception of man's rational soul has come into being through purely mechanical processes; the rational soul requires special creation because thinking cannot be understood as a modification of moved matter; rationality is the specific difference of man among the animals. Rousseau questions not only the creation of matter but likewise the traditional definition of man. Accepting the view that brutes are machines, he suggests that there is only a difference of degree between men and the brutes in regard to understanding or that the laws of mechanics explain the formation of ideas. It is man's power to choose and his consciousness of this freedom which cannot be explained physically and which proves the spirituality of his soul. "It is then not so much the understanding which constitutes the specific difference of man among the animals as his quality of a free agent." Yet, whatever Rousseau might have believed concerning this subject, the argument of the *Second Discourse* is not based on the assumption that freedom of the will is of the essence of man, or, more generally expressed, the argument is not based on dualistic metaphysics. Rousseau goes on to say that the cited definition of man is subject to dispute, and he therefore replaces "freedom" by "perfectibility"; no one can deny the fact that man is distinguished from the brutes by perfectibility. Rousseau means to put his doctrine on the most solid ground; he does not want to make it dependent on dualistic metaphysics, which is exposed to "insoluble objections," to "powerful objections," or to "insurmountable difficulties."[28] The argument of the *Second Discourse* is meant to be acceptable

28. *Second Discourse*, pp. 92–95, 118, 140, 166; *Julie*, p. 589 n.; *Émile*, II, 24, 37; *Beaumont*, pp. 461–63; *Rêveries*, III. Cf. *First Discourse*, p. 178.

to materialists as well as to others. It is meant to be neutral with regard to the conflict between materialism and antimaterialism, or to be "scientific" in the present-day sense of the term.[29]

The "physical" investigation[30] of the *Second Discourse* is meant to be identical with a study of the basis of natural right and therewith of morality; the "physical" investigation is meant to disclose the precise character of the state of nature. Rousseau takes it for granted that, in order to establish natural right, one must return to the state of nature. He accepts Hobbes's premise. Dismissing the natural right teaching of the ancient philosophers, he says that "Hobbes has seen very well the defect of all modern definitions of natural right." "The moderns" or "our jurists" (as distinguished from "the Roman jurists," i.e., Ulpian) erroneously assumed that man is by nature capable of the full use of his reason, i.e., that man as man is subject to perfect duties of natural law. Rousseau obviously understands by "the modern definitions of natural right" the traditional definitions which still predominated in the academic teaching of his time. He agrees, then, with Hobbes's attack on the traditional natural law teaching: natural law must have its roots in principles which are anterior to reason, i.e., in passions which need not be specifically human. He further agrees with Hobbes in finding the principle of natural law in the right of self-preservation, which implies the right of each to be the sole judge of what are the proper means for his self-preservation. This view presupposes, according to both thinkers, that life in the state of nature is "solitary," i.e., that it is characterized by the absence not only of society but even of sociability.[31] Rousseau expresses his loyalty to the

29. As regards the prehistory of this approach, see above, pp. 173–74 and 203–4.

30. *Second Discourse*, pp. 75, 173.

31. *Ibid.*, pp. 76, 77, 90, 91, 94–95, 104, 106, 118, 120, 151; *Julie*, p. 113; *C.S.*, I, 2; II, 4, 6; cf. also *Émile*, II, 45.

spirit of Hobbes's reform of the natural law teaching by sub-
stituting for "that sublime maxim of reasoned justice 'Do unto
others as you would have them to do unto you' . . . this much
less perfect, but perhaps more useful maxim 'Do good to your-
self with as little evil as possible to others.' " He tries no less
seriously than Hobbes to find the basis of justice by "taking
men as they are," and not as they ought to be. And he accepts
Hobbes's reduction of virtue to social virtue.[32]

Rousseau deviates from Hobbes for the same two reasons for
which he deviates from all previous political philosophers. In
the first place, "the philosophers who have examined the
foundations of society, have all of them felt the necessity to go
back to the state of nature, but not one of them has arrived
there." All of them have painted civilized man while claiming
to paint natural man or man in the state of nature. Rousseau's

32. *Second Discourse*, p. 110; cf. also *C.S.*, I (beginning); *D'Alembert*, pp. 246, 248; and
Confessions, II, 267. Rousseau was fully aware of the antibiblical implications of the
concept of the state of nature. For this reason, he originally presented his account of the
state of nature as altogether hypothetical; the notion that the state of nature was once
actual contradicts the biblical teaching which every Christian philosopher is obliged
to accept. But the teaching of the *Second Discourse* is not that of a Christian; it is the
teaching of a man addressing mankind; it is at home in the Lyceum at the time of
Plato and of Xenocrates, and not in the eighteenth century; it is a teaching arrived at
by applying the natural light to the study of man's nature, and nature never lies. In
accordance with these statements, Rousseau asserts later on that he has proved his
account of the state of nature. What remains hypothetical, or less certain than the
account of the state of nature, is the account of the development leading from the state
of nature to despotism, or "the history of governments." At the end of the First Part
of the bipartite work, Rousseau calls the state of nature a "fact": the problem consists
in linking "two facts given as real" "by a sequence of intermediate and actually or
supposedly unknown facts." The given facts are the state of nature and contemporary
despotism. It is to the intermediate facts, and not to the characteristics of the state of
nature, that Rousseau refers when he says in the first chapter of the *C.S.* that he does
not know them. If Rousseau's account of the state of nature were hypothetical, his
whole political teaching would be hypothetical; the practical consequence would be
prayer and patience and not dissatisfaction and, wherever possible, reform. Cf. *Second
Discourse*, pp. 75, 78–79, 81, 83–85, 104, 116–17, 149, 151–52, 165; cf. also the reference
to the "thousands of centuries" required for the development of the human mind (*ibid.*,
p. 98) with the biblical chronology; see also Morel, *op. cit.*, p. 135.

predecessors attempted to establish the character of natural man by looking at man as he is now. This procedure was reasonable as long as it was assumed that man is by nature social. Making this assumption, one could draw the line between the natural and the positive or the conventional by identifying the conventional with what is manifestly established by convention. One could take it for granted that at least all those passions which arise in man independently of the fiat of society are natural. But once one denies, with Hobbes, man's natural sociality, one must regard it as possible that many passions which arise in man as we observe him are conventional in so far as they originate in the subtle and indirect influence of society and hence of convention. Rousseau deviates from Hobbes because he accepts Hobbes's premise; Hobbes is grossly inconsistent because, on the one hand, he denies that man is by nature social and, on the other hand, he tries to establish the character of natural man by referring to his experience of men which is the experience of social man.[33] By thinking through Hobbes's critique of the traditional view, Rousseau was brought face to face with a difficulty which embarrasses most present-day social scientists: not the reflection on man's experience of men, but only a specifically "scientific" procedure, seems to be able to lead one to genuine knowledge of the nature of man. Rousseau's reflection on the state of nature, in contradistinction to Hobbes's reflection, takes on the character of a "physical" investigation.

Hobbes had identified natural man with the savage. Rousseau frequently accepts this identification and accordingly makes extensive use of the ethnographic literature of the age. But his doctrine of the state of nature is, in principle, independent of this kind of knowledge, since, as he points out, the savage is already molded by society and therefore no longer a natural man in the strict sense. He also suggests some experi-

33. *Second Discourse*, pp. 74–75, 82–83, 90, 98, 105–6, 137–38, 160, 175.

ments which might be helpful for establishing the character of natural man. But these experiments, being entirely a matter of the future, cannot be the basis of his doctrine. The method which he uses is a "meditation on the first and most simple operations of the human soul"; those mental acts which presuppose society cannot belong to man's natural constitution, since man is by nature solitary.[34]

The second reason why Rousseau deviates from Hobbes can be stated as follows. Hobbes had taught that if natural right is to be effectual, it must be rooted in passion. On the other hand, he had conceived of the laws of nature (of the rules prescribing man's natural duties), apparently in the traditional manner, as dictates of reason; he had described them as "conclusions or theorems." Rousseau draws the conclusion that, since Hobbes's criticism of the traditional view is sound, one must question Hobbes's conception of the laws of nature: not only the right of nature but the laws of nature or man's natural duties or his social virtues must be rooted directly in passion; they must have a much more powerful support than reasoning or calculation. By nature, the law of nature "must speak immediately with the voice of nature"; it must be prerational, dictated by "natural sentiment" or by passion.[35]

Rousseau has summed up the result of his study of natural man in the statement that man is by nature good. This result can be understood as the outcome of a criticism of Hobbes's doctrine which is based on Hobbes's premises. Rousseau argues as follows: Man is by nature asocial, as Hobbes admitted. But pride or *amour-propre* presupposes society. Hence natural man cannot be proud or vain, as Hobbes had contended that he is. But pride or vanity is the root of all viciousness, as Hobbes had also contended. Natural man is therefore free from all

34. *Ibid.*, pp. 74–77, 90, 94–95, 104, 124, 125, 174; cf. also Condorcet, *Esquisse d'un tableau historique des progrès de l'esprit humain*, Première Époque (beginning).

35. *Second Discourse*, pp. 76–77, 103, 107–10; cf. also *Émile*, I, 289.

viciousness. Natural man is swayed by self-love or the concern with self-preservation; he will therefore hurt others if he believes that by doing so he will preserve himself; but he will not be concerned with hurting others for its own sake, as he would be if he were proud or vain. Furthermore, pride and compassion are incompatible; to the extent to which we are concerned with our prestige, we are insensitive to the sufferings of others. The power of compassion decreases with the increase of refinement or convention. Rousseau suggests that natural man is compassionate: the human race could not have survived prior to the existence of any conventional restraints if the powerful promptings of the instinct of self-preservation had not been mitigated by compassion. He seems to assume that the instinctive desire for the preservation of the species bifurcates into the desire for procreation and compassion. Compassion is the passion from which all social virtues derive. He concludes that man is by nature good because he is by nature swayed by self-love and compassion and free from vanity or pride.[36]

For the same reason for which natural man lacks pride, he also lacks understanding or reason and therewith freedom. Reason is coterminous with language, and language presupposes society: being presocial, natural man is prerational. Here again Rousseau draws a necessary conclusion from Hobbes's premises which Hobbes had not drawn. To have reason means to have general ideas. But general ideas, as distinguished from the images of memory or imagination, are not the products of a natural or unconscious process; they presuppose definitions; they owe their being to definition. Hence they presuppose language. Since language is not natural, reason is not natural. From this we can understand best why Rousseau replaces the traditional definition of man as a rational animal by a new definition. Furthermore, since natural man is prerational, he is utterly incapable of any knowledge of the law of nature which

36. *Second Discourse*, pp. 77, 87, 90, 97–99, 104, 107–10, 116, 120, 124–25, 147, 151, 156–57, 160–61, 165, 176–77.

is the law of reason, although "he attributes to himself [in accordance] with reason the right to the things which he needs." Natural man is premoral in every respect: he has no heart. Natural man is subhuman.[37]

Rousseau's thesis that man is by nature good must be understood in the light of his contention that man is by nature subhuman. Man is by nature good because he is by nature that subhuman being which is capable of becoming either good or bad. There is no natural constitution of man to speak of: everything specifically human is acquired or ultimately depends on artifice or convention. Man is by nature almost infinitely perfectible. There are no natural obstacles to man's almost unlimited progress or to his power of liberating himself from evil. For the same reason, there are no natural obstacles to man's almost unlimited degradation. Man is by nature almost infinitely malleable. In the words of the Abbé Raynal, the human race is what we wish to make it. Man has no nature in the precise sense which would set a limit to what he can make out of himself.[38]

37. *Ibid.*, pp. 85, 89, 93–94, 98–99, 101, 102, 105–6, 109, 111, 115, 118, 157, 168. Morel (*op. cit.*, p. 156) points in the right direction by saying that Rousseau "substitue à la fabrication naturelle des idées générales, leur construction scientifiquement réfléchie" (cf. above, pp. 172–74). In Rousseau's model, Lucretius' poem (v. 1028–90), the genesis of language is described without any reference to a genesis of reason: reason belongs to man's natural constitution. In Rousseau, the genesis of language coincides with the genesis of reason (*C.S.*, I, 8; *Beaumont*, pp. 444, 457).

38. Rousseau's contention that man is by nature good is deliberately ambiguous. It expresses two incompatible views—a rather traditional view and a thoroughly antitraditional one. The first view can be stated as follows: Man is by nature good; he is bad through his own fault; almost all evils are of human origin: almost all evils are due to civilization; civilization has its root in pride, i.e., in the misuse of freedom. The practical consequence of this view is that men ought to bear the now inevitable evils of civilization in a spirit of patience and prayer. According to Rousseau, this view is based on belief in biblical revelation. In addition, natural man or man in the state of nature, as Rousseau describes him, is incapable of pride; hence pride cannot have been the reason for his leaving the state of nature (a state of innocence) or for his embarking on the venture of civilization. More generally expressed, natural man lacks freedom of will; hence he cannot misuse his freedom; natural man is characterized, not by freedom, but by perfectibility. Cf. *Second Discourse*, pp. 85, 89, 93–94, 102, 160; *C.S.*, I, 8; cf. above, n. 32.

If man's humanity is acquired, that acquisition must be explained. In accordance with the requirements of a "physical investigation," man's humanity must be understood as a product of accidental causation. This problem had hardly existed for Hobbes. But it arose necessarily on the basis of his premises. He had distinguished between the natural or mechanical production of natural beings and the voluntary or arbitrary production of human constructs. He had conceived of the world of man as a kind of universe within the universe. He had conceived of man's leaving the state of nature and establishing civil society as a kind of revolt of man against nature. His notion of the whole required, however, as Spinoza had indicated, that the dualism of the state of nature and the state of civil society, or the dualism of the natural world and the world of man, be reduced to the monism of the natural world or that the transition from the state of nature to civil society, or man's revolt against nature, be understood as a natural process.[39] Hobbes had concealed from himself this necessity, partly because he erroneously assumed that presocial man is already a rational being, a being capable of making contracts. The transition from the state of nature to civil society therefore coincided for him with the conclusion of the social contract. But Rousseau was forced by his realization of the necessary implications of Hobbes's premises to conceive of that transition as consisting in, or at least as decisively prepared by, a natural process: man's leaving the state of nature, his embarking on the venture of civilization, is due not to a good or a bad use of his freedom or to essential necessity but to mechanical causation or to a series of natural accidents.

Man's humanity or rationality is acquired. Reason comes later than the elementary wants of the body. Reason emerges in the process of satisfying these wants. Originally, these simple and uniform wants are easily satisfied. But this very

---

39. Cf. Spinoza's criticism of Hobbes in *Ep.* 50 with *Tr. theol.-pol.*, chap. iv (beginning) and *Ethics* III praef.; cf. above, chap. v, A, n. 9.

fact leads to an enormous increase in population and thus renders difficult the satisfaction of the elementary wants. Man is therefore forced to think—to learn to think—in order to survive. Furthermore, the elementary wants are satisfied in different manners under different climatic and other conditions. The mind develops, therefore, in exact proportion to the particular manner in which the basic wants or their satisfaction are modified by particular circumstances. These circumstances mold men's thinking. Once thus molded, men develop new wants, and, in attempting to satisfy them, the mind develops further. The progress of the mind is then a necessary process. It is necessary because men are forced to invent by changes (formation of islands, eruption of volcanoes, and the like) which, although not directed toward an end and hence accidental, are yet the necessary effects of natural causes. Accident forces understanding and its development upon man. This being the character especially of the transition from the state of nature to civilized life, it is perhaps not surprising that the process of civilization should have been destructive of the subhuman bliss of the state of nature or that men should have committed grave errors in organizing societies. Yet all this misery and all these blunders were necessary; they were the necessary outcome of early man's lack of experience and lack of philosophy. Still, in and through society, however imperfect, reason develops. Eventually, the original lack of experience and of philosophy is overcome, and man succeeds in establishing public right on solid grounds.[40] At that moment, which is Rousseau's moment, man will no longer be molded by fortuitous circumstances but rather by his reason. Man, the product of blind fate, eventually becomes the seeing master of his fate. Reason's creativity or mastership over the blind forces of nature is a product of those blind forces.

In Rousseau's doctrine of the state of nature, the modern

40. *Second Discourse*, pp. 68, 74-75, 91, 94-96, 98-100, 116, 118-19, 123, 125, 127, 128, 130, 133, 135, 136, 141, 142, 145, 179; *Narcisse*, p. 54; *Julie*, p. 633 n.

natural right teaching reaches its critical stage. By thinking through that teaching, Rousseau was brought face to face with the necessity of abandoning it completely. If the state of nature is subhuman, it is absurd to go back to the state of nature in order to find in it the norm for man. Hobbes had denied that man has a natural end. He had believed that he could find a natural or nonarbitrary basis of right in man's beginnings. Rousseau showed that man's beginnings lack all human traits. On the basis of Hobbes's premise, therefore, it became necessary to abandon altogether the attempt to find the basis of right in nature, in human nature. And Rousseau seemed to have shown an alternative. For he had shown that what is characteristically human is not the gift of nature but is the outcome of what man did, or was forced to do, in order to overcome or to change nature: man's humanity is the product of the historical process. For a moment—the moment lasted longer than a century—it seemed possible to seek the standard of human action in the historical process. This solution presupposed that the historical process or its results are unambiguously preferable to the state of nature or that that process is "meaningful." Rousseau could not accept that presupposition. He realized that to the extent to which the historical process is accidental, it cannot supply man with a standard, and that, if that process has a hidden purpose, its purposefulness cannot be recognized except if there are trans-historical standards. The historical process cannot be recognized as progressive without previous knowledge of the end or purpose of the process. To be meaningful, the historical process must culminate in perfect knowledge of the true public right; man cannot be, or have become, the seeing master of his fate if he does not have such knowledge. It is, then, not knowledge of the historical process but knowledge of the true public right which supplies man with the true standard.

It has been suggested that Rousseau's predicament was due

to mere misunderstanding. In the academic teaching of his
time, the state of nature was understood not as the condition
in which man had actually lived in the beginning but as a
mere "supposition": man in the state of nature is man with all
his essential faculties duly developed but "considered" as subject only to the natural law, and therefore as the bearer of all
those duties and rights and of only those duties and rights
which derive from natural law; whether man actually ever
lived in such a state in which he was not subject to any positive law is irrelevant. In the *Second Discourse* Rousseau himself
alludes to this conception of the state of nature and seems to
accept it. At the beginning of the *Social Contract* he seems to say
that knowledge of the "historical" state of nature is irrelevant
for the knowledge of natural right. Accordingly, his teaching
about the state of nature would seem to have no other merit
than that of having made abundantly clear the necessity of
keeping completely separate from each other the two wholly
unrelated meanings of the state of nature: the state of nature as
man's original condition (and hence as a fact of the past) and
the state of nature as the legal status of man as man (and hence
as an abstraction or a supposition). In other words, Rousseau
seems to be a somewhat unwilling witness to the fact that the
academic natural right teaching was superior to the teachings
of men like Hobbes and Locke.[41] This criticism disregards the
necessary connection between the question concerning the existence, as well as the content, of natural right and the question concerning the sanctions for natural right, the latter
question being identical with the question of the status of man
within the whole, or of man's origin. Rousseau is therefore
not altogether wrong in saying that all political philosophers
have felt the necessity to go back to the state of nature, i.e., to
man's original condition; all political philosophers are forced

41. Moses Mendelssohn, *Gesammelte Schriften* (Jubilaeums-Ausgabe), II, 92; cf.
Second Discourse, p. 83, and above, pp. 230–31.

to reflect upon whether and how far the demands of justice have a support which is independent of human enactments. Rousseau, could not have returned to the academic natural right teaching of his time except by simply adopting the traditional natural theology on which that teaching was explicitly or implicitly based.[42]

The character, as well as the content, of natural right may be decisively affected by the way in which the origin of man is conceived. This does not do away with the fact that natural right is addressed to man as he is now and not to the stupid animal which lived in Rousseau's state of nature. It is therefore difficult to understand how Rousseau could have based his natural right teaching on what he believed he knew of natural man or man in the state of nature. His conception of the state of nature points toward a natural right teaching which is no longer based on considerations of man's nature, or it points toward a law of reason which is no longer understood as a law of nature.[43] Rousseau may be said to have indicated the character of such a law of reason by his teaching concerning the general will, by a teaching which can be regarded as the outcome of the attempt to find a "realistic" substitute for the traditional natural law. According to that teaching, the limitation of human desires is affected, not by the ineffectual requirements of man's perfection, but by the recognition in all others of the same right which one claims for one's self; all others necessarily take an effective interest in the recognition of their rights, whereas no one, or but a few, take an effective interest in human perfection of other men. This being the case, my desire transforms itself into a rational desire by being "generalized," i.e., by being conceived as the content of a law which binds all members of society equally; a desire which survives

42. Cf. *C.S.*, II, 6 (see chap. iii, n. 18, above). As for the connection between the *C.S.* and the *Second Discourse*, see nn. 26 and 32 above.

43. Cf. *C.S.*, II, 4, and *Second Discourse*, p. 77

the test of "generalization" is, by this very fact, proved to be rational and hence just. By ceasing to conceive of the law of reason as a law of nature, Rousseau could have made his Socratic wisdom radically independent of natural science. Yet he did not take that step. The lesson which he had learned from Montesquieu counteracted in his thought the doctrinaire tendencies inherent in natural constitutional law; and extreme doctrinairism was the outcome of the attempt to make the law of reason radically independent of the knowledge of man's nature.[44]

The conclusions regarding the state of nature which Rousseau drew from Hobbes's premises seemed to suggest a return to the conception of man as a social animal. There was a further reason why Rousseau might have returned to that conception. According to Hobbes, all virtues and duties arise from the concern with self-preservation alone and hence immediately from calculation. Rousseau, however, felt that calculation or self-interest is not strong enough as the bond of society and not profound enough as the root of society. Yet he refused to admit that man is by nature a social being. He thought that the root of society can be found in human passions or sentiments as distinguished from a fundamental sociality of man. His reason can be stated as follows: If society is natural, it is not essentially based on the wills of the individuals; it is essentially nature, and not a man's will, which makes him a member of society. On the other hand, the primacy of the individ-

44. Rousseau agrees with the classics by explicitly agreeing with the "principle established by Montesquieu" that "liberty not being a fruit of all climates, is not within the reach of all peoples" (*C.S.*, III, 8). Acceptance of this principle explains the moderate character of most of Rousseau's proposals which were meant for immediate application. Deviating from Montesquieu and the classics, Rousseau teaches, however, that "every legitimate government is republican" (II, 6) and hence that almost all existing regimes are illegitimate: "very few nations have laws" (III, 15). This amounts to saying that in many cases despotic regimes are inevitable, without becoming, by this fact, legitimate: the strangling of a sultan is as lawful as all governmental actions of the sultan (*Second Discourse*, p. 149).

ual in relation to society is preserved if the place which Hobbes had assigned to calculation or self-interest is assigned to passion or sentiment. Rousseau refused, then, to return to the conception of man as a social animal because he was concerned with the radical independence of the individual, i.e., of every human being. He retained the notion of the state of nature because the state of nature guaranteed the individual's radical independence. He retained the notion of the state of nature because he was concerned with such a natural standard as favored in the highest possible degree the independence of the individual.[45]

Rousseau could not have maintained the notion of the state of nature if the depreciation or ex-inanition of the state of nature which he unintentionally effected had not been outweighed in his thought by a corresponding increase in the importance of independence or freedom, i.e., of the most characteristic feature of man in the state of nature. In Hobbes's doctrine, freedom, or the right of everyone to be the sole judge of the means conducive to his self-preservation, had been subordinate to self-preservation; in the case of conflict between freedom and self-preservation, self-preservation takes precedence. According to Rousseau, however, freedom is a higher good than life. In fact, he tends to identify freedom with virtue or with goodness. He says that freedom is obedience to the law which one has given to one's self. This means, in the first place, that not merely obedience to the law but legislation itself must originate in the individual. It means, secondly, that freedom is not so much either the condition or the consequence of virtue as virtue itself. What is true of virtue can also be said of goodness, which Rousseau distinguished from virtue: freedom is identical with goodness; to be free, or to be one's self, is to be good—this is one meaning of his thesis that man is by nature good. Above all, he suggests that the traditional defini-

45. Hachette, I, 374; *Émile*, I, 286–87, 306, II, 44–45.

tion of man be replaced by a new definition according to which not rationality but freedom is the specific distinction of man.[46] Rousseau may be said to have originated "the philosophy of freedom." The connection between the developed form of "the philosophy of freedom," i.e., German idealism, and Rousseau, and hence Hobbes, was realized by no one more clearly than by Hegel. Hegel noted the kinship between Kant's and Fichte's idealism and "the anti-socialistic systems of natural right," i.e., those natural right doctrines which deny man's natural sociality and "posit the being of the individual as the first and highest thing."[47]

"The anti-socialistic systems of natural right" had emerged by virtue of a transformation of Epicureanism. According to the Epicurean doctrine, the individual is by nature free from all social bonds because the natural good is identical with the pleasant, i.e., fundamentally with what is pleasant to the body. But, according to the same doctrine, the individual is by nature kept within definite bounds because there is a natural limit to pleasure, namely, the greatest or highest pleasure: endless striving is against nature. Hobbes's transformation of Epicureanism implied the liberation of the individual not only from all social bonds which do not originate in his will but also from any natural end. Rejecting the notion of a natural end of a man, he no longer understood by the "good life" of the individual his compliance with, or assimilation to, a universal pattern which is apprehended before it is willed. He

46. *Second Discourse*, pp. 93 (cf. Spinoza, *Ethics*, III, 9 schol.), 116, 130, 138, 140–41, 151; *C.S.*, I, 1 (beginning), 4, 8, 11 (beginning); III, 9 n. (end). Cf. the headings of the first two parts of Hobbes's *De cive;* also Locke, *Treatises*, II, secs. 4, 23, 95, 123.

47. "Wissenschaftliche Behandlungsarten des Naturrechts," *Schriften zur Politik und Rechtsphilosophie*, ed. Lasson, pp. 346–47: "In einer niedrigern Abstraktion ist die Unendlichkeit zwar auch als Absolutheit des Subjekts in der Glückseligkeitslehre überhaupt, und im Naturrecht insbesondere von den Systemen, welche anti-sozialistisch heissen und das Sein des einzelnen als das Erste und Höchste setzen, herausgehoben, aber nicht in die reine Abstraktion, welche sie in dem Kantischen oder Fichteschen Idealismus erhalten hat." Cf. Hegel's *Encyclopädie*, secs. 481–82.

conceived of the good life in terms of man's beginnings or of man's natural right as distinguished from his duty or perfection or virtue. Natural right, as he understood it, canalizes rather than limits infinite desire: that infinite desire for power after power which originates in the concern with self-preservation becomes identical with the legitimate pursuit of happiness. Natural right thus understood leads only to conditional duties and to mercenary virtue. Rousseau was satisfied that happiness as Hobbes understood it is indistinguishable from constant misery[48] and that Hobbes's and Locke's "utilitarian" understanding of morality is inadequate: morality must have a more solid support than calculation. In trying to restore an adequate understanding of happiness and of morality, he had recourse to a considerably modified version of traditional natural theology, but he felt that even that version of natural theology was exposed to "insoluble objections."[49] To the extent to which he was impressed by the power of these objections, he was compelled to attempt to understand human life by starting from the Hobbesian notion of the primacy of right or of freedom as distinguished from the primacy of perfection or virtue or duty. He attempted to graft the notion of unconditional duties and of nonmercenary virtue onto the Hobbesian notion of the primacy of freedom or of rights. He admitted, as it were, that duties must be conceived of as derivative from rights or that there is no natural law, properly speaking, which antedates the human will. Yet he sensed that the basic right in question cannot be the right of self-preservation, i.e., a right which leads only to conditional duties and which is itself derivative from an impulse that man shares with the brutes. If morality or humanity were to be understood adequately, they had to be traced to a right or a freedom which is radically and specifically human. Hobbes had implicitly ad-

48. *Second Discourse*, pp. 104–5, 122, 126, 147, 160–63; cf. also *Émile*, I, 286–87.
49. Cf. n. 28 above.

mitted the existence of such a freedom. For he had implicitly admitted that if the traditional dualism of substances, of mind and of body, is abandoned, science cannot be possible except if meaning, order, or truth originates solely in man's creative action, or if man has the freedom of a creator.[50] Hobbes was, in fact, compelled to replace the traditional dualism of body and mind, not by materialistic monism, but by the novel dualism of nature (or substance) and freedom. What Hobbes had, in fact, suggested in regard to science was applied by Rousseau to morality. He tended to conceive of the fundamental freedom, or of the fundamental right, as such a creative act as issues in the establishment of unconditional duties and in nothing else: freedom is essentially self-legislation. The ultimate outcome of this attempt was the substitution of freedom for virtue or the view that it is not virtue which makes man free but freedom which makes man virtuous.

It is true that Rousseau distinguishes true freedom or moral freedom, which consists in obedience to the law that one has given to one's self and which presupposes civil society, not only from civil freedom but, above all, from the natural freedom which belongs to the state of nature, i.e., to a state characterized by the rule of blind appetite and hence by slavery in the moral sense of the term. But it is also true that he blurs these distinctions. For he also says that in civil society everyone "obeys only himself and remains as free as he was before," i.e., as he was in the state of nature. This means that natural freedom remains the model for civil freedom, just as natural equality remains the model for civil equality.[51] Civil freedom, in its turn, being in a way obedience to one's self alone, certainly comes very close to moral freedom. The blurring of the distinctions between natural freedom, civil freedom, and moral

50. See pp. 172–74 above.

51. *C.S.*, I, 6, 8; *Second Discourse*, p. 65. As for the ambiguity of "freedom," cf. also *Second Discourse*, pp. 138–41.

freedom is no accidental error: the novel understanding of moral freedom originated in the notion that the primary moral phenomenon is the freedom of the state of nature. At any rate, the enhancement of the status of "freedom" gives the almost exploded notion of the state of nature a new lease on life in Rousseau's doctrine.

In Hobbes's and Locke's doctrines, the state of nature had been, as one might say, a negative standard: the state of nature is characterized by such a self-contradiction as points to one and only one sufficient solution, which is "the mighty leviathan" whose "blood is money." Rousseau, however, thought that civil society as such, to say nothing of civil society as Hobbes and Locke had conceived of it, is characterized by a fundamental self-contradiction and that it is precisely the state of nature which is free from self-contradiction; man in the state of nature is happy because he is radically independent, whereas man in civil society is unhappy because he is radically dependent. Civil society must therefore be transcended in the direction not of man's highest end but of his beginning, of his earliest past. Thus the state of nature tended to become for Rousseau a positive standard. Yet he admitted that accidental necessity had forced man to leave the state of nature and has transformed him in such a manner as to incapacitate him forever for a return to that blessed state. Hence Rousseau's answer to the question of the good life takes on this form: the good life consists in the closest approximation to the state of nature which is possible on the level of humanity.[52]

On the political plane that closest approximation is achieved by a society which is constructed in conformity with the requirements of the social contract. Like Hobbes and Locke, Rousseau starts from the premise that in the state of nature all men are free and equal and that the fundamental desire is the

52. *Second Discourse*, pp. 65, 104–5, 117–18, 122, 125–26, 147, 151, 160–63, 177–79; *Julie*, p. 385; *C.S.*, II, 11; III, 15; *Émile*, II, 125.

desire for self-preservation. Deviating from his predecessors, he contends that at the beginning, or in the original state of nature, the promptings of the desire for self-preservation were tempered by compassion and that the original state of nature was considerably changed through accidental necessity, prior to man's entering civil society; civil society becomes necessary or possible only in a very late stage of the state of nature. The decisive change which took place within the state of nature consisted in the weakening of compassion. Compassion was weakened because of the emergence of vanity or pride and ultimately because of the emergence of inequality and therefore of the dependence of man on his fellows. As a consequence of this development, self-preservation became increasingly difficult. Once the critical point is reached, self-preservation demands the introduction of an artificial substitute for natural compassion, or of a conventional substitute for that natural freedom and that natural equality which existed at the beginning. It is the self-preservation of everyone which requires that the closest possible approximation to original freedom and equality be achieved within society.[53]

The root of civil society must then be sought exclusively in the desire for self-preservation or in the right of self-preservation. The right to self-preservation implies the right to the means required for self-preservation. Accordingly, there exists a natural right to appropriation. Everyone has by nature the right to appropriate to himself what he needs of the fruits of the earth. Everyone may acquire through his labor, and only through his labor, an exclusive right to the produce of the land which he has cultivated, and therewith an exclusive right to the land itself, at least until the next harvest. Continuous cultivation may even legitimate continuous possession of the land cultivated, but it does not create property right in that

53. *Second Discourse*, pp. 65, 75, 77, 81, 109–10, 115, 118, 120, 125, 129, 130, 134; *C.S.*, I, 6 (beginning); I, 2.

land; property right is the creation of positive law; prior to the sanction by positive law, land is usurped, i.e., acquired by force, and not truly owned. Otherwise, natural right would hallow the right of the first occupier to the detriment of the right of self-preservation of those who, perhaps through no fault of their own, failed to take possession of land; the poor retain the natural right to acquire as free men what they need for self-preservation. If they are unable to appropriate what they need by cultivating a plot of their own because everything has already been appropriated by others, they may use force. Thus a conflict arises between the right of the first occupiers and the right of those who must rely on force. The need for appropriation of the necessities of life transforms the latest stage of the state of nature into the most horrible state of war. Once this point has been reached, it is to the interest of everyone, of the poor as well as of the rich, that right should succeed to violence, i.e., that peace be guaranteed through convention or compact. This amounts to saying that "according to the maxim of the wise Locke, there could not be injustice where there is no property" or that in the state of nature everyone has "an unlimited right to everything which tempts him and which he can get." The compact which is at the basis of factual societies transformed men's factual possessions as they existed at the end of the state of nature into genuine property. It therefore sanctioned earlier usurpation. Factual society rests on a fraud perpetrated by the rich against the poor: political power rests on "economic" power. No improvement can ever cure this original defect of civil society; it is inevitable that the law should favor the haves against the have-nots. Yet, in spite of this, the self-preservation of everyone requires that the social contract be concluded and kept.[54]

The social contract would endanger the individual's self-preservation if it did not allow him to remain the judge of the

54. *Second Discourse*, pp. 82, 106, 117, 118, 125, 128–29, 131–35, 141, 145, 152; *C.S.*, I, 2, 8, 9; II, 4 (toward the end); *Émile*, I, 309; II, 300.

means required for his self-preservation or to remain as free as he was before. On the other hand, it is of the essence of civil society that private judgment be replaced by public judgment. These conflicting demands are reconciled, as far as they can be reconciled, if those public judgments which issue in executive action conform strictly with law, if those public judgments which are laws are the work of the citizen body, and if every adult male who is subject to the laws can have influenced their content through his vote. Voting on a law means to conceive of the object of one's private or natural will as the object of a law which is binding on all equally and benefits all equally, or to restrict one's selfish desire by considering the undesirable consequences which would follow if everyone else indulged his selfish desire as well. Legislation by the all-inclusive citizen body is therefore the conventional substitute for natural compassion. The citizen is indeed less free than man in the state of nature, since he cannot follow his unqualified private judgment, but he is freer than man in the state of nature, since he is habitually protected by his fellows. The citizen is as free as man in the (original) state of nature, since, being subject only to the law or to the public will or to the general will, he is not subject to the private will of any other man. But if every kind of personal dependence or of "private government" is to be avoided, everyone and everything must be subject to the general will; the social contract requires "the total alienation of each associate, with all his rights, to the whole community" or the transformation of "every individual who by himself is a perfect and solitary whole into a part of a greater whole from which, in a sense, that individual receives his life and his being." In order to remain as free in society as he was before, man must become completely "collectivized" or "denaturalized."[55]

55. *C.S.*, I, 6, 7; II, 2-4, 7; *Émile*, I, 13. The discussion of the social contract in the *Second Discourse* is admittedly provisional (p. 141).

Freedom in society is possible only by virtue of the complete surrender of everyone (and in particular of the government) to the will of a free society. By surrendering all his rights to society, man loses the right to appeal from the verdicts of society, i.e., from the positive law, to natural right: all rights become social rights. Free society rests and depends upon the absorption of natural right by positive law. Natural right is legitimately absorbed by the positive law of a society which is constructed in accordance with natural right. The general will takes the place of the natural law. "By the very fact that he is, the sovereign is always what he ought to be."[56]

Rousseau sometimes called the free society as he conceived of it a "democracy." Democracy is closer to the equality of the state of nature than is any other regime. Yet democracy must be "wisely tempered." While everyone must have a vote, the votes must be "arranged" in such a manner as to favor the middle class and the rural population as against *la canaille* of the big towns. Otherwise, those who have nothing to lose might sell freedom for bread.[57]

The absorption of natural right by the positive law of a properly qualified democracy would be defensible if there were a guaranty that the general will—and this means, for all practical purposes, the will of the legal majority—could not err. The general will or the will of the people never errs in so far as it always wills the good of the people, but the people do not always see the good of the people. The general will is therefore in need of enlightenment. Enlightened individuals may see the good of society, but there is no guaranty that they will espouse it if it conflicts with their private good. Calculation

---

56. *C.S.*, I, 7; II, 3, 6. Cf. *ibid.*, II, 12 ("Division of Laws") with the parallels in Hobbes, Locke, and Montesquieu, to say nothing of Hooker and Suarez; Rousseau does not even mention natural law.

57. *Second Discourse*, pp. 66, 143; *Julie*, pp. 470–71; *C.S.*, IV, 4; *Montagne*, pp. 252, 300–301. Cf. Rousseau's criticism of the aristocratic principle of the classics in *Narcisse*, pp. 50–51, and in the *Second Discourse*, pp. 179–80.

and self-interest are not strong enough as social bonds. Both the people as a whole and the individuals are then equally in need of a guide; the people must be taught to know what it wills, and the individual, who as a natural being is concerned exclusively with his private good, must be transformed into a citizen who unhesitatingly prefers the common good to his private good. The solution of this twofold problem is supplied by the legislator, or the father of a nation, i.e., by a man of superior intelligence, who, by ascribing divine origin to a code which he has devised or by honoring the gods with his own wisdom, both convinces the people of the goodness of the laws which he submits to its vote and transforms the individual from a natural being into a citizen. Only by the action of the legislator can the conventional acquire, if not the status, at least the force, of the natural. It goes without saying that the arguments by which the legislator convinces the citizens of his divine mission or of the divine sanction for his code are necessarily of doubtful solidity. One might think that, once the code were ratified, a "social spirit" developed, and the wise legislation accepted on account of its proved wisdom rather than its pretended origin, the belief in the superhuman origin of the code would no longer be required. But this suggestion overlooks the fact that the living respect for old laws, "the prejudice of antiquity" which is indispensable for the health of society, can only with difficulty survive the public questioning of the accounts regarding their origin. In other words, the transformation of natural man into a citizen is a problem coeval with society itself, and therefore society has a continuous need for at least an equivalent to the mysterious and awe-inspiring action of the legislator. For society can be healthy only if the opinions and sentiments engendered by society overcome and, as it were, annihilate the natural sentiments. That is to say, society must do everything possible to render the citizens oblivious of the very facts that political philosophy brings to the center of their attention as the foundations of society. Free society stands or falls by a specific obfuscation against which philosophy necessarily revolts. The problem posed by political philosophy must be forgotten if the solution to which political philosophy leads is to work.[58]

It is true, no doubt, that Rousseau's doctrine of the legislator is meant to clarify the fundamental problem of civil society rather than to suggest a practical solution, except in so far as that doctrine adumbrates Rousseau's own function. The precise reason why he had to abandon the classical notion of the legislator was that that notion is liable to obscure the sovereignty of the people, i.e., to lead, for all practical purposes, to the substitution of the supremacy of the law for the full sovereignty of the people. The classical notion of the legislator is irreconcilable with Rousseau's notion of freedom which leads to the demand for periodic appeals from the whole established order to the sovereign will of the people or from the will of past generations to the will of the living generation. Rousseau, therefore, had to find a substitute for the action of the legislator. According to his final suggestion, the function originally intrusted to the legislator must be discharged by a civil religion described from somewhat different points of view in the *Social Contract*, on the one hand, and the *Émile*, on the other. Only the civil religion will engender the sentiments required of the citizen. We need not go into the question of whether Rousseau himself fully subscribed to the religion which he presented in the profession of faith of the Savoyard vicar, a question that cannot be answered by reference to what he said when he was persecuted on account of that profession. What is decisive is the fact that, according to his explicit views about the relation of knowledge, faith, and the people,

58. *Narcisse*, p. 56; *Second Discourse*, pp. 66–67, 143; *C.S.*, II, 3, 6–7; III, 2, 11. Compare the reference to miracles in the chapter on the legislator (*C.S.*, II, 7) with the explicit discussion of the problem of miracles in *Montagne*, ii–iii.

the people cannot have more than opinion regarding the truth of this or any other religion. One may even wonder whether any human being can have any genuine knowledge in this respect, since the religion preached by the Savoyard vicar is exposed to "insoluble objections." Therefore, every civil religion would seem, in the last analysis, to have the same character as the legislator's account of the origin of his code, at least in so far as both are essentially endangered by the "dangerous pyrrhonism" fostered by science; the "insoluble objections" to which even the best of all religions is exposed are dangerous truths. Precisely a free society cannot exist if he who doubts the fundamental dogma of the civil religion does not outwardly conform.[59]

Apart from the civil religion, the equivalent to the action of the early legislator is custom. Custom, too, socializes the wills of the individuals independently of the generalization of the wills which takes place in the act of legislation. Law is even preceded by custom. For civil society is preceded by the nation or the tribe, i.e., a group which is kept together by customs arising from the fact that all members of the group are exposed to, and molded by, the same natural influences. The prepolitical nation is more natural than civil society, since natural causes are more effective in its production than in the genesis of civil society, which is produced by contract. The nation is closer to the original state of nature than is civil society, and therefore it is in important respects superior to civil society. Civil society will approximate the state of nature on the level of humanity to a higher degree, or it will be more healthy, if it rests on the almost natural basis of nationality or if it has a national individuality. National custom or national cohesion is a deeper root of civil society than are calculation and self-interest and hence than the social contract. National

---

59. *Julie*, pp. 502–6; *C.S.*, IV, 8; *Beaumont*, p. 479; *Montagne*, pp. 121–36, 180; cf. also n. 28 above.

custom and national "philosophy" are the matrix of the general will, just as feeling is the matrix of reason. Hence the past, and especially the early past, of one's own nation tends to become of higher dignity than any cosmopolitan aspirations. If man's humanity is acquired by accidental causation, that humanity will be radically different from nation to nation and from age to age.[60]

It is not surprising that Rousseau did not regard the free society as he conceived of it as the solution to the human problem. Even if that society met the requirements of freedom more nearly than did any other society, what would follow would simply be that true freedom must be sought beyond civil society. If civil society and duty are coextensive, as Rousseau suggests, human freedom must be sought even beyond duty or virtue. With a view to the connection between virtue and civil society, as well as to the problematic character of the relation between virtue and happiness, Rousseau made a distinction between virtue and goodness. Virtue presupposes effort and habituation; it is primarily a burden, and its demands are harsh. Goodness, i.e., the desire to do good or at least the complete absence of a desire to do harm, is simply natural; the pleasures of goodness come immediately from nature; goodness is immediately connected with the natural sentiment of compassion; it belongs to the heart rather than to conscience or reason. Rousseau taught, indeed, that virtue is superior to goodness. Yet the ambiguity of his notion of freedom, or, in other words, his longing for the happiness of prepolitical life, makes that teaching questionable from his own point of view.[61]

60. *Narcisse*, p. 56; *Second Discourse*, pp. 66–67, 74, 123, 125, 150, 169–70; *C.S.*, II, 8, 10, 12; III, 1; *Émile*, II, 287–88; *Pologne*, chaps. ii–iii; cf. also Alfred Cobban, *Rousseau and the Modern State* (London, 1934), p. 284.

61. Cf. especially *C.S.*, I, 8, and II, 11; *Second Discourse*, pp. 125–26, 150; *Julie*, pp. 222, 274, 277; *Émile*, II, 48, 274–75; *Confessions*, II, 182, 259, 303; III, 43; *Rêveries*, vi.

From this we can understand Rousseau's attitude toward the family or, more precisely, toward conjugal and paternal love as well as toward heterosexual love simply. Love is closer to the original state of nature than is civil society, duty, or virtue. Love is simply incompatible with compulsion and even self-compulsion; it is free or it is not. It is for this reason that conjugal and paternal love can be "the sweetest sentiments," or even "the sweetest sentiments of nature," "which are known to man" and that heterosexual love simply can be "the sweetest of passions" or "the most delicious sentiment which can enter the human heart." These sentiments give rise to "rights of the blood" and "rights of love"; they create bonds which are more sacred than any man-made bonds. Through love, man achieves a closer approximation to the state of nature on the level of humanity than he does through a life of citizenship or virtue. Rousseau returns from the classical city to the family and the loving couple. Using his own language, we may say that he returns from the concern of the citizen to the noblest concern of the bourgeois.[62]

Yet, at least according to that writing of Rousseau in which he revealed his principles "with the greatest boldness, not to say audacity," there is an element of the conventional or of the factitious even in love.[63] Love being a social phenomenon and man being by nature asocial, it becomes necessary to consider whether the solitary individual is not capable of the closest approximation to the state of nature which is possible on the level of humanity. Rousseau has spoken in glowing terms of the charms and raptures of solitary contemplation. By "solitary contemplation" he does not understand philosophy or the culmination of philosophy. Solitary contemplation, as he understands it, is altogether different from, not to say hostile to,

---

62. *Second Discourse*, pp. 122, 124; *D'Alembert*, pp. 256–57; *Julie*, pp. 261, 331, 392, 411 (cf. also pp. 76, 147–48, 152, 174 n., 193, 273–75); *Rêveries*, x (p. 164).

63. *Second Discourse*, pp. 111, 139.

thinking or observation. It consists of, or it leads up to, "the feeling of existence," i.e., the pleasant feeling of one's own existence. If man has withdrawn from everything outside himself, if he has emptied himself of every affection other than the feeling of existence, he enjoys the supreme felicity—godlike self-sufficiency and impassibility; he finds consolation only in himself by being fully himself and by belonging fully to himself, since the past and the future are extinguished for him. It is in giving himself completely to this feeling that civilized man completes the return to the primitive state of nature on the level of humanity. For, whereas sociable man derives the feeling of his existence, as it were, exclusively from the opinions of his fellows, natural man—indeed even the savage—feels his existence naturally; he gives himself "to the sole feeling of his present existence without any idea of the future." The feeling of existence is "man's first feeling." It is more fundamental than the desire for self-preservation; man is concerned with the preservation of his existence because existence itself, mere existence, is by nature pleasant.[64]

The feeling of existence as Rousseau experienced and described it has a rich articulation which must have been lacking in the feeling of existence as it was experienced by man in the state of nature. Here at last civilized man or those civilized men who have returned from civil society to solitude reach a degree of happiness of which the stupid animal must have been utterly incapable. In the last analysis it is only this superiority of civilized man, or of the best among civilized men, which permits Rousseau to contend without hesitation that, while the emergence of civil society was bad for the human species or for the common good, it was good for the individual.[65] The ultimate justification of civil society is, then, the fact that it allows a certain type of individual to enjoy the supreme felicity by withdrawing from civil society, i.e., by living at its

64. *Ibid.*, pp. 96, 118, 151, 165; *Émile*, I, 286; *Rêveries*, V and VII. See above, pp. 261–62.

65. *Second Discourse*, pp. 84, 116, 125–26; *Beaumont*, p. 471.

fringes. Whereas in the earliest of his important writings the citizen of Geneva had said that "every useless citizen may be regarded as a pernicious man," he says in his last writing that he himself always was indeed a useless citizen, yet that his contemporaries have done wrong in proscribing him from society as a pernicious member, instead of merely removing him from society as a useless member.[66] The type of man foreshadowed by Rousseau, which justifies civil society by transcending it, is no longer the philosopher but what later came to be called the "artist." His claim to privileged treatment is based on his sensitivity rather than on his wisdom, on his goodness or compassion rather than on his virtue. He admits the precarious character of his claim: he is a citizen with a bad conscience. Yet, since his conscience accuses not merely himself but at the same time the society to which he belongs, he is inclined to regard himself as the conscience of society. But he is bound to have a bad conscience for being the bad conscience of society.

One must contrast the dreamlike character of Rousseau's solitary contemplation with the wakefulness of philosophic contemplation. In addition, one must take into consideration the insoluble conflict between the presuppositions of his solitary contemplation and his natural theology (and therewith the morality based on that theology). Then one realizes that the claim which he raises on behalf of the individual, or of some rare individuals, over against society lacks clarity and definiteness. More precisely, the definiteness of the act of claiming contrasts sharply with the indefiniteness of the content of the claim. This is not surprising. The notion that the good life consists in the return on the level of humanity to the state of nature, i.e., to a state which completely lacks all human traits, necessarily leads to the consequence that the individual claims such an ultimate freedom from society as lacks any definite human content. But this fundamental defect of the

66. *First Discourse*, p. 131; *Rêveries*, VI (end).

state of nature as the goal of human aspiration was in Rousseau's eyes its perfect justification: the very indefiniteness of the state of nature as a goal of human aspiration made that state the ideal vehicle of freedom. To have a reservation against society in the name of the state of nature means to have a reservation against society without being either compelled or able to indicate the way of life or the cause or the pursuit for the sake of which that reservation is made. The notion of a return to the state of nature on the level of humanity was the ideal basis for claiming a freedom from society which is not a freedom for something. It was the ideal basis for an appeal from society to something indefinite and undefinable, to an ultimate sanctity of the individual as individual, unredeemed and unjustified. This was precisely what freedom came to mean for a considerable number of men. Every freedom which is freedom for something, every freedom which is justified by reference to something higher than the individual or than man as mere man, necessarily restricts freedom or, which is the same thing, establishes a tenable distinction between freedom and license. It makes freedom conditional on the purpose for which it is claimed. Rousseau is distinguished from many of his followers by the fact that he still saw clearly the disproportion between this undefined and undefinable freedom and the requirements of civil society. As he confessed at the end of his career, no book attracted and profited him as much as the writings of Plutarch.[67] The solitary dreamer still bowed to Plutarch's heroes.

B. BURKE

The difficulties into which Rousseau was led by accepting and thinking through the modern natural right teaching might have suggested a return to the premodern conception of natural right. Such a return was attempted, at the last minute,

---

67. *Rêveries*, IV (beginning).

as it were, by Edmund Burke. Burke sided with Cicero and with Suarez against Hobbes and against Rousseau. "We continue, as in the last two ages, to read, more generally than I believe is now done on the Continent, the authors of sound antiquity. These occupy our minds." Burke sided with "the authors of sound antiquity" against "the Parisian philosophers" and especially against Rousseau, the originators of a "new morality" or "the bold experimenters in morality." He repudiated with scorn "that philosophy which pretends to have made discoveries in the *terra australis* of morality.[68] His political activity was indeed guided by devotion to the British constitution, but he conceived of the British constitution in a spirit akin to that in which Cicero had conceived of the Roman polity.

Burke did not write a single theoretical work on the principles of politics. All his utterances on natural right occur in statements *ad hominem* and are meant to serve immediately a specific practical purpose. Accordingly, his presentation of political principles changed, to a certain degree, with the change of the political situation. Hence he might easily appear to have been inconsistent. In fact, he adhered throughout his career to the same principles. A single faith animated his actions in favor of the American colonists, in favor of the Irish Catholics, against Warren Hastings, and against the French Revolution. In accordance with the eminently practical bent of his thought, he stated his principles most forcefully and most clearly when such a statement was most urgently needed, i.e., when these principles were attacked both most intransigently and most effectively—after the outbreak of the French Revolution. The French Revolution affected his expectations in regard to the future progress of Europe; but it hardly af-

68. *The Works of Edmund Burke* ("Bohn's Standard Library"), II, 385, 529, 535, 541; VI, 21–23. Cited hereafter as "*Works*."

fected, it hardly did more than confirm, his views of what is right or wrong both morally and politically.[69]

The practical character of Burke's thought partly explains why he did not hesitate to use the language of modern natural right whenever that could assist him in persuading his modern audience of the soundness of a policy which he recommended. He spoke of the state of nature, of the rights of nature or of the rights of man, and of the social compact or of the artificial character of the commonwealth.[70] But he may be said to integrate these notions into a classical or Thomistic framework.

We must confine ourselves to a few examples. Burke is willing to grant that men in the state of nature, "uncovenanted" men, have natural rights; in the state of nature, everyone has "the right of self-defense, the first law of nature," the right to govern himself, i.e., "to judge for himself, and to assert his own cause," and even "a right to every thing." But "by having a right to every thing, they want every thing." The state of nature is the state of "our naked, shivering nature" or of our nature not yet affected in any way by our virtues, or of original barbarism. Hence the state of nature and "the full rights of men" which belong to it cannot supply the standard for civilized life. All wants of our nature—certainly, all higher wants of our nature—point away from the state of nature toward civil society: not "the state of rude nature" but civil society is the true state of nature. Burke grants that civil society is "the offspring of convention" or "a contract." But it is "a contract," "a partnership" of a particular kind—"a partnership in every virtue, and in all perfection." It is a contract in

69. *Ibid.*, II, 59–62; III, 104; VI, 144–53. As regards the issue of progress, cf. II, 156; III, 279, 366; VI, 31, 106; VII, 23, 58; VIII, 439; *Letters of Edmund Burke: A Selection*, ed. Harold J. Laski, p. 363 (cited hereafter as "*Letters*"); cf. also *Burke, Select Works*, ed. E. J. Payne, II, 345.

70. Cf., e.g., *Works*, I, 314, 348, 470; II, 19, 29–30, 145, 294–95, 331–33, 366; III, 82; V, 153, 177, 216; VI, 29.

almost the same sense in which the whole providential order, "the great primeval contract of eternal society," can be said to be a contract.[71]

Burke admits that the purpose of civil society is to safeguard the rights of man and especially the right to the pursuit of happiness. But happiness can be found only by virtue, by the restraints "which are imposed by the virtues upon the passions." Hence the subjection to reason, to government, to law, or "the restraints on men, as well as their liberties, are to be reckoned among their rights." Man can never act "without any moral tie," since "men are never in a state of total independence of each other." Man's will must always be under the dominion of reason, prudence, or virtue. Burke therefore seeks the foundation of government "in a conformity to our duties" and not in "imaginary rights of men." Accordingly, he denies the contention that all our duties arise from consent or from contract.[72]

The discussion regarding the "imaginary rights of men" centers on the right of everyone to be the sole judge of what is conducive to his self-preservation or to his happiness. It was this alleged right which seemed to justify the demand that everyone must have some share, and, in a sense, as large a share as anyone else, in political power. Burke questions this demand by going back to the principle on which the alleged basic right is founded. He grants that everyone has a natural right to self-preservation and to the pursuit of happiness. But he denies that everyone's right to self-preservation and to the pursuit of happiness becomes nugatory if everyone does not have the right to judge of the means conducive to his self-preservation and to his happiness. The right to the satisfaction of wants or to the advantages of society is therefore not necessarily a right to participation in political power. For the judg-

71. *Ibid.*, II, 220, 332–33, 349, 368–70; III, 82, 86; V, 212, 315, 498.
72. *Ibid.*, II, 310, 331, 333, 538; III, 109; V, 80, 122, 216, 424.

ment of the many, or "the will of the many, and their interest, must very often differ." Political power or participation in political power does not belong to the rights of man, because men have a right to good government, and there is no necessary connection between good government and government by the many; the rights of man, properly understood, point toward the predominance of the "true natural aristocracy" and therewith to the predominance of property and especially landed property. In other words, everyone is indeed able to judge properly of grievances by his feelings, provided that he is not seduced by agitators into judging of grievances by his imagination. But the causes of grievances "are not matters of feeling, but of reason and foresight, and often of remote considerations, and of a very great combination of circumstances, which [the majority] are utterly incapable of comprehending." Burke therefore seeks the foundation of government not in "imaginary rights of men" but "in a provision for our wants, and in a conformity to our duties." Accordingly, he denies that natural right by itself can tell much about the legitimacy of a given constitution: that constitution is legitimate in a given society which is most suitable to the provision for human wants and to the promotion of virtue in that society; its suitability cannot be determined by natural right but only by experience.[73]

Burke does not reject the view that all authority has its ultimate origin in the people or that the sovereign is ultimately the people or that all authority is ultimately derived from a compact of previously "uncovenanted" men. But he denies that these ultimate truths, or half-truths, are politically relevant. "If civil society be the offspring of convention, that convention must be its law." For almost all practical purposes,

73. *Ibid.*, I, 311, 447; II, 92, 121, 138, 177, 310, 322–25, 328, 330–33, 335; III, 44–45, 78, 85–86, 98–99, 109, 352, 358, 492–93; V, 202, 207, 226–27, 322–23, 342; VI, 20–21, 146.

the convention, the original compact, i.e., the established constitution, is the highest authority. Since the function of civil society is the satisfaction of wants, the established constitution derives its authority less from the original convention or from its origin than from its beneficent working through many generations or from its fruits. The root of legitimacy is not so much consent or contract as proved beneficence, i.e., prescription. Only prescription, as distinguished from the original compact of "uncovenanted" savages, can reveal the wisdom of the constitution and therefore legitimate the constitution. The habits produced on the basis of the original compact, and especially the habits of virtue, are infinitely more important than the original act itself. Only prescription, as distinguished from the original act, can hallow a given social order. The people is so little the master of the constitution that it is its creature. The strict notion of the sovereignty of the people implies that the present generation is sovereign: "present conveniency" becomes the only "principle of attachment" to the constitution. "The temporary possessors and life-renters" in the commonwealth, "unmindful of what they have received from their ancestors," inevitably become unmindful "of what is due to their posterity." The people, or for that matter any other sovereign, is still less master of the natural law; natural law is not absorbed by the will of the sovereign or by the general will. As a consequence, the distinction between just and unjust wars retains its full significance for Burke; he abhors the notion that one should determine the foreign policy of a nation exclusively in terms of its "material interest."[74]

Burke does not deny that under certain conditions the people may alter the established order. But he admits this only as an

74. *Ibid.*, II, 58, 167, 178, 296, 305–6, 331–32, 335, 349, 359–60, 365–67, 422–23, 513–14, 526, 547; III, 15, 44–45, 54–55, 76–85, 409, 497, 498; V, 203–5, 216; VI, 3, 21–22, 145–47; VII, 99–103.

ultimate right. The health of society requires that the ultimate sovereignty of the people be almost always dormant. He
opposes the theorists of the French Revolution because they
turn "a case of necessity into a rule of law" or because they regard as normally valid what is valid only in extreme cases.
"But the very habit of stating these extreme cases is not very
laudable or safe." Burke's opinions, on the other hand, "never
can lead to an extreme, because their foundation is laid in an
opposition to extremes."[75]

Burke traces the extremism of the French Revolution to a
novel philosophy. "The old morality" was a morality "of
social benevolence and of individual self-denial." The Parisian
philosophers deny the nobility of "individual self-restraint"
or of temperance or of "the severe and restrictive virtues."
They recognize only the "liberal" virtues: "a virtue which
they call humanity or benevolence."[76] Humanity thus understood goes well with dissoluteness. It even fosters it; it fosters
the loosening of the marriage bonds and the substitution of the
theater for the church. In addition, "the same discipline
which . . . relaxes their morals," "hardens their hearts": the
extreme humanitarianism of the theorists of the French Revolution necessarily leads to bestiality. For that humanitarianism is based on the premise that the fundamental moral facts
are rights which correspond to the basic bodily wants; all
sociability is derivative and, in fact, artificial; certainly, civil

75. *Ibid.*, I, 471, 473, 474; II, 291, 296, 335–36, 468; III, 15–16, 52, 81, 109; V, 120.
Cf. G. H. Dodge, *The Political Theory of the Huguenots of the Dispersion* (New York, 1947), p.
105: Jurieu held that it is better "for public peace" that the people do not know the true
extent of their powers; the rights of the people are "remedies which must not be wasted
or applied in the case of minor wrongs. They are mysteries which must not be profaned
by exposing them too much before the eyes of the common herd." "When it comes to
the destruction of the state or religion, then [these remedies] can be produced; beyond
that I do not think it evil that they should be covered with silence."

76. Letter to Rivarol of June 1, 1791 (cf. *Works*, I, 130–31, 427; II, 56, 418), *Works*,
V, 208, 326. Cf. Montesquieu, *De l'esprit des lois*, XX, 1 (and XIX, 16) on the connection
between commerce and the mildness of manners as distinguished from their purity.

society is radically artificial. Hence the virtues of the citizen cannot be grafted "on the stock of the natural affections." But civil society is assumed to be not only necessary but noble and sacred. Accordingly, the natural sentiments, all natural sentiments, must be ruthlessly sacrificed to the alleged requirements of patriotism or of humanity. The French revolutionists arrive at these requirements by approaching human affairs in the attitude of scientists, of geometricians or of chemists. Hence, they are, from the outset, "worse than indifferent about those feelings and habitudes, which are the support of the moral world." They "consider men in their experiments, no more than they do mice in an air pump, or in a recipient of mephitic gas." Accordingly, "they are ready to declare that they do not think two thousand years too long a period for the good that they pursue." "Their humanity is not dissolved. They only give it a long prorogation. . . . Their humanity is at their horizon—and, like the horizon, it always flies before them." It is this "scientific" attitude of the French revolutionists or of their teachers which also explains why their dissoluteness, which they oppose as something natural to the conventions of earlier gallantry, is "an unfashioned, indelicate, sour, gloomy, ferocious medley of pedantism and lewdness."[77]

Burke opposes, then, not merely a change in regard to the substance of the moral teaching. He opposes likewise, and even primarily, a change in regard to its mode: the new moral teaching is the work of men who think about human affairs as geometricians think about figures and planes rather than as acting men think about a business before them. It is this fundamental change from a practical to a theoretical approach which, according to Burke, gave the French Revolution its unique character.

"The present revolution in France seems to me . . . to bear

77. *Works*, II, 311, 409, 419, 538–40; V, 138, 140–42, 209–13.

little resemblance or analogy to any of those which have been brought about in Europe, upon principles merely political. It is a revolution of doctrine and theoretic dogma. It has a much greater resemblance to those changes which have been made upon religious grounds, in which a spirit of proselytism makes an essential part." The French Revolution, therefore, has a certain resemblance to the Reformation. Yet "this spirit of general political faction," or this "armed doctrine," is "separated from religion" and is, in fact, atheistic; the "theoretic dogma" guiding the French Revolution is purely political. But, since that revolution extends the power of politics to religion and "even to the constitution of the mind of man," it is the first "*complete* revolution" in the history of mankind. Its success cannot be explained, however, by the political principles which animate it. Those principles have at all times had a powerful appeal, since they are "most flattering to the natural propensities of the unthinking multitude." Hence there have been earlier insurrectionary attempts "grounded on these rights of men," like the Jacquerie and John Ball's insurrection in the Middle Ages and the efforts of the extreme wing during the English Civil War. But none of these attempts was successful. The success of the French Revolution can be explained only by that one among its features which distinguishes it from all parallels. The French Revolution is the first "philosophic revolution." It is the first revolution which was made by men of letters, philosophers, "thoroughbred metaphysicians," "not as subordinate instruments and trumpeters of sedition, but as the chief contrivers and managers." It is the first revolution in which "the spirit of ambition is connected with the spirit of speculation."[78]

In opposing this intrusion of the spirit of speculation or of

78. *Ibid.*, II, 284–87, 299, 300, 302, 338–39, 352, 361–62, 382–84, 403–5, 414, 423–24, 527; III, 87–91, 164, 350–52, 354, 376, 377, 379, 442–43, 456–57; V, 73, 111, 138, 139, 141, 245, 246, 259 (the italics are in the original).

theory into the field of practice or of politics, Burke may be said to have restored the older view according to which theory cannot be the sole, or the sufficient, guide of practice. He may be said to have returned to Aristotle in particular. But, to say nothing of other qualifications, one must add immediately that no one before Burke had spoken on this subject with equal emphasis and force. One may even say that, from the point of view of political philosophy, Burke's remarks on the problem of theory and practice are the most important part of his work. He spoke more emphatically and more forcefully on this problem than Aristotle in particular had done because he had to contend with a new and most powerful form of "speculatism," with a political doctrinairism of philosophic origin. That "speculatist" approach to politics came to his critical attention a considerable time before the French Revolution. Years before 1789, he spoke of "the speculatists of our speculating age." It was the increased political significance of speculation which, very early in his career, most forcefully turned Burke's attention to "the old quarrel between speculation and practice."[79]

It was in the light of that quarrel that he conceived his greatest political actions: not only his action against the French Revolution but his action in favor of the American colonists as well. In both cases the political leaders whom Burke opposed insisted on certain rights: the English government insisted on the rights of sovereignty and the French revolutionists insisted on the rights of man. In both cases Burke proceeded in exactly the same manner: he questioned less the rights than the wisdom of exercising the rights. In both cases he tried to restore the genuinely political approach as against a legalistic approach. Now he characteristically regarded the legalistic approach as one form of "speculatism," other forms being the approaches of the historian, the meta-

79. *Ibid.*, I, 311; II, 363; III, 139, 356; V, 76; VII, 11.

physician, the theologian, and the mathematician. All these approaches to political matters have this in common—that they are not controlled by prudence, the controlling virtue of all practice. Whatever might have to be said about the propriety of Burke's usage, it is here sufficient to note that, in judging the political leaders whom he opposed in the two most important actions of his life, he traced their lack of prudence less to passion than to the intrusion of the spirit of theory into the field of politics.[80]

It has often been said that Burke, in the name of history, attacked the theories which prevailed in his age. As will appear later, this interpretation is not altogether unjustified. But, in order to see its limited correctness, one must start from the fact that what appeared to the generations after Burke as a turn to History, not to say as the discovery of History, was primarily a return to the traditional view of the essential limitations of theory as distinguished from practice or prudence.

"Speculatism" in its most thoroughgoing form would be the view that all the light which practice needs is supplied by theory or philosophy or science. Over against this view Burke asserts that theory is insufficient for the guidance of practice and, in addition, has essentially a tendency to mislead practice.[81] Practice and hence practical wisdom or prudence are distinguished from theory, in the first place, by the fact that they are concerned with the particular and changeable, whereas theory is concerned with the universal and unchangeable. Theory, "which regards man and the affairs of men," is primarily concerned with the principles of morality as well as with "the principles of true politics [which] are those of morality en-

80. *Ibid.*, I, 257, 278, 279, 402, 403, 431, 432, 435, 479–80; II, 7, 25–30, 52, 300, 304; III, 16; V, 295; VII, 161; VIII, 8–9; cf. also Ernest Barker, *Essays on Government* (Oxford, 1945), p. 221.

81. *Works*, I, 259, 270–71, 376; II, 25–26, 306, 334–35, 552; III, 110; VI, 148; *Letters*, p. 131.

larged" or with "the proper ends of government." Knowing the proper ends of government, one does not know anything of how and to what extent those ends can be realized here and now, under these particular circumstances both fixed and transitory. And it is the circumstances which give "to every political principle its distinguishing colour and discriminating effect." Political freedom, for example, may be a blessing or a curse, according to the difference of circumstances. "The science of constructing a commonwealth, or renovating it, or reforming it," as distinguished from the knowledge of the principles of politics, is therefore an "experimental science, not to be taught *a priori*." Theory, then, deals not merely with the proper ends of government but also with the means to those ends. But there is hardly any rule regarding those means which is universally valid. Sometimes one is confronted even "with the dreadful exigence in which morality submits to the suspension of its own rules in favour of its own principles."[82] Since there are many rules of this kind which are sound in most cases, they have a plausibility that is positively misleading in regard to the rare cases in which their application would be fatal. Such rules do not make proper allowance for chance, "to which speculators are rarely pleased to assign that very large share to which she is justly entitled in all human affairs." Disregarding the power of chance and thus forgetting that "perhaps the only moral trust with any certainty in our hands, is the care of our own time," "they do not talk as politicians, but as prophets." The concern with the universal or the general is likely to create a kind of blindness in regard to the particular and the unique. Political rules derived from experience express the lessons drawn from what has succeeded or failed down to the present. They are therefore inapplicable to new situations. New situations sometimes arise

82. *Works*, I, 185, 312, 456; II, 7–8, 282–83, 333, 358, 406, 426–27, 431, 520, 533, 542–43, 549; III, 15–16, 36, 81, 101, 350, 431–32, 452; V, 158, 216; VI, 19, 24, 114, 471; VII, 93–94, 101.

in reaction to the very rules which uncontradicted previous experience pronounced to be universally valid: man is inventive in good and in evil. Therefore it may happen that "experience upon other data [than the actual circumstances of the case], is of all things the most delusive."[83]

It follows from this that history is only of very limited value. From history "much political wisdom may be learned," but only "as habit, not as precept." History is liable to turn man's understanding from "the business before him" to misleading analogies, and men are naturally inclined to succumb to that temptation. For it requires a much greater effort to articulate a hitherto unarticulated situation in its particular character than to interpret it in the light of precedents which have been articulated already. "I have constantly observed," Burke says, "that the generality of people are fifty years, at least, behind hand in their politics . . . in books everything is settled for them, without the exertion of any considerable diligence or sagacity." This is not to deny that the politician sometimes needs history for the sake of "the business before him." Reason and good sense absolutely prescribe, e.g., "whenever we are involved in difficulties from the measures we have pursued, that we should take a strict review of those measures" or that we should "enter into the most ample historical detail." History has this in common with practical wisdom—that both are concerned with particulars; and it has this in common with theory—that the objects of history, i.e., past actions or transactions (*acta*), are not objects of action proper (*agenda*), i.e., things which we have to do now. Thus history, or "retrospective wisdom," creates the delusion that it could "serve admirably to reconcile the old quarrel between speculation and practice."[84]

Another way in which men try to evade the hardship in-

83. *Ibid.*, I, 277–78, 312, 365; II, 372, 374–75, 383; III, 15–17; V, 78, 153–54, 257.
84. *Ibid.*, I, 311, 384–85; II, 25; III, 456–57; V, 258.

volved in articulating and handling difficult situations is legalism. They sometimes act on the assumption that political questions proper, which, as such, concern the here and now, can be fully answered by recourse to law, which, as such, is concerned with universals. It is with a view to this difference between the prudential and the legal that Burke calls the legal approach sometimes "speculative" or "metaphysical." He contrasts "the limited and fixed" character of the legal, which is "adapted to ordinary occasions," with the prudential, which alone can guide men "when a new and troubled scene is opened."[85]

Theory, then, is capable of a simplicity, uniformity, or exactness which practical wisdom necessarily lacks. It is characteristic of the theory which regards man and the affairs of men that it be primarily concerned either with the best or simply just order or with the state of nature. In both forms theory is primarily concerned with the simplest case. This simple case never occurs in practice; no actual order is simply just, and every social order is fundamentally different from the state of nature. Therefore, practical wisdom always has to do with exceptions, modifications, balances, compromises, or mixtures. "These metaphysical rights entering into common life, like rays of light which pierce into a dense medium are, by the laws of nature, refracted from their straight line." Since "the objects of society are of the greatest possible complexity," "the primitive rights of men" cannot continue "in the simplicity of their original direction"; "and in proportion as [these rights] are metaphysically true, they are morally and politically false." Practical wisdom, in contradistinction to theory, requires, therefore, "the most delicate and complicated skill," a skill which arises only from long and varied practice.[86]

85. *Ibid.*, I, 199, 406–7, 431, 432; II, 7, 25, 28; V, 295.
86. *Ibid.*, I, 257, 336–37, 408, 433, 500–501; II, 29–30, 333–35, 437–38, 454–55, 515; III, 16; V, 158; VI, 132–33.

On the other hand, Burke characterizes theory as "subtle" or "refined" and sees in simplicity or plainness an essential character of sound politics: "refined policy has ever been the parent of confusion." The wants for which society has to provide and the duties to which it has to conform may be said to be known to everyone through his feelings and his conscience. Political theory raises the question regarding the best solution to the political problem. For this purpose, to say nothing of others, it transcends the limits of common experience: it is "refined." The man of civil discretion is vaguely aware of the best solution but is clearly aware of which modification of the best solution is appropriate in the circumstances. To take an example from the present day, he is aware of the fact that at present only "a wider, if a simpler culture"[87] is possible. The clarity required for sound action is not necessarily enhanced by enhanced clarity about the best solution or by enhanced theoretical clarity of any other kind: the clear light of the ivory tower or, for that matter, of the laboratory obscures political things by impairing the medium in which they exist. It may require "the most delicate and complicated skill" to devise a policy which agrees tolerably well with the ends of government in a given situation. But such a policy is a failure if the people cannot see its soundness: "refined policy" is destructive of trust and hence of full obedience. Policy must be "plain" as regards "all broader grounds of policy," whereas it is not necessary that "the ground of a particular measure, making a part of a plan" should "suit the ordinary capacities of those who are to enjoy it" or even that that ground should be divulged to them. "In the most essential point," "the less inquiring" can be and ought to be, by virtue of "their feelings and their experience," "on a par with the most wise and knowing."[88]

87. Winston S. Churchill, *Blood, Sweat, and Tears* (New York, 1941), p. 18.

88. *Works*, I, 337, 428-29, 435, 454, 489; II, 26, 30, 304, 358, 542; III, 112, 441; V, 227, 278; VI, 21, 24; VII, 349.

Furthermore, practice presupposes attachment to a particular or, more precisely, to "one's own" (one's country, one's people, one's religious group, and the like), whereas theory is detached. To be attached to something means to care for it, to have a concern with it, to be affected by it, or to have a stake in it. Practical matters, as distinguished from theoretical ones, "come home to the business and bosoms of men." The theoretician as such is no more interested in his own case or in the case of his own group than in any other. He is impartial and neutral, not to say "cold and languid." "Speculators ought to be neutral. A minister cannot be so." Acting man is necessarily and legitimately partial to what is his own; it is his duty to take sides. Burke does not mean that the theoretician must not pass "value judgments" but that, as theoretician, he is a partisan of excellence regardless of when and where it is found; he unqualifiedly prefers the good to what is his own. Acting man, however, is primarily concerned with what is his own, with what is nearest and dearest to him, however deficient in excellence it may be. The horizon of practice is necessarily narrower than that of theory. By opening up a larger vista, by thus revealing the limitations of any practical pursuit, theory is liable to endanger full devotion to practice.[89]

Practice lacks the freedom of theory also because it cannot wait: "we must submit . . . affairs to time." Practical thought is thought with a view to some deadline. It is concerned with the most imminent rather than with the most eligible. It lacks the ease and the leisure of theory. It does not permit man "to evade an opinion" or to suspend his judgment. Therefore, it must rest satisfied with a lower degree of clarity or certainty than theoretical thought. Every theoretical "decision" is reversible; actions are irreversible. Theory can and must ever again begin from the beginning. The very question of the best social order means that one "moots cases . . . on the supposed

89. *Ibid.*, I, 185–86, 324, 501; II, 29, 120, 280–81, 548; III, 379–80; VI, 226; VIII, 458.

ruin of the constitution," i.e., that one does something which in practical thought would bespeak "a bad habit." In contradistinction to theory, practice is limited by past decisions and, therefore, by what is established. In human affairs, possession passes for a title, whereas there is no presumption in favor of the accepted view in theoretical matters.[90]

Speculation, being essentially "private," is concerned with the truth without any regard to public opinion. But "national measures" or "political problems do not primarily concern truth or falsehood. They relate to good or evil." They relate to peace and "mutual convenience," and their satisfactory handling requires "unsuspecting confidence," consent, agreement, and compromise. Political action requires "a judicious management of the temper of the people." Even in giving "a direction . . . to the general sense of the community," it must "follow . . . the public inclination." Regardless of what one might have to think of "the abstract value of the voice of the people, . . . opinion, the great support of the State, [depends] entirely upon that voice." Hence it may easily happen that what is metaphysically true is politically false. "Established opinions," "allowed opinions which contribute so much to the public tranquillity," must not be shaken, although they are not "infallible." Prejudices must be "appeased." Political life requires that fundamental principles proper, which, as such, transcend the established constitution, be kept in a state of dormancy. Temporary solutions of continuity. must be "kept from the eye," or a "politic, well-wrought veil" must be thrown over them. "There is a sacred veil to be drawn over the beginnings of all governments." Whereas speculation is "innovating," whereas the "waters" of science "must be troubled, before they can exert their virtues," practice must keep as closely as possible to precedent, example, and tradition: "old custom . . . is the great support of all the govern-

90. *Ibid.*, I, 87, 193, 323, 336, 405; II, 26, 427–28, 548, 552; VI, 19; VII, 127.

ments in the world." Society rests, indeed, on consent. Yet the consent cannot be achieved by reasoning alone, and in particular not by the mere calculation of the advantages of living together—a calculation which may be completed in a brief span of time—but solely by habits and prejudices which grow up only in long periods. Whereas theory rejects error, prejudice, or superstition, the statesman puts these to use.[91]

The intrusion of theory into politics is liable to have an unsettling and inflaming effect. No actual social order is perfect. "Speculative inquiries" necessarily bring to light the imperfect character of the established order. If these inquiries are introduced into political discussion, which, of necessity, lacks "the coolness of philosophic inquiry," they are liable "to raise discontent in the people" in regard to the established order, discontent which may make rational reform impossible. The most legitimate theoretical problems become, in the political arena, "vexatious questions" and cause "a spirit of litigation" and "fanaticism." Considerations transcending "the arguments of states and kingdoms" must be left "to the schools; for there only they may be discussed with safety."[92]

As may be inferred from the preceding paragraphs, Burke is not content with defending practical wisdom against the encroachments of theoretical science. He parts company with the Aristotelian tradition by disparaging theory and especially metaphysics. He uses "metaphysics" and "metaphysician" frequently in a derogatory sense. There is a connection between this usage and the fact that he regards Aristotle's natural philosophy as "unworthy of him," whereas he considers Epicurean physics to be "the most approaching to rational."[93]

91. *Ibid.*, I, 87, 190, 257, 280, 307, 352, 375, 431, 432, 471, 473, 483, 489, 492, 502; II, 27–29, 33–34, 44, 292, 293, 306, 335, 336, 349, 429–30, 439; III, 39–40, 81, 109, 110; V, 230; VI, 98, 243, 306–7; VII, 44–48, 59, 60, 190; VIII, 274; *Letters*, pp. 299–300.

92. *Works*, I, 259–60, 270–71, 432; II, 28–29, 331; III, 12, 16, 25, 39, 81, 98–99, 104, 106; VI, 132.

93. *Ibid.*, VI, 250–51.

There is a connection between his strictures on metaphysics and the skeptical tendencies of his contemporaries Hume and Rousseau. At least so much must be said that Burke's distinction between theory and practice is radically different from Aristotle's, since it is not based on a clear conviction of the ultimate superiority of theory or of the theoretical life.

For the support of this contention, we do not have to rely entirely on a general impression derived from Burke's usage and the bent of his thought. He wrote one theoretical work: *A Philosophical Inquiry into the Origin of Our Ideas of the Sublime and Beautiful*. In that work he speaks in a nonpolemical tone about the limitations of theoretic science: "When we go but one step beyond the immediate sensible qualities of things, we go out of our depth. All we do after is but a faint struggle, that shows we are in an element which does not belong to us." Our knowledge of bodily and mental phenomena is limited to the manner of their operation, to their How; it can never reach their Why. The very title of the inquiry reveals the ancestry of Burke's sole theoretic effort; it is reminiscent of Locke and of Burke's acquaintance, Hume. Of Locke, Burke says that "the authority of this great man is doubtless as great as that of any man can be." The most important thesis of the *Sublime and Beautiful* is in perfect agreement with British sensualism and in explicit opposition to the classics; Burke denies that there is a connection between beauty, on the one hand, and perfection, proportion, virtue, convenience, order, fitness, and any other such "creatures of the understanding," on the other. That is to say, he refuses to understand visible or sensible beauty in the light of intellectual beauty.[94]

The emancipation of sensible beauty from its traditionally assumed directedness toward intellectual beauty foreshadows or accompanies a certain emancipation of sentiment and instinct from reason, or a certain depreciation of reason. It is this

94. *Ibid.*, I, 114 ff., 122, 129, 131, 143–44, 155; II, 441; VI, 98.

novel attitude toward reason which accounts for the nonclassical overtones in Burke's remarks on the difference between theory and practice. Burke's opposition to modern "rationalism" shifts almost insensibly into an opposition to "rationalism" as such.[95] What he says about the deficiencies of reason is indeed partly traditional. On some occasions he does not go beyond depreciating the judgment of the individual in favor of "the judgment of the human race," the wisdom of "the species" or "the ancient, permanent sense of mankind," i.e., the *consensus gentium*. On other occasions he does not go beyond depreciating the experience which the individual can acquire in favor of the much more extensive and varied experience of "a long succession of generations" or of "the collected reason of ages."[96] The novel element in Burke's critique of reason reveals itself least ambiguously in its most important practical consequence: he rejects the view that constitutions can be "made" in favor of the view that they must "grow"; he therefore rejects in particular the view that the best social order can be or ought to be the work of an individual, of a wise "legislator" or founder.[97]

To see this more clearly, it is necessary to contrast Burke's view of the British constitution, which he regarded, to say the

95. In the *Sublime and Beautiful*, Burke says that "our gardens, if nothing else, declare we begin to feel that mathematical ideas are not the true measures of beauty," and that this wrong view "arose from the Platonic theory of fitness and aptitude" (*Works*, I, 122). In the *Reflections on the Revolution in France*, he compares the French revolutionists to the French "ornamental gardeners" (*Works*, II, 413). Cf. *ibid.*, II, 306, 308; I, 280.

96. *Works*, II, 359, 364, 367, 435, 440; VI, 146–47.

97. Friedrich von Gentz, the German translator of the *Reflections on the Revolution in France*, says: "Konstitutionen können schlechterdings nicht gemacht werden, sie müssen sich, wie Natur-Werke, durch allmähliche Entwicklung von selbst bilden. . . . Diese Wahrheit ist die kostbarste, *vielleicht die einzige wirklich neue* (*denn höchstens geahnt, aber nicht vollständig erkannt wurde sie zuvor*), um welche die französische Revolution die höhere Staatswissenschaft bereichert hat" (*Staatsschriften und Briefe* [Munich, 1921], I, 344) (the italics are not in the original).

least, as second to none, with the classical view of the best constitution. According to the classics, the best constitution is a contrivance of reason, i.e., of conscious activity or of planning on the part of an individual or of a few individuals. It is in accordance with nature, or it is a natural order, since it fulfils to the highest degree the requirements of the perfection of human nature, or since its structure imitates the pattern of nature. But it is not natural as regards the manner of its production: it is a work of design, planning, conscious making; it does not come into being by a natural process or by the imitation of a natural process. The best constitution is directed toward a variety of ends which are linked with one another by nature in such a manner that one of these ends is the highest end; the best constitution is therefore directed particularly toward that single end which is by nature the highest. According to Burke, on the other hand, the best constitution is in accordance with nature or is natural also and primarily because it has come into being not through planning but through the imitation of natural process, i.e., because it has come into being without guiding reflection, continuously, slowly, not to say imperceptibly, "in a great length of time, and by a great variety of accidents"; all "new fancied and new fabricated republics" are necessarily bad. The best constitution is therefore not "formed upon a regular plan or with any unity of design" but directed toward "the greatest variety of ends."[98]

One goes beyond what Burke himself says if one ascribes to him the view that a sound political order must be the product of History. What came to be called "historical" was, for Burke, still "the local and accidental." What came to be called "historical process" was for him still accidental causation or accidental causation modified by the prudential handling of situations as they arose. Accordingly, the sound political order for him, in the last analysis, is the unintended out-

98. *Works*, II, 33, 91, 305, 307-8, 439-40; V, 148, 253-54.

come of accidental causation. He applied to the production of the sound political order what modern political economy had taught about the production of public prosperity: the common good is the product of activities which are not by themselves ordered toward the common good. Burke accepted the principle of modern political economy which is diametrically opposed to the classical principle: "the love of lucre," "this natural, this reasonable . . . principle," "is the grand cause of prosperity to all states."[99] The good order or the rational is the result of forces which do not themselves tend toward the good order or the rational. This principle was first applied to the planetary system and thereafter to "the system of wants," i.e., to economics.[100] The application of this principle to the genesis of the sound political order was one of the two most important elements in the "discovery" of History. The other, equally important, element was supplied by the application of the same principle to the understanding of man's humanity; man's humanity was understood as acquired by virtue of accidental causation. This view, of which the classic exposition is to be found in Rousseau's *Second Discourse,* led to the consequence that "the historical process" was thought to culminate in an absolute moment: the moment in which man, the product of blind fate, becomes the seeing master of his fate by understanding for the first time in an adequate manner what is right and wrong politically and morally. It led to a "complete revolution," to a revolution extending "even to the constitution of the mind of man." Burke denies the possibility of an absolute moment; man can never become the seeing master of

99. *Ibid.,* II, 33; V, 313; VI, 160; *Letters,* p. 270. As for Burke's agreement with the modern "economical politicians," see especially *Works,* I, 299, 462; II, 93, 194, 351, 431–32; V, 89, 100, 124, 321; VIII, 69. One of the few things which Burke seems to have learned through the French Revolution is that power and influence do not necessarily go with property. Compare *Works,* III, 372, 456–57; V, 256, with VI, 318; see also Barker, *op. cit.,* p. 159.

100. Cf. Hegel, *Rechtsphilosophie,* sec. 189 Zusatz.

his fate; what the wisest individual can think out for himself is always inferior to what has been produced "in a great length of time, and by a great variety of accidents." He denies therefore, if not the feasibility, at least the legitimacy, of a "complete revolution"; all other moral or political errors almost fade into insignificance if compared with the error underlying the French Revolution. The age of the French Revolution, far from being the absolute moment, is "the most unenlightened age, the least qualified for legislation that perhaps has been since the first formation of civil society." One is tempted to say that it is the age of perfect sinfulness. Not admiration, but contempt of the present; not contempt, but admiration of the ancient order and eventually of the age of chivalry, is the sound attitude—everything good is inherited. What is needed is not "metaphysical jurisprudence" but "historical jurisprudence."[101] Thus Burke paves the way for "the historical school." But his intransigent opposition to the French Revolution must not blind us to the fact that, in opposing the French Revolution, he has recourse to the same fundamental principle which is at the bottom of the revolutionary theorems and which is alien to all earlier thought.

It almost goes without saying that Burke regards the connection between "the love of lucre" and prosperity, on the one hand, and "a great variety of accidents" and a healthy political order, on the other, as part of the providential order; it is because the processes which are not guided by human reflection are part of the providential order that their products are infinitely superior in wisdom to the products of reflection. From a similar point of view, Kant has interpreted the teaching of Rousseau's *Second Discourse* as a vindication of Providence.[102] Accordingly, the idea of History, precisely like mod-

---

101. *Works*, II, 348–49, 363; VI, 413; see also Thomas W. Copeland, *Edmund Burke: Six Essays* (London, 1950), p. 232.

102. *Works*, II, 33, 307; V, 89, 100, 321; Kant, *Sämtliche Werke*, ed. Karl Vorländer, VIII, 280.

ern political economy, could appear to have emerged through a modification of the traditional belief in Providence. That modification is usually described as "secularization." "Secularization" is the "temporalization" of the spiritual or of the eternal. It is the attempt to integrate the eternal into a temporal context. It therefore presupposes that the eternal is no longer understood as eternal. "Secularization," in other words, presupposes a radical change of thought, a transition of thought from one plane to an entirely different plane. This radical change appears in its undisguised form in the emergence of modern philosophy or science; it is not primarily a change within theology. What presents itself as the "secularization" of theological concepts will have to be understood, in the last analysis, as an adaptation of traditional theology to the intellectual climate produced by modern philosophy or science both natural and political. The "secularization" of the understanding of Providence culminates in the view that the ways of God are scrutable to sufficiently enlightened men. The theological tradition recognized the mysterious character of Providence especially by the fact that God uses or permits evil for his good ends. It asserted, therefore, that man cannot take his bearings by God's providence but only by God's law, which simply forbids man to do evil. In proportion as the providential order came to be regarded as intelligible to man, and therefore evil came to be regarded as evidently necessary or useful, the prohibition against doing evil lost its evidence. Hence various ways of action which were previously condemned as evil could now be regarded as good. The goals of human action were lowered. But it is precisely a lowering of these goals which modern political philosophy consciously intended from its very beginning.

Burke was satisfied that the French Revolution was thoroughly evil. He condemned it as strongly and as unqualifiedly as we today condemn the Communist revolution. He regarded it as possible that the French Revolution, which conducted "a war against all sects and all religions," might be victorious and thus that the revolutionary state might exist "as a nuisance on the earth for several hundred years." He regarded it, therefore, as possible that the victory of the French Revolution might have been decreed by Providence. In accordance with his "secularized" understanding of Providence, he drew from this the conclusion that "if the system of Europe, taking in laws, manners, religion and politics" is doomed, "they, who persist in opposing this mighty current in human affairs . . . will not be resolute and firm, but perverse and obstinate."[103] Burke comes close to suggesting that to oppose a thoroughly evil current in human affairs is perverse if that current is sufficiently powerful; he is oblivious of the nobility of last-ditch resistance. He does not consider that, in a way which no man can foresee, resistance in a forlorn position to the enemies of mankind, "going down with guns blazing and flag flying," may contribute greatly toward keeping awake the recollection of the immense loss sustained by mankind, may inspire and strengthen the desire and the hope for its recovery, and may become a beacon for those who humbly carry on the works of humanity in a seemingly endless valley of darkness and destruction. He does not consider this because he is too certain that man can know whether a cause lost now is lost forever or that man can understand sufficiently the meaning of a providential dispensation as distinguished from the moral law. It is only a short step from this thought of Burke to the supersession of the distinction between good and bad by the distinction between the progressive and the retrograde, or between what is and what is not in harmony with the historical process. We are here certainly at the pole opposite to Cato, who dared to espouse a lost cause.

Whereas Burke's "conservatism" is in full agreement with classical thought, his interpretation of his "conservatism"

103. *Works*, III, 375, 393, 443; VIII, 510; *Letters*, p. 308.

prepared an approach to human affairs which is even more foreign to classical thought than was the very "radicalism" of the theorists of the French Revolution. Political philosophy or political theory had been from its inception the quest for civil society as it ought to be. Burke's political theory is, or tends to become, identical with a theory of the British constitution, i.e., an attempt to "discover the latent wisdom which prevails" in the actual. One might think that Burke would have to measure the British constitution by a standard transcending it in order to recognize it as wise, and to a certain extent he undoubtedly does precisely this: he does not tire of speaking of natural right, which, as such, is anterior to the British constitution. But he also says that "our constitution is a prescriptive constitution; it is a constitution whose sole authority is that it has existed time out of mind" or that the British constitution claims and asserts the liberties of the British "as an estate especially belonging to the people of this kingdom, without any reference whatever to any other more general or prior right." Prescription cannot be the sole authority for a constitution, and therefore recourse to rights anterior to the constitution, i.e., to natural rights, cannot be superfluous unless prescription by itself is a sufficient guaranty of goodness. Transcendent standards can be dispensed with if the standard is inherent in the process; "the actual and the present is the rational." What could appear as a return to the primeval equation of the good with the ancestral is, in fact, a preparation for Hegel.[104]

We have noted before that what appeared later on as the discovery of History was originally rather the recovery of the distinction between theory and practice. That distinction had been blurred by the doctrinairism of the seventeenth and eighteenth centuries or, what is fundamentally the same thing, by

104. *Works*, II, 306, 359, 443; III, 110, 112; VI, 146; Hegel, *op. cit.*, Vorrede; cf. also Barker, *op. cit.*, p. 225.

the understanding of all theory as essentially in the service of practice (*scientia propter potentiam*). The recovery of the distinction between theory and practice was from the outset modified by skepticism in regard to theoretical metaphysics, a skepticism which culminated in the depreciation of theory in favor of practice. In accordance with these antecedents, the highest form of practice—the foundation or formation of a political society—was viewed as a quasi-natural process not controlled by reflection; thus it could become a purely theoretical theme. Political theory became understanding of what practice has produced or of the actual and ceased to be the quest for what ought to be; political theory ceased to be "theoretically practical" (i.e., deliberative at a second remove) and became purely theoretical in the way in which metaphysics (and physics) were traditionally understood to be purely theoretical. There came into being a new type of theory, of metaphysics, having as its highest theme human action and its product rather than the whole, which is in no way the object of human action. Within the whole and the metaphysic that is oriented upon it, human action occupies a high but subordinate place. When metaphysics came, as it now did, to regard human action and its product as the end toward which all other beings or processes are directed, metaphysics became philosophy of history. Philosophy of history was primarily theory, i.e., contemplation, of human practice and therewith necessarily of completed human practice; it presupposed that significant human action, History, was completed. By becoming the highest theme of philosophy, practice ceased to be practice proper, i.e., concern with *agenda*. The revolts against Hegelianism on the part of Kierkegaard and Nietzsche, in so far as they now exercise a strong influence on public opinion, thus appear as attempts to recover the possibility of practice, i.e., of a human life which has a significant and undetermined future. But these attempts increased the confusion, since they destroyed, as far as in them lay, the very possibility of theory. "Doctrinairism" and "existentialism" appear to us as the two faulty extremes. While being opposed to each other, they agree with each other in the decisive respect—they agree in ignoring prudence, "the god of this lower world."[105] Prudence and "this lower world" cannot be seen properly without some knowledge of "the higher world"—without genuine *theoria*.

Among the great theoretical writings of the past, none seems to be nearer in spirit to Burke's statements on the British constitution than Cicero's *Republic*. The similarity is all the more remarkable since Burke cannot have known Cicero's masterpiece, which was not recovered until 1820. Just as Burke regards the British constitution as the model, Cicero contends that the best polity is the Roman polity; Cicero chooses to describe the Roman polity rather than to invent a new one, as Socrates had done in Plato's *Republic*. These contentions of Burke and of Cicero are, if taken by themselves, in perfect agreement with the classical principles: the best polity being essentially "possible," it could have become actual at some place and at some time. One should note, however, that, whereas Burke assumed that the model constitution was actual in his time, Cicero assumed that the best polity had been actual in the past but was no longer actual. Above all, Cicero made it perfectly clear that the characteristics of the best polity can be determined without regard to any example, and especially to the example of the Roman polity. In the respect under discussion, there is no difference between Cicero and Plato in particular; Plato commenced a sequel to his *Republic*, namely the *Critias*, in which the "invented" polity of the *Republic* was to be shown to have been actual in the Athenian past. The following agreement between Burke and Cicero seems to be more important: just as Burke traced the excellence of the British constitution to the fact that it had come into

105. *Works*, II, 28.

being "in a great length of time" and thus embodies "the collected reason of ages," Cicero traced the superiority of the Roman polity to the fact that it was not the work of one man or of one generation but of many men and many generations. Cicero calls the way in which the Roman order developed into the best polity, "some natural road." Still, "the very idea of the fabrication of a new government" did not fill Cicero, as it did Burke, "with disgust and horror." If Cicero preferred the Roman polity, which was the work of many men and many generations, to the Spartan polity, which was the work of one man, he did not deny that the Spartan polity was respectable. In his presentation of the origins of the Roman polity, Romulus appears almost as the counterpart of Lycurgus; Cicero did not abandon the notion that civil societies are founded by superior individuals. It is "counsel and training" as opposed to chance that Cicero understands to be the "natural road" by which the Roman polity reached its perfection; he does not understand the "natural road" to be processes unguided by reflection.[106]

Burke disagreed with the classics in regard to the genesis of the sound social order because he disagreed with them in regard to the character of the sound social order. As he saw it, the sound social or political order must not be "formed upon a regular plan or with any unity of design" because such "systematical" proceedings, such "presumption in the wisdom of human contrivances," would be incompatible with the highest possible degree of "personal liberty"; the state must pursue "the greatest variety of ends" and must as little as possible "sacrifice any one of them to another, or to the whole." It must be concerned with "individuality" or have the highest possible regard for "individual feeling and individual interest." It is for this reason that the genesis of the sound social

106. Cicero *Republic* i. 31–32, 34, 70–71; ii. 2–3, 15, 17, 21–22, 30, 37, 51–52, 66; v. 2; *Offices* i. 76. Consider also Polybius vi. 4. 13, 9. 10, 10. 12–14, 48. 2.

order must not be a process guided by reflection but must come as close as possible to natural, imperceptible process: the natural is the individual, and the universal is a creature of the understanding. Naturalness and free flowering of individuality are the same. Hence the free development of the individuals in their individuality, far from leading to chaos, is productive of the best order, an order which is not only compatible with "some irregularity in the whole mass" but requires it. There is beauty in irregularity: "method and exactness, the soul of proportion, are found rather prejudicial than serviceable to the cause of beauty."[107] The quarrel between the ancients and the moderns concerns eventually, and perhaps even from the beginning, the status of "individuality." Burke himself was still too deeply imbued with the spirit of "sound antiquity" to allow the concern with individuality to overpower the concern with virtue.

107. *Works*, I, 117, 462; II, 309; V, 253-55.

INDEX

✸

Thrasymachus, 6, 107 n., 114
Thucydides, 58, 109 n., 134 n.
Troeltsch, Ernst, 2 n., 61 n.

Ulpian, 144, 266

Voltaire, 22, 207

Weber, Max, 36–78

Whitehead, A. N., 89 n.

Wyclif, 185 n.

Xenocrates, 267 n.

Xenophon, 84 n., 86 n., 97 n., 101 nn.,
105 n., 106 n., 107 n., 109 n., 119 n.,
121 nn., 122 n., 129 n., 134 n., 135 n.,
137 n., 140 n., 143 n., 148 n., 150 n.